Further Steps 2

Further Steps brings together New York's foremost choreographers—among them MacArthur "Genius" award winners Meredith Monk and Bill T. Jones—to discuss the past, present and future of dance in the US. In a series of exclusive and enlightening interviews, this diverse selection of artists discuss the changing roles of race, gender, politics, and the social environment on their work.

Bringing her own experience of the New York dance scene to her study, Constance Kreemer traces the lives and works of the following choreographers: Lucinda Childs, Douglas Dunn, Molissa Fenley, Rennie Harris, Bill T. Jones, Kenneth King, Nancy Meehan, Meredith Monk, Rosalind Newman, Gus Solomons jr, Doug Varone, Dan Wagoner, Mel Wong and Jawole Zollar.

Constance Kreemer is a dancer, teacher, dance historian, dance critic and founder of the Society of Dance History Scholars. She has taught at universities throughout the USA and Hong Kong, and danced with the Nancy Meehan and Mel Wong Dance Companies.

Further Steps 2

Fourteen choreographers
on what's the RAGE in dance?

Constance Kreemer

Routledge
Taylor & Francis Group

LONDON AND NEW YORK

First published 2008
by Routledge
2 Park Square, Milton Park, Abingdon, Oxon OX14 4RN

Simultaneously published in the US
by Routledge
270 Madison Avenue, New York, NY 10016

Routledge is an imprint of the Taylor & Francis Group, an informa business

© 2008 Constance Kreemer

Typeset in Minion and Stone by
Keystroke, 28 High Street, Tettenhall, Wolverhampton

Printed and bound in the UK by TJ International Ltd, Padstow, Cornwall

British Library Cataloguing in Publication Data
A catalogue record for this book is available from the British Library

Library of Congress Cataloging in Publication Data
    Further steps : fourteen choreographers on what's the R.A.G.E. in dance?/
    [edited by] Constance Kreemer.
        p. cm.
    Includes bibliographical references and index.
    ISBN 978–0–415–96906–2 (hb: alk. paper) – ISBN 978–0–415–96907–9 (pb: alk. paper)
    1. Choreographers–Interviews. 2. Modern dance. 3. Choreography.
    I. Kreemer, Connie.
    GV1785.A1F87 2008
    792.8'2092–dc22   2007028699

ISBN 10: 0–415–96906–9 (hbk)
ISBN 10: 0–415–96907–7 (pbk)

ISBN 13: 978–0–415–96906–2 (hbk)
ISBN 13: 978–0–415–96907–9 (pbk)

This book is dedicated to my mother, Martha Kreemer,
whose love of the arts inspired mine. It is also dedicated to Mel Wong,
whose art is eternally inspirational, and to our daughters
Anika, Kira, and Suzanna Wong

Contents

Illustrations

Acknowledgments

First, I honor the late Selma Jeanne Cohen, whose dedication to preserving the history of dance through scholarship created the field of dance history in the USA. I thank her for her teachings and for her support and belief in me. Her generosity and love of dance had no limits, and her spirit lives on through the field of dance history.

I would like to thank all of the choreographers for their time, effort, and honesty. Each of their statements is unique and helps to make this book a strong contribution to the history of modern dance in the USA. Most of the photographers donated their photos out of respect to these artists, and to them I am extremely grateful. A dance book should have visual examples, and it would not have been possible without their generosity. Filming the interviews, Ted Timreck, Christopher Beaver, and Julia Dengel were invaluable, professional, and keenly sensitive as videographers. To them I am grateful as well.

In addition, my heartfelt thanks is extended to Wendy Shifrin for her critical eye, invaluable help, organizational direction, and loving friendship. Rob Kaplan, Patty Bryan, Dion Farquhar, John Boardman, and Marsh Leicester were also instrumental in providing help, feedback, friendship, and support.

My greatest thanks goes to my loving children, Anika, Kira, and Suzanna Wong, for their absolute, unfailing belief in me. I thank them for their understanding, their patience, and everlasting love.

Introduction
What's the RAGE in dance?

Sitting on a plane flying from Hawaii to New York in the summer of 1978, the seeds for my first book were planted. Next to me sat Selma Jeanne Cohen, noted dance historian, who had written *The Modern Dance: Seven Statements of Belief*. We were returning from a conference of the Congress on Research in Dance (CORD), where I had just delivered my first paper entitled, "The Stigma of Women in Dance." Initially I had written it as a final project for Selma Jeanne when I studied with her at the University of Chicago during the summer of 1976.

As the plane flew back to New York, I was telling Selma Jeanne that I used her book, with choreographers of the 1950s and 1960s, to teach dance history but thought the book should be updated to include choreographers of the 1970s. She looked at me and surprisingly said, "Connie, I've written my book, now it's *your* turn." She asked what I would do if I were to write a book about modern dance, and when I told her my ideas, she said she would help make it happen.

Further Steps: Fifteen Choreographers on Modern Dance was published in 1987, by Harper & Row, Inc. In it were fifteen interviews with prominent and emerging New York choreographers. Almost thirty years after those first interviews, the contemporary dance scene is vastly different. Of course, the world has changed too. What has changed? It seems like just about everything.

My first book was written entirely on a typewriter. Some forward thinkers, like choreographer Kenneth King, may have known what was technologically in store for us, but, at that time, how many of us could imagine what computer technology and the introduction of the Internet would bring? Back then, the only web we knew had to do with spiders, and "on line" meant hanging clothes. Spam came in a can; pods contained peas; and a blackberry grew on a bush.

The world has drastically shrunk due to the web. In the age of information, it's just a google away. Travel and globalization are intermeshing cultures. Our sense of time has speeded up. We've gone from three television stations to cable television with over 200 channels. The five-second attention span demands images almost faster than the eye can blink. Videogames,

Xboxes, PlayStations, cybernetics, digital technology, iPods, and now iPhones . . . we are plugged in and connected like never before—and possibly disconnected in ways never before imagined.

Twenty years ago, snail mail was the norm, a postage stamp was 15 cents, bread cost 48 cents, and gas averaged 1 dollar and 3 cents a gallon. Today, email and text-messaging have accelerated communication to an instant. Cell phones with cameras and videos are now ubiquitous. Cash at ATM machines, credit cards, and online banking have changed the way we deal with money. Outsourcing of jobs and telecommuting have changed the way we work.

Our lives have become very fast, very convenient, and very isolated. Most people now spend eight to ten hours a day in front of a machine and less than two to three hours with other humans. Values have changed as well. In 1970, a survey of college freshman revealed their primary goal to be "developing a meaningful philosophy of life." By 2005, 75 percent said their goal was to be financially "very well off" (Roberts 2006).

MTV culture and reality shows were unheard of twenty-five years ago. Hip-hop, then on the fringes, but around for three decades, is now a generation lifestyle and a culture for people across the globe. It has permeated youth culture beyond the music, as an attitude, a style, and a language, entering the mainstream in commercialized forms. Corporate giants such as Nike, Coca-Cola, Tommy Hilfiger, and McDonald's have capitalized on the phenomenon, which has spread from the ghettos, into the suburbs, and on into corporate boardrooms.

Many of these technological and cultural changes, like them or not, have seeped into the world of art and concert dance. So what *are* the changes in modern dance? Let's start with the name. Has it become an old-fashioned term? Some no longer use it, except to refer to a specific time period within concert dance, corresponding to the period of modernism in art. Others use the terms "postmodern" or "contemporary dance," but many dancers in the USA use all three terms interchangeably when referring to concert dance as art. What are the differences? That requires examining the term "modernism" and "postmodernism" as well as looking back at the history of modern dance. Space limitations preclude a detailed analysis in this book, but highlighting important sequences of the progression of choreographers will attempt to provide a sense of modern dance's development.

Around the turn of the twentieth century in the USA, three revolutionary white women, Loie Fuller, Isadora Duncan, and Ruth St. Denis, began dancing to express themselves in ways never before viewed on a concert stage. Rebelling against many of the customs of their time, these impassioned women threw off their corsets and shoes, danced in revealing costumes, simultaneously shocking and enthralling audiences, while communicating physically in an artistic expression never before attempted.

These early pioneers danced in the name of art, to express themselves by making a statement through their own unique, "natural" movement. They were rebelling against the tasteless dance of their times, which, according to Reynolds and McCormick, existed "to titillate, decorate, or entertain—never to edify" (Reynolds and McCormick 2003: 2). Chorus-line dance and ballet were about the only theatrical dance offered back then. At the time, ballet tried to defy gravity by giving the illusion of sylphs, nymphs, and fairies flitting above the world in fantasy. Many twenty-first-century feminists now look at those ballets as displaying ballerinas as sex objects in a male-dominated world. These pioneer women danced to reclaim dignity for the art of dancing from being equated with prostitution, by reinstating spirituality and by striving to make dance a serious art form.

They hailed from all across the nation: Duncan was from the San Francisco Bay area, Fuller from Fullersburg, Illinois, while St. Denis was from a New Jersey farm. These women shared a fierce independence, since they had each been raised predominantly by their mothers and were compelled to work at an early age.

As strong, independent, daring women, they danced to be a part of the earth and to express feelings and emotions, which came from their inner beings. These founding modern-dance women wanted to express what was natural to them. They didn't need binding corsets or pointe shoes, or forcing the five turned-out positions of the arms and legs. They strove to change the female dancing image by presenting women who were powerful, expressive, sensual, and spiritual, declaring modern dance to be high art.

Around 1892, this movement started with Loie Fuller throwing off her corset and shoes. With nature as an inspiration, she whirled and swirled long yards of China silk wrapped around sticks, creating the illusion of butterflies, lilies, and flames. Combined with the modern innovation of theatrical electric colored lights, Fuller seemed to make the lighted material magically dance, offering a picturesque presentation that made her the rage of Europe, a superstar in the art-nouveau movement. Toulouse-Lautrec painted posters of her, while products like lamps, furniture, and fashion were sold, capitalizing on her fame. With the industrial revolution and "La Loie," as she was often called, so the commodification of art became intensified.

Fuller introduced both Ruth St. Denis and Isadora Duncan to European audiences. Although Duncan toured with Fuller for a brief time in 1902, she had her own ideas about dance as a serious art. Believing the body was beautiful in its natural form, Isadora also threw off the suffocating, binding corset. She dared to dance solo on a bare stage to major symphonic music, barefoot in a silk, diaphanous Grecian gown. Thinking of dance as an expression of the soul, her inspiration came from nature—the movement of ocean waves, the wind, the earth—and she strove to communicate the connection she felt by seeking movement that was natural but not imitative. "Humanism, populism, and feminism" were key aspects to Isadora's expression promoting social change (Reynolds and McCormick 2003: 19).

It is often incorrectly stated that Duncan did not develop a technique. Her method may not have been codified by her or documented in print, but it was passed down bodily through generations. I learned her idiom by studying with Kay Bardsley, a second-generation Duncan dancer who had studied dance from childhood, exclusively with Maria Theresa Duncan, one of the Isadorables (Isadora's "adopted" daughters).

Isadora had taught Maria Theresa a solo entitled *Angel at the Tomb*, which she had choreographed during World War I, in 1914, in recognition of the Tomb of the Unknown Soldier. The music was Chopin's *Étude in E Flat Major*. The dance was about an angel who sees a tomb on Earth and floats down to urge the soul to come up to Heaven. Since Isadora taught Maria Theresa, and Maria Theresa taught Kay, I felt honored to be the third in a direct lineage to that dance.

Working with Kay enabled me to realize much about Duncan technique. Kay would say to me, "Connie, be more feminine." I would look back at her puzzled, wondering what she meant. What did it mean to be feminine in the early twentieth century compared to what it means to be feminine in the twenty-first century? Finally, I asked her how I could become more visibly feminine to suit the dance's needs. Her reply was that I must never stand in a parallel position, with my feet apart facing the audience straight on. For this dance, an early twentieth-century woman would stand with her knees touching, one leg bent, with the body twisted, to what Kay called "on the bias." The torso of the body was slightly rotated, with the head leaning more to one shoulder, projecting a softer image. *That* was feminine!

In addition to learning how to be "feminine" for *Angel at the Tomb*, I also learned that there were some very definite prescribed movements at certain points in the music. Kay pointed out that Isadora had such a thorough knowledge of the music, she would know where she was to be in space and what gesture she wanted to execute at certain precise moments. In between those music cues, she would let herself feel the music and dance in the moment according to whatever moved her.

For me, it was like a map with certain signposts. As long as I arrived at the point at the right moment, the rest of the timing and gestures could differ whenever I danced the solo. However, the improvisation had to be in keeping with Isadora's idiom and her movement style, which was slow and sustained. The more I could become that celestial angel, looking down on Earth, coaxing the soul, the more successful the solo.

Ruth St. Denis was the third founding mother of modern dance. As a disenchanted chorus-girl dancer, Ruthie Dennis, canonized "St. Denis" by impresario David Belasco, was inspired one day while sitting in a drugstore when she saw a poster of the Egyptian goddess Isis. She decided she wanted to dance the way she envisioned Isis and set out to create exotic expression. This led to further creations of "oriental" dances, later nicknamed the "eeses" since she explored Japanese, Javanese, Chinese, and Burmese dance, along with other Eastern dance forms. Although she did study some authentic Eastern dance, she borrowed, picked, and chose movements without trying to present authentic replications.

St. Denis had a savvy, entrepreneurial way of mixing dance with spirituality and entertainment while simultaneously titillating audiences with flesh revealed in colorful exotic costumes. Although she was successful in Europe, she returned to the USA, where she also gained fame, thus beginning the canon of modern dance.

Ted Shawn, who had seen St. Denis dance, set out to dance himself, and he ended up becoming known as the father of modern dance. His mission was to reinstate virile male dancing. Having studied to enter the ministry, he switched gears and took ballroom lessons until he worked his way to New York, where he met St. Denis. It was practically love at first sight. They married and, combining names, set up the Denishawn School in Los Angeles in 1915, training the first generation of modern dancers.

Doris Humphrey, Charles Weidman, and Martha Graham were three of those dancers who trained at, and performed the spectacles and exotic, theatrical dances of, the Denishawn Company. Eventually, each broke away to find a personal movement style. They wanted to find movement natural to their own body, not an invention based on the impression of another country's dance. No more "eeses." Psychological and sociological issues, emotions, and investigations of movement itself were topics for their dance explorations.

Louis Horst, who had been Music Director at Denishawn for ten years, left as well, eventually becoming Graham's mentor, composer, and lover for twenty-seven years. Having studied in Europe, Horst was introduced to, recognized the innovation of, and was interested in the new developments of modern art and German *Ausdruckstanz*. Upon his return, he showed photographs of them to Graham.

In Germany beginning in 1912, Rudolf Laban led a movement to express feelings, cultural tensions, and important ideas. This effort was continued by his student, Mary Wigman, who came to study with him in 1913 at the age of twenty-seven. She went on to inspire the development of European modern dance by using body projection and intense awareness of space and raw emotion. Using drums, silence, masks, gesture, and extreme concentration, her dances often appeared harsh, ugly, and intense, even when they were lyrical and tender. Her ability to create a dynamic relationship to the space around her became the impetus for further explorations from her student, Hanya Holm, who in turn influenced Alwin Nikolais and Murray Louis, among others in the USA. Scores of other European modern dancers benefited from Wigman's creative explorations and teachings as well, but that is another branch of history.

Attracted to Wigman's approach of developing movement independent of music, Horst composed music specifically for Graham's dances after they were choreographed, and they collaborated on Graham's first New York solo performance in 1926. Although, at first, some dances were reminiscent of the same kinds of dances she'd been doing with Denishawn, with Horst's prodding and criticism, she soon began developing her own movement explorations. Graham went on to create a vocabulary of movement derived from emotion. Believing that life was nervous, sharp, and zig-zag, Graham set out initially in parallel stance with flexed feet. She felt no compunction to hide the darker side of life and used percussive, angular, bound movement, which revealed the effort required for its execution.

For sixty-five years, until her death in 1991, Graham often choreographed dances centered on exceptional women, where she herself played the protagonist role. Although she never professed to being a feminist, she turned the gender tables on the ballet world, accustomed to seeing a prince with a female *corps de ballet* dancing around him, by having her own chorus of dancing women and often bare-chested men dancing around her.

Freudian and Jungian psychological dances, Greek myths, biblical, Native American, American pioneer, and literary themes served as Graham's subject matter. From her teaching and choreography she developed a distinct vocabulary, based on the breath and contraction and release, which became codified and is now institutionalized and taught around the world. As the first modern dancer to visit the White House in 1937, and the first American modern dancer to leave a codified dance technique, Martha Graham's extensive contributions have made her the matriarch of American modern dance.

The other Denishawn dancers, Doris Humphrey and Charles Weidman, left in 1928 to create the Humphrey–Weidman school. Charles Weidman had an affinity for comic dancing while Doris Humphrey began to explore movement "from the inside out," playing with how gravity effected movement in fall and recovery. She believed the most exciting movement was the moment of suspension just before the fall. Humphrey focused on abstract dance, music visualization, and experimentation with choreographic principles. These explorations culminated in her book, *The Art of Making Dances*, published a year after her death in 1958.

Hanya Holm, who had come to the USA to teach in Mary Wigman's New York City school, created her own style of dance based on the spatial concerns of her predecessors, which emphasized kinaesthetic awareness over emotionality. Graham, Humphrey, Weidman, and Holm, known as the Big Four, spent summers teaching and creating dances at Bennington College, beginning in 1934.

Another woman who created dances around the same time of the Big Four was Helen Tamiris. She had danced with the Metropolitan Opera, studying ballet with Michel Fokine, but renounced her classical training and set out to create social and political dances for the working-class and middle-class audiences. Today, she is remembered for her dances based on "Negro spirituals." In 1927, she presented her first solo program and then, believing everyone would benefit from joining together to share production expenses, initiated the Dance Repertory Theater. Tamiris invited Graham, Humphrey, and Weidman to take part but, probably due to conflict between artistic temperaments, it lasted only from 1930 to 1931.

A pioneer working outside of the New York modern dance scene was an African-American woman in Chicago named Katherine Dunham. She had studied ballet and character dance, performed in 1933 in Ruth Page's *Le Guiablesse*, and tried unsuccessfully to found her own black ballet company. As a student of anthropology at the University of Chicago, Dunham combined her love of dance with her studies and received a grant to go to the West Indies to research rituals and dances of Haiti in 1936–7.

When she returned, Dunham made her New York debut at the 92nd Street Y in 1937, in the "Negro Dance Evening" directed by Edna Guy and Allison Burroughs, where she combined elements of ballet, modern dance, Caribbean, and African movement. Dunham went on to be recognized for her talents and made it to Broadway, where she danced in and co-choreographed, with George Balanchine, *Cabin in the Sky*, a black musical.

Dunham's amazing career spanned six decades. In the 1940s and 1950s she ran the Dunham School of Dance, which became the training ground for African-American dancers. The Katherine Dunham Dance Company toured over fifty-seven countries, and she received ten honorary doctorates, as well as the Medal of the Arts, the Albert Schweitzer Prize at the Kennedy Center Honors, among others. As a political activist, she worked tirelessly to educate and spread understanding about racism and opened the Performing Arts Training Center for disadvantaged children in East Saint Louis.

As a dancer, choreographer, author, and political activist, Dunham is known as the matriarch of black dance, who went to her roots and to ritual to promote racial equality by showing that the African-American heritage is beautiful. Her groundbreaking work in directing theater, musicals, and education is unparalleled. She died in her Manhattan assisted living facility on May 21, 2006.

Pearl Primus was a Trinidadian-American dancer-choreographer who began dancing in the 1940s, sharing an interest in African dances and rituals similar to Dunham's. Primus graduated from Hunter College with a degree in biology and premedical studies and eventually completed her doctorate in anthropology at New York University in 1978. Her first dances, presented at the 92nd Street Y in 1943, showed a range of talent and interest in both African dancing as well as in the African-American experience. She performed dances that dealt with racial inequality (*Strange Fruit* [1943] and *The Negro Speaks of Rivers* [1944]) as well as dances that were based on her knowledge of African and Caribbean dance. She had a dance school in New York City, choreographed for Alvin Ailey, performed in Broadway musicals, and had her own dance company. She died October 29, 1994.

Neither Dunham nor Primus was readily accepted into the art world in the same way that Graham, Humphrey–Weidman and Holm had been. Although modern dance appeared to be more accepting than other occupations (Graham had a racially integrated company), times were still racially segregated. Due to the color of their skin, Dunham and Primus could find themselves barred from walking in the front door of the very theater in which they were performing. It was an altogether different ball game for black directors of modern dance companies.

Another dancer, who was not white but of Mexican heritage, was José Limón. He had studied with Humphrey–Weidman and grew under the tutelage of Humphrey's use of the breath and curvilinear movement. He created his own technique while attempting to reestablish virility and complexity for the role of male dancers. Limón formed his own company in 1946 and named Humphrey as the Artistic Director until her death in 1958. In 1954, the Limón Dance Company was the first modern dance group to be selected by the State Department to travel abroad for cultural exchange. Limón died of cancer in 1972. With the artistic direction taken over first by Ruth Currier, and then by Carla Maxwell in 1978, his company was the first to survive without its namesake.

Except for Katherine Dunham in Chicago, and a few summer dance programs in the 1930s, most of modern dance we learn about in the history books was centered in New York City. One known exception to this was on the West Coast, in Los Angeles, where Lester Horton began his own movement investigations. Fascinated by Native American, Aztec, African, and Haitian cultures, Horton developed his own technique while creating a racially mixed company. He died at the age of forty-seven in 1953.

Bella Lewitsky, Horton's lead dancer, remained on the West Coast in Los Angeles and continued his legacy for thirty-one years, with her own company founded in 1966. On the East Coast, some of Horton's other dancers who preserved his lineage were Alvin Ailey, Joyce Trisler, and James Truitte. Alvin Ailey's American Dance Center school in New York continues to offer a course in Horton technique.

The same year that Horton died, a young Alvin Ailey debuted in New York with a small group of other Horton dancers. In 1958, he formed what became known as the Alvin Ailey American Dance Theater, a New York-based company, preserving Horton's idea of a racially mixed company inclusive of black, Hispanic, and Asian dancers. In 1960, Ailey created his signature piece, *Revelations*, to spirituals, which are a series of dances, humorous, poignant, and utterly captivating to audiences. This piece has probably been performed more times and in more places than any other modern dance in existence. His company has continued to thrive, even after his death in 1989.

The first generation of modern dance choreographers developed their own technique, their own vocabulary of dancing. This was often done without knowledge of proper alignment or scientific base, but it was done as a means to find a distinctive way to move, creating personal expression. Their way of moving was then taught to eager students who wanted to perform with them.

Hundreds of people studied and danced with the first generation of artists, which then produced a second generation of modern dancers and choreographers. Although the techniques of the first generation were ingrained in the bodies of the second, individuals set out to transform movement into their own personal style. They were successful to various degrees, but each eventually had their own company. From Graham came Anna Sokolow, Sophie Maslow, Jane Dudley, May O'Donnell, Jean Erdman, and Pearl Lang, Erick Hawkins, Merce Cunningham, and Paul Taylor, among others. Humphrey–Weidman produced Eleanor King, Sybil Shearer, William Bales, and José Limón, and from the Holm school came Vallerie Bettis and Alwin Nikolais.

Some of these students who had studied and performed with the Big Four diverged from their teachers and radically changed the direction of modern dance. They wanted to dance about what seemed natural to them in the 1950s, which involved investigating movement itself, rather than exploring emotional content within movement. They asked why every movement always had to mean something. To them, the act of moving itself was enough to hold interest.

Merce Cunningham, who studied ballet at Balanchine's School of American Ballet and had danced with Martha Graham, broke away from her company in 1945. He had become friends with musician and composer John Cage, and the two of them set out to forge new theories. Cage, who had studied with Henry Cowell and Arnold Schoenberg, proclaimed that any sound, even stillness, could be music. His interest in Zen Buddhism, Eastern philosophy, and the *I Ching* (*The Book of Changes*), propelled the idea that anything, even if organized by chance, could be viewed as art. Cunningham paralleled these ideas in his approach to dancing, insisting that any movement could be dance. He asserted that movement, in and of itself, naturally had meaning if a human was performing it. Thus, all movement elicits emotion. He experimented with tossing coins to the *I Ching* for chance procedures to determine movement sequences in his choreography.

Believing that music, dance, lighting, and set design could exist independently as equal but separate arts, Cunningham juxtaposed these elements in the same time and space in his dance concerts. He appreciated the random, indeterminate possibilities that occurred when theatrical elements were interdependent on stage. That there was no predetermined conjoined idea left it up to the audience to find their own meaning or to focus attention on whatever they chose.

Much like walking down a city street, one person might focus on a truck honking, while another observed potted plants on a windowsill of a second-story building. Yet another might be walking along, absorbed by his or her own thoughts, oblivious to the surroundings, while someone else was tuning into the sounds and movements of nearby pigeons. Reflecting life's multiplicities, these things existed in the same time and space, and no one incident was "right" or should necessarily have more value than the other. And so it was for the viewer to watch Cunningham's dances. The meaning was whatever he or she gave to it.

In *The Art of Making Dances*, Doris Humphrey (1959) had assigned significance to certain areas of the stage, like the center, which she viewed as the most powerful place. Cunningham alleged that wherever someone was dancing was important, because the eye would naturally follow, so he gave equal value to every place onstage. Likewise, he veered from the frontal positioning of the body in choreography, believing that movement was interesting from all sides.

Cunningham's movement included a vertical balletic vocabulary, but it entailed isolation of body parts, "moving separately and sometimes in opposition to one another" (Reynolds and McCormick 2003: 361) with tilts, arches, curves, twists, and "rapid shifts of weight and direction" (ibid.: 361). What Graham had called the spinal contraction, Cunningham called a curve, separating it into three parts: a shoulder curve, middle-spine curve, and pelvic curve. He said the curve initiated from the back of the spine instead of Graham's image of "up the front."

Cunningham wanted his dancers to appear "natural" on stage, without emoting. He wanted his dancers to have genuine facial expressions, rather than forcing a smile or a superimposed emotion. Likewise, there was no star system among his dancers, but every dancer was viewed as a soloist. The women's hair didn't have to be tied back in a tight bun, giving them all the same look; dancers were individuals.

In 1954, the painter Robert Rauschenberg joined Cunningham as Designer and Production Manager, followed by avant-garde painter Jasper Johns. Thus began collaborations with cutting-edge composers and artists, such as Andy Warhol, David Tudor, Gordon Mumma, Pauline Oliveros, Charles Atlas, Mark Lancaster, Marsha Skinner, and Takehisa Kosugi, to name a few.

Cunningham created what he called an "Event," which involved taking excerpts from different dances, stringing them together without a pause, like a collage. This allowed him to be able to perform in any kind of space, from gymnasiums to proscenium stages, without requiring the theatrical effects of lighting, costuming, or proscenium seating. Often the dancers would be surrounded by the audience, and this created a more intimate atmosphere. Lasting about ninety minutes, "Events" became so popular that there have been hundreds of them.

As Cunningham aged, he changed his choreographic methods so that movement was not necessarily created on his own body. He was a pioneer in the computerized technology, Life Forms, beginning in 1989, premiering his first computer-choreographed dance, *Trackers*, in 1991. Probably Roger Copeland is correct in saying that Cunningham's approach to life and art would have led him to the use of computer technology even if his severe arthritis hadn't made it too difficult for him to physically choreograph standing up (Copeland 2004: 184). His experiments with technology have opened up a vast explorational artistic frontier.

In 1978, when I asked choreographers from *Further Steps* who had been the greatest influence on their art, without hesitation the majority said Merce Cunningham. This was surprising to me, given that some choreographers, like Louis Falco, hadn't even studied with him. Still, they had been exposed to his ideas and methodology, and that had left an indelible impression on their own thinking and creativity. Along with Isadora Duncan and Martha Graham, Merce Cunningham has had the greatest influence on modern dance in the twentieth century.

Around the same time that Cunningham began experimenting with new choreographic principles, another former Graham dancer broke away to begin forming his own theories of modern dance. His name was Erick Hawkins. He had studied Greek at Harvard, had been inspired by Isadora Duncan's *The Art of the Dance*, and had studied in Salzburg with Harald Kreutzberg and Yvonne Georgi. In 1934, Hawkins enrolled in the School of American Ballet, and two years later, he became an original member of Lincoln Kirstein's Ballet Caravan (Reynolds and McCormick 2003: 370).

Hawkins studied at Bennington with Graham, and, in 1938, he invaded the tight-knit female body of dancers to become the first male to join the Graham Company. For thirteen years, he partnered her, creating new roles in her dances. He also influenced her to expand her use of contemporary scores, to collaborate with sculptor Isamu Noguchi, and to use Greek themes. The two married in 1948.

In 1950, on their first London tour, Hawkins and Graham ended their marriage. Having sustained injuries while dancing in Ballet Caravan and in Graham's company, at the age of forty-one, Hawkins set out to find a more natural, less injurious way to dance. He had an idea to soften Graham's movement. Like Cunningham, Hawkins believed that dance didn't have to "mean" anything. Combining ideas from the influence of Zen, plus from the Yale philosopher F. S. C. Northrop, and from scientific principles of anatomy and movement, Hawkins created a new and distinct approach to modern dance.

Using a Zen-like idea to create unity of body and soul, Hawkins decided that dance should be effortless, without revealing tension or rigidity. From Northrop, he developed a normative theory of dance and concluded that just because movement is possible does not make it desirable. He would use the example of lifting the leg to over 180 degrees: Just because it was humanly possible did not make it necessarily aesthetically desirable or worthy of choreographic inclusion. Athletic tricks were not impressive to Hawkins, quality of movement was.

He set out to understand scientific principles of movement, based on anatomy and kinesiology. Mabel Ellsworth Todd's book from 1937, *The Thinking Body: A Study of the*

Balancing Forces of Dynamic Man, and later, Lulu E. Sweigard's *Human Movement Potential*, published in 1975, were key contributions to Hawkins' theory that movement should be executed in accordance with alignment while using the least amount of effort possible to execute the movement beautifully and precisely. He based his movement technique on the idea that there are no straight lines in the universe, so why should there be in dance? In order to get to a place, one moved either in undercurves or overcurves, and the extremities were viewed as tassels to the core of the body. Pelvic and spinal initiation and movement from the center became key elements to his technique.

In keeping with the wholeness of Eastern philosophy, in direct contrast to Cunningham, who separated the various theatrical elements (dance, music, lighting, costumes, and set design), Hawkins integrated them. He insisted that music was composed specifically for his choreography and was always performed live. This led to a partnership with composer Lucia Dlugoszewski, whom he eventually married. He saw to it that the sets, costumes, props, and masks were created beforehand so that the choreography could synthesize the elements into a unified whole, and he found designer-sculptor Ralph Dorazio to create them.

In addition, he went back to Isadora Duncan's beliefs in "natural dancing" to find "the true nature of the human body and of human movement in order to find beautiful dance art" (Brown 1971/2: 8). In keeping with Duncan's beliefs, he wrote that dance should use "virtuosity only in the service of 'poetry,' not as acrobatics misconceived as art" (Hawkins 1979: 33).

Critics often labeled his sustained movement presentation as "noodling about." Some even called it boring. Hawkins' technique is one of the most misunderstood and underappreciated techniques in modern dance. By concentrating on noninjurious movement and creating another approach to dancing, in the form of free-flow technique, Hawkins influenced enormous numbers of dancers. Today's look of uncontrolled abandon, easy, throw-away movement stems from his free-flow technique, now popularly called "release technique."

Perhaps more appreciated for his technique than choreography, Hawkins taught and choreographed for over forty years. He died at the age of eighty-five in 1994. Dlugoszewski died in 2000, and, since her death, the company has disbanded.

Another choreographer of the same generation as Cunningham and Hawkins was Alwin Nikolais. He had seen a performance in 1933 by Mary Wigman, then studied dance with Truda Kashman, a Wigman disciple, in Hartford, Connecticut, before studying with the Big Four at Bennington. He gravitated to the teachings of Hanya Holm and became her teaching assistant, before being appointed in 1948 as Codirector of the modern dance program at the Henry Street Playhouse. There he trained a group of dancers, among whom was Murray Louis. Louis eventually became his partner and collaborator for forty-four years, until Nikolais' death in 1993.

Nikolais was best known for his dance philosophy, promoting dance as motion, not emotion. His choreography emphasized clarity of spatial, temporal, and sculptural components. He integrated all theatrical elements, creating a multimedia phantasmagoria of motion, where all the elements (light, sound, color, shapes, movement, props, costumes) had equal importance, fusing into total theater. Early on, he created taped sound music and worked with multiple slide projections, designing everything himself. Often the dancers would be enveloped in fabric or obscured by props or masks, which presented magical illusions devoid of recognizable bodies.

Though some critics found his work dehumanizing, others found the illusionist effects wildly entertaining and creative. His work appeared on television in 1959, and the company achieved popularity in the USA and Europe throughout the 1970s. Nikolais greatly increased the popularity of modern dance by making it more accessible and entertaining to a wide audience.

Someone who briefly danced with Merce Cunningham in 1953 and who began his own experimentation with stretching the definition of dance was Paul Taylor. He also had danced off and on with Martha Graham from 1955 to 1962, before breaking away to form his own company in 1962. Taylor created *Duet*, during which he stood onstage in stillness next to the equally still but seated Toby Armour, for four minutes. The review Louis Horst wrote for *Dance Observer* mimicked the dance in that it was four inches of blank space, with the initials "L.H." at the bottom of the review.

After testing the waters of radicalism, Taylor returned to his roots and created more traditional pieces with his own piquant twist. He has choreographed over 100 dances, and his company continues to travel the world as a preeminent representative of American modern dance.

The definition of modern dance was continually tested, stretched, and radicalized. On July 6, 1962, a series of free dance performances began at the Judson Memorial Church in Greenwich Village that has been called "the most radical dance movement since the late 1920's" (Reynolds and McCormick 2003: 383). The Judson Dance Theater was a collective of dancers, artists, and musicians "whose sometimes outrageous experimentation changed the course of modern dance" (Perron 2001: 25), and was the fomentation of what came to be called "postmodern dance."

Influences leading up to the Judson performances included the Cage–Cunningham idea that any sound could be music or any movement could be dance. Anna Halprin, from the West Coast, influenced many dancers, including Yvonne Rainer, Simone Forti, Trisha Brown, and, later, Meredith Monk and Sally Gross, with her "task dances" and "celebration of the ordinary human body"(Perron 2001: 25). She created happening-like events on city streets or in natural surroundings and used improvisation as a creative source.

Absurdist ballet choreographer James Waring developed an avant-gardist following due to his inane juxtapositioning of the serious, the irreverent, and nonsensical humor, accompanied by outlandish costumes and crazy props of his own design. Rainer and David Gordon studied with him.

In 1960, pianist Robert Dunn was asked by John Cage to teach a composition class at the Cunningham studio. Rainer, Forti, and Steve Paxton were among the first students. Dunn's approach picked up on Cage's and Cunningham's experimental methods, as well as their embrace of Eastern philosophies. His teachings stressed process compared to what Horst had taught as more traditional, formulaic compositional procedures.

By 1962, students wanted a place to perform and share their work. Associate minister, Al Carmines, who was already providing facilities for poetry readings, happenings, and other controversial art activities, was approached and offered the use of Judson Church. Thus began a series of free concerts that lasted until 1964.

> The Judson Dance Theatre evolved into a democratic group committed to breaking the rules of conventional theatrical dance. Rehearsing and performing in the Judson Memorial Church, dancers, visual artists, poets, and musicians concerned themselves

with movement from everyday life; there was often no emphasis on technique. Structure could come from a children's game, from play or sports, or from any movement, gesture, or posture, and it could use total energy exertion (Carol Schneemann's *Lateral Splay*, 1963) or little at all (Steve Paxton's *Transit*, 1962, or David Gordon's *Mannequin Dance*, 1962). The dancers could perform in street clothes or in the nude (*Word Words*, 1963, by Steve Paxton and Yvonne Rainer); they could be barefoot or wear sneakers. They performed in parks, churches, museums, outdoors, or in any available space. By incorporating ordinary gestures and mundane events, such as putting on plastic curlers or moving furniture, by bringing what was previously thought of as nondance onto the performance space (whatever the surface), the choreographers turned conventional reality into unconventional dance.

(Kreemer 1987: 4)

The legacy of Judson Dance Theater, as Perron so aptly put it, "is the possibility of total permissiveness and freedom, on one hand, and the wish to pare down to essentials, on the other" (Perron 2001: 28). Yvonne Rainer's now monumentally important treatise on modern dance, *Trio A* (1966), embodied the new postmodern dance aesthetics by saying no to almost everything modern dance represented up until that point. Rainer influenced a whole genre of dance-makers.

Next came the Grand Union—a collective group consisting of Rainer and dancers who worked with her: Becky Arnold, Douglas Dunn, David Gordon, Barbara Dilley Lloyd, Steve Paxton, and additional dancers Trisha Brown, Nancy Lewis (Green), and Lincoln Scott. This was a group that took turns leading, by often conducting "anarchic games that were boring or dissatisfying in their lack of resolution" (Reynolds and McCormick 2003: 406).

Steve Paxton, colleague of Rainer and participant of Judson and Grand Union, had also danced with Limón and Cunningham. He continued his own explorations and went on to found contact improvisation in 1972. "Contact improv" involved partnering someone and improvising together while maintaining bodily contact with a give and take of weight, lifting and being lifted, and using the floor in rolls, tumbles, falls, and balances that resembled wrestling. The emphasis was on the performers sensing each other's weight as well as their own, and, in so doing, the process of improvising became more important than communicating or performing to an audience. This "technique" has directly influenced today's look in dance because so many choreographers use it as a way to find movement.

Trisha Brown, David Gordon, Twyla Tharp, and Mark Morris are other choreographers who have made significant contributions to furthering the contemporary look of dance today. Reductive, accumulative movement, equipment dances, and formal patterns were explored by Brown, while Gordon pursued more theatrical "performance art"-like events, sometimes with text.

Twyla Tharp, who had danced with Paul Taylor, struck out on her own, first exploring minimalism but then going on to combine other dance forms such as jazz, tap, ballroom, ballet, and popular dances. Her eclectic choices in popular music from Jelly Roll Morton (*Eight Jelly Rolls*, 1971), or the Beach Boys (*Deuce Coupe*, 1973), to David Byrne of Talking Heads (*The Catherine Wheel*, 1981), to Frank Sinatra (*Nine Sinatra Songs*, 1982), along with her loose, throwaway movement, which was so precise it could stop on a dime, provided entertainment and accessibility that popularized modern dance and expanded over into the ballet world.

Like Tharp, Mark Morris embraced a pluralism of dance idioms by combining his early studies of folk dance, flamenco, and fencing with ballet and modern dance. Unlike his predecessors of the Judson era, he reintroduced a respect for musicality and tradition, but he added his own touch of humor and irreverence. For this, he was greeted as a breath of fresh air by the dance world, weary of the dry tediousness of the preceding postmodern dance.

With the advent of contact improvisation, more and more technique incorporated use of the floor. Gymnastic handstands and rolls were introduced from the influence of yoga, aikido, and capoeira. Pilates, Klein floor barre, Feldenkrais, Alexander Technique, rolfing, acupuncture, and tai chi also melded philosophies and movement into modern dance techniques. With the Judson and Grand Union's pedestrian explorations interweaving with the free-flow technique of Erick Hawkins, the philosophies of Merce Cunningham, Nikolais-Louis, Hawkins, Limón's movement with breath, along with the loose and fast-flung movement of Twyla Tharp and Tricia Brown, these movement disciplines furthered the distinctive look to modern dance.

Even in the 1970s, during the postmodern phase of labeling dance "movement for movement's sake," "what you see is what you get," many choreographers were communicating meaning through symbolism and gesture in their movements. Postmodern dance was never entirely "one thing," one presentation of an idea, but perhaps the press emphasized and promoted it that way. Certainly, Kei Takei, Mel Wong, Meredith Monk, Kenneth King, and Nancy Meehan were communicating something beyond pure movement. In the early 1980s, most dance reviews stated that the movement wasn't supposed to mean anything, and that would frequently puzzle me because when I saw performances I would often come away uplifted in a metaphoric, emotional, or spiritual way. Many dances had communicated more to me than just movement.

The above history is the Eurocentric (or should I say US-centric?) linear version of modern/postmodern/contemporary dance. What about the sociocultural/political version? Rock 'n' roll also played a large part in influencing modern dance. Twyla Tharp used the music of the Beach Boys and hip movement got looser, but who most influenced the movement of rock 'n' roll? African Americans. What roles have James Brown and Eleo Pomare played in our dance history? Elvis and other white musicians may have popularized and legitimized it, but African Americans were the originators. The history of dance in the USA still needs more research and incorporation of all branches of dance, regardless of race.

With the above chronological, linear historical overview, where does that leave us in terms of the words "modern dance," "postmodern" or "contemporary dance?" What is it called now? Modern dance has always been a relatively obscure art form. As I travel around the country meeting people from different walks of life, I find that the majority of Americans do not have a clue about what modern dance is. I am usually greeted with fascinated or quizzical blank stares when I tell them I teach and write about modern dance. "Modern dance? What is that?" Many think modern dance means popular dance—whatever the current dance fad is—from salsa to hip-hop, swing, or tango. Students can be very surprised when they've enrolled in a modern-dance class only to learn that it isn't "popular dance"— the current fashionable steps young people do at clubs, parties, or raves. So, if it's not popular dance, what is modern dance? That begins the process of explaining what it is or isn't.

I usually ask if they've heard of Martha Graham. If people haven't heard of her, and increasingly unfortunately they haven't, then we must start at the beginning. Some have heard of her but offer stereotyped ideas about what she represented. Students will say that modern dance is "free form," or "ugly." Often they will say that ballet is "strict and formal," while modern is "free," "uncontrolled," "improvisational," or "loose." Or, they say that modern dance has "no technique." These stereotypes incorrectly imply that modern dance is somehow "easier" than ballet and often unattractive and undesirable.

From there, I usually begin describing what modern dance "isn't," because, without seeing it, it's perhaps easier for people to understand what it *isn't*, rather than what it *is*. Modern dance is not jazz, tap, social dance, African, any national dance, or ballet, but it can use or borrow steps from all of the above. It often uses the same five positions as ballet, as well as the same turn-out from the hip socket, but it doesn't have to. Modern dance can be improvisational, but it is not always improvised; in fact, usually it is choreographed. And modern dance most definitely involves technique and requires training and extreme control and knowledge of the body.

From this conversation, students will then ask how it differs from Broadway dance or dancing in musicals. Those questions lead to a discussion of art and how modern dance comes closer to the sensibility of a modern or contemporary art painting. I usually end the discussion by saying that it's difficult to describe modern dance, but Selma Jeanne Cohen's definition in *Modern Dance: Seven Statements of Belief* sums it up, stating "modern dance is a point of view," "an art of iconoclasts" (Cohen 1965: 14).

Is modern dance a period in time that began with the early pioneers (Fuller, Duncan, St. Denis) which continued up until the Cunningham era? Beginning with Judson in the 1960s, is everything else postmodern dance? These are easy and convenient chronological categorizations—if life could be so neatly packaged—but what then is contemporary dance? Is it twenty-first-century concert dance? Or, are the words "modern dance," a loose term, interchangeably connecting and connoting concert dance?

I decided to conduct a little research on my own, to see what labels the major dance universities use. Most of the major dance schools in the USA still list their courses as "modern dance." A few call it "contemporary dance." Some have a postmodern dance course, but, for the most part, technique classes continue to be called "modern dance."

Concert dance today, regardless of what it's called, is distinguishable from the look of earlier modern-dance techniques because there can be a throwaway looseness to it, an ease with the floor, with upside-down limbs and head, and curvilinear movement in contrast to the more vertical, bound, and shaped movement from the first two generations of modern dance.

Another major difference today is that students no longer study with just one choreographer to learn their mentor's technique. Instead, all of the above-mentioned somatic classes can be explored, along with ballet and almost any other kind of dance form, from African, Middle Eastern, to flamenco, Balinese, and beyond. Globalization has increased the fusion of cultures, art, world music, and dance.

So, rather than study one technique, students now investigate many dance and somatic possibilities and, thus, bring their own body explorations to the choreographer. In the twenty-first century, technical codified dance that is choreographer-led is perhaps no longer the norm. Much work now is site-specific rather than made for the theater, cross-disciplinary, and it can be devised in collaboration among all the participating artists, including the dancers.

The next generation of postmodern dancers were the choreographers who I included in the first edition of *Further Steps*, which was published in 1987. Most of the original participants have remained in New York, but Kei Takei returned to live in her native Japan. Gail Conrad is in Los Angeles. Mel Wong moved to Hong Kong, then Boulder, Col. before finally settling in Santa Cruz, Calif. Rosalind Newman also moved to Hong Kong for ten years, then to London, but recently she returned to New York, while Dan Wagoner went first to London, then to New London, Conn., and eventually down to Tallahassee, Fla. Lucinda Childs moved to Martha's Vineyard, but works predominantly in Europe, while Molissa Fenley divides her time between New York and Oakland, Calif. each year.

Eleven of the choreographers included in this book were selected because they participated in interviews in *Further Steps* twenty-five to thirty years ago. Due to distance and time constraints, Kei Takei and Gail Conrad, both of whom also participated in the first book, were unable to be included.

Sadly, three of the original fifteen, Louis Falco, Arnie Zane, and Mel Wong, passed away since the first publication. When Routledge first contracted me to write this book, in 2003, I knew that I would reinterview all the initial choreographers from *Further Steps*. I asked my husband, Mel Wong, if I could interview him, and he replied, "How many have you done already?" I said, "None, you'd be the first." He retorted, "Get a few under your belt before you interview me." Tragically, he died suddenly of a heart attack before I had a chance to interview him. Having known each other for twenty-five years, married for almost twenty, as mother of our three daughters, dancer with, manager of, and Associate Director of the Mel Wong Dance Company, I have written for him, how I think he would have responded, using his words wherever possible.

To provide a broader perspective of the developments in modern dance, three more choreographers were added: Rennie Harris, Doug Varone, and Jawole Zollar. These three have emerged since the 1980s as innovators in the field and were selected because of the new directions they have taken. Varone is based in New York; Zollar rehearses there but teaches in Tallahassee, Fla.; and Harris is based in Philadelphia.

Each of these fourteen choreographers has at one time been the rage in the contemporary dance world. Those who were part of the first edition of *Further Steps* have been around for several decades now, and, as they have aged, they have achieved various degrees of success. Of the three newly added choreographers, all are either in their forties or beyond, so they are "seasoned" artists as well.

In hindsight, the 1970s and 1980s were the golden age of dance for this country, and New York was viewed as the center of the dance world. I thought it would be interesting to trace the changes in dance over the past thirty years, by looking at where these choreographers are today.

Although the reasons to pare down or leave New York are as varied as the choreographers, many of their choices were dictated by financial concerns. Some of the artists found themselves recognized no longer as the "flavor of the month," as Rosalind Newman so aptly put it. In addition to that, in 1990, the National Endowment for the Arts (NEA), which had been a major support for so many of these artists, found itself involved in a major controversy, which ultimately resulted in the diminution of its support base (see *National Endowment for the Arts* vs. *Finley*). This caused artists to have to scramble for funds, to increase private donorship, and to run dance companies more like business corporations with an active board of directors. Of the original fifteen choreographers, only Bill T. Jones and Meredith Monk, both of whom have won MacArthur Awards, have continued to expand their companies. The rest have either scaled back or reconfigured.

As in the first book, the choreographers participated in a two-hour taped interview, which was then transcribed. Using only their words, I wrote up a statement for each, which was then approved by them. Due to the many questions, the statements may not appear to flow as seamlessly as in a written essay. The text reads like a conversation. It is not intended to be formal, as if each person wrote a literary statement. For me, the conversational tone conveys more intimacy, because it's as if the reader is there in the room, listening to each artist speak.

As in the first edition of *Further Steps*, there were some who wanted to write their own statements, so the formality is more evident. Kenneth King wrote his own statement, and Douglas Dunn participated in an interview but rewrote his own version based on the interview, sometimes making up the questions (and attributing them to me) for his own purposes.

I asked each choreographer the same questions so that the reader can compare the responses and draw conclusions. The questions were:

1. During the past twenty-five to thirty years, what major events in your life or in the world have affected your art? How?
2. How has your work evolved and changed from twenty-five years ago?
3. What are your thoughts on the following in relation to creating dances, and how have these thoughts or situations affected your art?

    (a) Race
    (b) Age
    (c) Gender
    (d) Environment (choose any or all to comment on):

        (i) Political
        (ii) Economic
        (iii) Geographic
        (iv) Social.

4. How have your ideas about the body and dance changed over the years?

As in any conversation, the discussion took on its own path, depending on what particularly interested the artists, so the emphasis and direction of each interview are varied.

It is evident from my questions that I have an interest in how race, age, gender, and environment affected each choreographer. This is the origin of the acronym "RAGE." Rage also suggests the idea of "what is hot" (popular), or it can refer to anger or disgust with current realities of the dance world. It is up to the reader to discern which rage prevails.

Concerning many of the questions, I kept being reminded of Don Miguel Ángel Ruiz's book, *The Four Agreements*, where he urged the reader, as part of the second agreement, not to take anything personally, because what someone says is more about themselves than it is about the person to whom they are speaking. When each artist answered the questions, they were speaking about themselves and their own experience. Often those experiences differed vastly from choreographer to choreographer, regardless of skin color. A perfect example of this had to do with the topic of race.

Gus Solomons jr was a case in point. As an African American, he gave the reverse answer of what would be expected concerning racism. (Perhaps it was racist of me, just because he is African American, to have expected him to answer otherwise.) He said that "race is not an issue in downtown Manhattan," where most modern dance takes place. He thought since Martha Graham had integrated her company early on, there was a "tradition" of mixed races, and there was no problem in his eyes. In fact, he said he had been criticized for not having a more racially mixed company, but since he wasn't "dancing about being black, didn't feel compelled to seek out black dancers." Perhaps this positive step, exhibited in modern dance, should be acknowledged as an affirmation that change is beginning to happen. That an African-American male would not feel racism in his profession is grounds for celebration.

Many of these choreographers shared his opinion. In their minds, modern dance always had been racially mixed since Graham's era. Seeing Horton's and Graham's integrated companies created an acceptance in this generation of dancers, so no problem was perceived, and they believed there never had been one within modern dance. Some said they were not affected by race because they were not dancing about it. Doug Varone pointed out that "the physical nature of how we move and how we speak" is a "universal thing" and that dance reflects the diversity in life. Another artist commented that he had never noticed racist behavior among dancers, nor did he "experience the scene as racist, or even 'racial.'"

As Zollar said, "Race is a difficult subject for this country to tackle, and it will probably continue to be until we come to terms with it." It is a very awkward subject, and no one wants to get caught saying something that could be construed as racist. Unfortunately, many of the choreographers rescinded much of what they said about race, not wanting it published. Fortunately, it is true that for a long time much of modern dance has been racially integrated, and, on a one-to-one basis, overt racism may not be apparent. Further steps, concerning racism, are forging ahead.

In the past, I would have blithely agreed with the above ideas that racism is nonexistent within modern dance, because I am a blonde, blue-eyed, Caucasian American female who never encountered it. My naive eyes were jarringly opened to a vastly different world by living with and being married to a Chinese-American dancer/choreographer. I learned that as a white person my privilege was such that it only *felt* like there was no racism around me. What I experienced living with Mel Wong was an entirely different story.

We all know that racism and discrimination have existed and continue to exist in the USA. All we have to do is watch the news (in December 2006, and April 2007 as I write this) to see *Seinfeld*'s television star Michael Richards mouthing off at African Americans, calling them the "N" word; Rosie O'Donnell making fun of the Chinese language; or Don Imus calling the Rutgers girls basketball team a group of "nappy-headed hos" to realize that racism (and sexism) is still prevalent. Racism and discrimination are insidious. Prevalent but difficult to prove without hard facts, the situations encountered in racism often make the facts elusive; they remain intangible feelings and suspicions. An example of this nebulous gray area is grant-funding and touring for dance companies.

Jawole Zollar differed from the choreographers who said there was never a problem of racism in modern dance.

> Dance can't exist outside society, and we are subject to all of the same issues that are in the larger society. Racism is white skin privilege, and you can't not have your privilege. It's just there and it's part of the picture. It's about power and who protects that power.

In *The Black Dancing Body*, Brenda Dixon Gottschild wrote:

> Race is not a biological imperative but a social construct convenient for purposes of classification and differentiation [. . .] We need to address peoples in terms of context, culture, and attitudes, not race.
>
> (Dixon Gottschild 2003: 5)

> Here we are living in the twenty-first century, talking about black dance and black dancers! What are we really talking about? A prejudice? A stereotype? An ideal? A limitation? And if I speak of black dance and a black dancing body, then is there also a white dancing body, an Asian dancing body, and so on? How and what differentiates these separate bodies? Who has the final word on what it is they do? Who is studying them? Where? And to what end? How is the information being gathered? If we let go of the concept of race, then where would we hang our racism?
>
> (Dixon Gottschild 2003: 6)

In *Butting Out*, Ananya Chatterjea wrote: "Racial and cultural difference are matters neither personal nor ontological, but of construction, and need to be understood through critical engagement" (Chatterjea 2004: xiv). She wrote about conversations taking place in

> bichromatic terms; white versus the rest, a tendency that only reifies the picture and prevents vital dialogues across populations of color. It is important not to write about artists of color only reactively, only in terms of an over-arching racism where one dominant culture dictates the terms of dialogue between all other cultures. Ultimately, this creates a reductive picture where the only conversation of race relations is one where the struggle is always to assert one's identity against the dominance of whiteness.
>
> (Chatterjea 2004: 13)

Halifu Osumare suggested that the label of "black dance" is divisive because it creates a racial continuum of white versus black. Mel Wong would say that there should be other colors besides black and white in this discussion, because the reds, browns, and yellows get left out.

It is not my intention to write a Eurocentric historiography, but I also realize that it's difficult for me not to, because Eurocentrism is engrained in my every fiber. Up until very recently, it has been the silent, unquestioned, standard educational approach in the USA. I recognize that white privilege prevails and, as the dominant culture in the hegemony, dictates the dialogue. Other races in this country are always struggling against the white dominant hierarchy. I agree with Chatterjea that the history of dance should not be learned as straight chronology and linearity. Subaltern studies need to be expanded. The window to that has been opened, and history is unfolding in a new way with important research changing and offering different interpretations and perspectives.

Even within the field of dance history, up until recently, racism has been discussed in hushed, behind-the-scenes tones, but, gradually, an alternative dance history is being formulated. After all, dance history is still a young field. It is up to all scholars to enrich our history by broadening the perspectives, exposing and celebrating cultural diversity. Thankfully, that is beginning to happen.

It is my intention in this book to present many points of view, knowing full well that no one book can contain the entire elusive history of modern dance. For example, to date, there is no history of Asian-American modern dance in the USA. We may never know of the Asian Americans, if there were any, who struggled to produce modern dance in the 1940s or 1950s in the USA, because there was no press coverage of their attempts. The same goes for other Mexican Americans or Latinos who were perhaps not as fortunate as José Limón to be able to take modern dance classes and pursue choreography.

Racism has always existed within the dance world, just like in the rest of American culture. Even as a revolutionary woman at the forefront of "modernism," Isadora Duncan still was not above being a product of her times when she expressed sentiments of racism by writing: "It seems to me monstrous for anyone to believe that the Jazz rhythm expresses America. Jazz rhythm expresses the South African savage" (Duncan 1928: 49). She continued by comparing the Charleston to "ape-like convulsions" and then asserting that American dance "will have nothing in it, either of the servile coquetry of the ballet or the sensual convulsion of the South African Negro. It will be clean" (Duncan 1928: 49).

Likewise, the circumstances surrounding the racial interactions of Ruth St. Denis and Ted Shawn reveal the prevailing prejudices of the time. Edna Guy, a young African-American woman from Summit, NJ, began contacting St. Denis by letter, beginning in 1922. She wanted to study at Denishawn to "be the first colored girl to make the world see that a little Negro girl, an American, can do beautiful and creative dances" (Lacy and Zucker 2001). St. Denis first told her to get more dance training, then put her off a second time, dodging her request by telling her how gifted she was (Lacy and Zucker 2001).

Edna Guy then tried to train in a new school of aesthetic dance, "beyond Harlem" but was told "some of the girls didn't like to have a colored girl in their class," and she was not allowed to take dance lessons there. St. Denis replied to Guy's second request by writing, "Dear Girlie, Concerning conditions in the big city, you are a very ignorant little girl and some things cannot be forced or hurried"(Lacy and Zucker 2001).

To give St. Denis the benefit of the doubt, perhaps she realized that most of America was not ready for integrated dance classes or performances, and it was not she, herself, who was against it. Either way, the situation kept Guy from breaking the barriers she so desired and attempted to traverse. In *Divine Dancer*, Suzanne Shelton stated that St. Denis was "vaguely anti-Semitic."

> Her only mention of anti-Semitism was an entry in her diary in which she told of defending a Denishawn dancer whom Ted alleged was undermining the school because of her Jewishness. Ruth might well have approved of a quota system as part of public policy, however [but she] did not display any sort of bigotry in her private behavior.
>
> (Shelton 1981: 222)

The above does not necessarily mean that St. Denis and Shawn were not racist. Perhaps being racist against African Americans was considered so "normal" at the time that it was only against lighter-skinned Jews that it seemed discriminatory. Zollar pointed out that there are "degrees of racism, degrees of acceptance within the construct." In fact, journalist Lynne Conner said that Guy was "not pretty enough or light enough in color. She never got a job dancing. She was too dark for the chorus line and the wrong color for modern dance" (Lacy and Zucker 2001). Skin color is something Zollar brought up in reference to Katherine

Dunham and Pearl Primus, believing that lighter skin for blacks was more acceptable and helpful in getting ahead in the entertainment world as well.

Guy was finally admitted into the Denishawn school in 1924, but, after three years of training, was only able to perform in the in-house recitals. By 1930, it became evident to Guy that she would never be allowed to dance in the company of St. Denis when she was eventually given the more servile role of Seamstress and Wardrobe Assistant. Disheartened, she left and went on with Hemsley Winfield to organize the "First Negro Dance Recital in America" in 1931, which consisted of shared programming by African-diaspora artists (DeFrantz 2002: 27).

Ted Shawn and Ruth St. Denis reinforced the prevailing racist attitudes of their time. Martha Graham commented in her autobiography that Miss Ruth didn't find her attractive enough because she had dark hair and eyes. "I wasn't beautiful. I was not blond and I did not have curly hair. These were the Denishawn ideals" (Graham 1991: 66). That description sounds almost Aryan in preference, or white Protestant Anglo-Saxon at the very least.

Shawn likewise revealed his evolutionist theory about the "primitive simplicity" of the "savage," and the "unsophistication of the Negroes" in regard to their "emotional structure and in their mental and spiritual development." He apparently believed that the Negro was less evolved, and there was a "great naiveté" in the race, concluding it meant that "the natural movements of the body are not sinful to them," and "their dances are innocently sensual" (Foster 1986: 162).

There is evidence as well that the early dance critics perpetuated racism by referring to "primitive dance." Writers such as deMille, Sorell, Terry, Martin, and Haskell wrote many of the first dance-history books, which contained sections on primitive dance, with a separate section of "black dance history". It was up to the anthropologist Joann Kealiinohomoku, in 1969, to finally dispel the myth by stating that "there is no such thing as a 'primitive dance' form" and that "those who teach courses called 'primitive dance' are perpetuating a dangerous myth" (Dils and Albright 2001: 37).

Just as there are degrees of racism in terms of skin color, so there are degrees of racism towards different races. Since 9/11, and as the Iraq war continues, Muslims in the USA have been seen in a different light. Asian and black communities are also "racialized differently in the United States," and "necessarily cast in a 'pecking' hierarchical order in a sociopolitical structure that is predicated upon a pernicious racism" (Chatterjea 2004: 17).

Mel Wong spoke about Asian Americans as the "silent minority." He felt they were overlooked and underappreciated. On the one hand, they are exploited for working hard for little pay, while at the same time detested for undercutting white peoples' jobs by working hard. He felt that Asian Americans had not been welcomed or assimilated into Western culture, and I witnessed this attitude one evening in 1983, when a man in the Pocono Mountains in Buck Hill Falls, Pa., asked Mel, quite literally, "When did you get off the boat?" The man was merely making conversation and seemed oblivious to or unconcerned about the fact that he was condescending to Mel. Mel was a fourth-generation American. Did the man ask me, the blonde, blue-eyed Caucasian, when I got off the boat? Certainly not.

Rennie Harris spoke about realizing that racism had affected his whole life and art. From going into prisons where the inmates told him racism was the reason they were there, to feeling like his hip-hop dancing was being viewed and judged as mere entertainment not meant to be political, Harris stated that hip-hop "is just another extension of Black African-

American culture in this country." The "good and the bad" are always there, and "we can't not acknowledge that it doesn't exist. You can't have the one without the other. If you're going to see the greatness and beauty of what it is, you have to see the death, pain and suffering, because they both go hand in hand." With this in mind, along with fantastic athleticism of dancing, Harris has sometimes presented the darker side of life, like when he had his dancers fall to the floor every time the poem said, "Die nigga."

By going back into his culture to "learn, be proactive and proud about the culture," as his company performs, Harris is helping others learn and be proud as well. For him, that idea expanded beyond skin color to "being human," which resulted in him trying to acknowledge being present now, aware that we are "unevolved humans on the planet."

Both Bill T. Jones and Gus Solomons jr said that being a black man was much more complex than the color of skin. If a black man has Eurocentric cultural tastes and doesn't fit in to the stereotypic black dance scene, is he less black? Jones pointed out that skin color is only the superficial outer layer and that the nuances of a person are what make him whole, though the nuances may not be immediately perceivable. When queried by the *San Francisco Chronicle* about black dance, Donald Byrd said that if you're African American and you make work, it's African American, but "presenters and funders tend to think that if it doesn't look like the African diaspora maybe it's not African American" (Howard 2007). He further stated that if choreographers do not fulfill the preconceptions of what "black dance" is, they "can find their accomplishments minimized" (Howard 2007). He believed subtle racist factors remain, which expect African Americans to "just get out there and dance," without any "choreography or intellect behind it" (Howard 2007).

The idea prevails today that people of color must fit into their cultural stereotype, and yet, other assumptions are made within categorizations. Because Mel Wong came from the Cunningham company, he was judged as descending from the same Eurocentric aesthetic, and critics incorrectly categorized his dances as "Mercist." Wong's cultural heritage, which played an important role in his art, went unrecognized.

Categorizations and preconceptions feed racism. When Alonzo King, of Lines Ballet, was asked whether racism existed in dance he replied, "Oh, my God, yes! Why do the large ballet companies look like they do in 2007, with one or two token blacks, when we have stellar black dancers who have to go to Europe? Because the companies say one or two is enough" (Howard 2007). King's solution was, "You have to obliterate any 'ism,'" by starting with the self and peeling away the layers of the "onion of identity" that include age, sex, race, and gender (Howard 2007).

Lucinda Childs brought up the idea of racism concerning the possibility of children having access to dance class. Minority children may not have access to dance class due to living in inner-city ghettos. Doesn't that have even more to do with classism? Doesn't that really speak to both racism and classism? Jawole Zollar lived in a segregated neighborhood, but, with a father in real estate, she was still afforded the opportunity of dance classes. Those who are impoverished have little possibility for dance training. Then, of course, with Rennie Harris, being impoverished in Philadelphia meant that the whole culture danced, and his dancing and lifestyle are now part of what corporate America has capitalized on. As Chatterjea alleged, the "most progressive and avant-garde edge in mainstream culture has continued to borrow consciously or unconsciously from the inescapable lived realities of peoples who form its underclass" (Chatterjea 2004: 102). The commodification of the hip-hop culture is a perfect example.

In Robert Jensen's book, *The Heart of Whiteness*, he suggests "some of what we white people have is unearned" (Jensen 2005: 53). Some of what white people have is a "product of the work of others, distributed unevenly across society." (Jensen 2005: 53.) Walter Benn Michaels confirms this through research and concludes in his book, *The Trouble with Diversity: How We Learned to Love Identity and Ignore Inequality*, that "the single best predictor of someone's net worth is not their race or their current salary, but the net worth of their parents." (Michaels 2006: 99) The problem, he pointed out, is that "we would much rather get rid of racism than get rid of poverty" (ibid: 12).

Classism is perhaps the last of the "isms" to be addressed, probably because, as Jensen stated, "the deepest fear that lives in the heart of whiteness is a system in which white people become the minority and could be treated as whites have long treated non-whites" (Jensen 2005: 54) Modern dance may have been in the forefront of integration, but it is time dance history caught up to reflect its heritage. There is no clear-cut history of racism/no racism, or segregation/integration. It's a continuum going back and forth in degrees, as it progresses onward.

Zollar mentioned that power bases are difficult to challenge, because power rarely concedes itself. She spoke of the human impulse to create exclusionary bases, to "take care of what I view as my own."

> It's what happens with any power base. Any power base wants to perpetuate itself until it's challenged. If it's a smart power base, when it's challenged, it figures out that it will be stronger by opening up, not by closing ranks. It becomes strengthened by opening out, not by closing in.

Dan Wagoner acknowledged that in our society, "all of the prejudices are still there. Perhaps there is no way for a white person to know about African American heritage."

Molissa Fenley stepped up to the plate to recognize white privilege and said she is willing to step aside in order to even the field of opportunity to enable change to occur:

> The white culture has to agree that is the case because we have to get on equal ground and we never will if everyone is angry and can't budge. Equal ground means that yes, people who have not had the opportunities have to be given more opportunity because white culture always has opportunity. Now women in the white culture don't always have opportunity, but that's another issue.

Rosalind Newman turned the racial tables by becoming the "other," albeit privileged other, in another culture. As a white in Asia, she experienced people's stereotypical ideas towards whites, and that led her to realize, "You're never going to be part of that world, in a true deep sense." It had "a very strange kind of repercussion emotionally," and her experience points out how people of color must feel as minorities in the USA.

Douglas Dunn was aware of racial difference in looking at his dancing bodies but chose not to manipulate the movement to make any kind of "meaningful" statement, because he would like conclusions to be drawn naturally. When a white woman was on a black man's shoulders with a black woman circling them, Dunn ignored it as a racial moment, wanting to "let the possible narrative play itself out without conscious manipulation on my part." His interests lie more in the formal spatial configurations, shapes, and rhythms than in superimposing meaning onto movement.

Meredith Monk is conscious of trying to make work that transcends race and is "accessible to any human being on the planet." Others voiced similar ideas.

Lynne Fauley Emery stated that the development of journalistic criticism that engages the complexities of "black dance" and its political dimensions has been slow to emerge. There have been few African-American critics to begin with, but with the decline of arts criticism and column space in national decline, few dance critics are seemingly prepared "to meet the challenge of chronicling performance while illuminating its cultural underpinnings" (DeFrantz 2002: 22). According to DeFrantz,

> In 1980, critic Zita Allen described the severity of this cultural divide in which "white critics seem so totally unfamiliar with Afro-American cultural heritage and history and ignorant of the processes of their interaction with, and influence on, their own" that they were "ill-equipped to either identify those roots or determine when they are being demeaned and denied or drawn from for inspiration." Two decades later this cultural divide persists.
>
> (DeFrantz 2002: 22)

The above statement could also be true of critics who viewed Mel Wong's Asian-influenced choreography back in the 1970s and early 1980s. Even an African-American critic, who presumably should have had more sensitivity to minority dance-making, apparently did not have enough understanding of Asian-American culture to be able to recognize the cultural underpinnings in the choreography. However, this situation was one of those elusive, intangible, and unprovable examples of what may or may not be racism (or simply unintended naivety). A negative review does not necessarily indicate racism, but, rather, it could reflect sour grapes on the part of the receiver/artist suggesting that it was racist or ignorant.

Dance history is expanding with a growing awareness that "any discussions of 'Dance History' that do not immediately negotiate differential understandings of organizing concepts and genres such that they do not only reinforce Eurocentric hierarchies, tend to repeat the Orientalist move Edward Said talks about" (Chatterjea 2004: 7).

> European modernity comes to be constructed suggesting that only in Europe and America can dance be said to have reached pinnacles of "development," having passed through the classical and the modern to the postmodern eras . . . one cannot be modern without implicating an other in "primitive" . . . thus non-Western cultures are seemingly stuck in antiquity.
>
> (Chatterjea 2004: 8)

Chatterjea stated as well, "Choreographers from non-white and non-Western contexts are often misread by critics and audiences here. The issue is even more urgent when the choreographers are working in ways that deviate from 'traditional' practice" (Chatterjea 2004: xiii).

During the past thirty years, the field of dance history has gone from being a marginal study to one where there are now departments offering Ph.D.s. Methods of looking at history are changing to allow more awareness and acknowledgment of the bias and constructions, the Eurocentric dominant perspective, patriarchal, racial hierarchies, class and gender differences. History is being reconsidered, deconstructed, even rewritten. In the 1970s, this awareness was germinating. Now, as the world seems to be getting smaller and smaller, while access to it is faster and more comprehensive, a different consciousness is taking root across the country. A more inclusive realization has begun.

Awareness and inclusion has begun to extend beyond the issue of race, in other areas as well, with plenty of room still left for expansion. Perhaps with the baby boomers turning sixty there is a new consciousness about aging. Aging is something most people will experience and yet a negative, harmful conception about it prevails. According to Dr. Andrew Weil, the public is bombarded with "unrelenting images and messages from the media telling us that youth is where it's at, that growing old is a disaster, that the worth of life peaks early (Weil 2005: 120). Our culture finds little value in aging. Ironically, teenagers are trying to look older and grow up before their time so they can pass for adults in order to drink and do other "adult things," while the rest of us want to look younger because the media, fashion, and entertainment industries glorify tight skin and supple young, sexualized bodies.

Dance is one of the most youthful professions, even more concentrated on the young than many professional sports such as football or baseball. Most dancers stop dancing by the time they reach forty, and it is exceptional to see someone dancing on stage over forty. As Rosalind Newman said, "Dance is particularly cruel because what's impressive to an audience is who has the hottest young body and who can do the tricks."

Comments by critics exulting youthful dancers don't help society to change views about aging. In 2006, Tobi Tobias wrote:

> Dance fans are forever complaining about dancing stars who refuse to recognize when the time has come to call it quits and retire from the stage [. . .] One of the tragic ironies of a career in dance, especially in ballet, is that the body's glory years are already winding down just as the soul fully awakens. There's no simple or single solution for dancers whose athletic prowess is waning; their dilemma (and the anguish that must accompany it) is part of the career they've bought into. But for us, members of the tribe of dedicated onlookers, I have an idea. If the artist who probably should retire won't, the viewer must decide when enough is enough and retire the artist.
>
> (Tobias 2007)

She then went on to write that viewers either can read a book or go out in the lobby to have a cocktail while the older dancer is performing, or "just close your eyes and remember" what they used to look like. As Andrew Weil suggested, "nonacceptance of aging seems to be the rule in our society, not the exception" (Weil 2005: 86). People only see the negative aspects of aging, so their perception is skewed, because they never consider the positive side. Rather than place all the blame on and try to get rid of the aging dancer, why not try to change aesthetic values to include virtuosity of the soul? Is technique the only thing Americans value? What would Isadora Duncan think? She would stand in stillness until encouraged by the music, slowly raise her arms, gesturing up to the heavens, and move an audience to tears. Her simple gesture communicated a timeless connection to the universe beyond glitzy technique.

New York Times critic John Rockwell wrote,

> Part of what makes dance so seductive is its inevitable celebration of youth and youthful bodies. People often look back on their first flush of adulthood as a time of happy

memories: first real loves, first realizations of self through work, health and energy. The eternal youth of dance reminds us of what we once were.

(Rockwell 2006)

In statements such as this, Rockwell perpetuates the belief that dancing not only already is but should also continue to be a youthful profession.

The choreographers in RAGE have three situations to deal with in relation to aging. One, their own bodies are getting older; two, their companies have been in existence a long time; and three, their dancers are generally much younger than they are. These choreographers are adapting to their aging bodies with their increasing limitation of mobility and flexibility. As Bill T. Jones so aptly put it, "Age happens." Nancy Meehan commented that she wasn't going into old age happily and that aging is definitely a problem in the performing arts. Dan Wagoner said he couldn't move the way he used to, and it was "harder to get out of bed."

Gus Solomons jr admitted that aging and injuries had affected his art more than anything in the past few decades. He didn't consider aging as bad as the injuries, which are due to "time and wear," as well as lack of knowledge about correct body alignment when dancing as a youth. Thankfully, over the years, there has been increased scientific information about body mechanics, and hopefully that will extend the performing lives of other dancers.

Since nonacceptance of aging dominates society's thinking, people only see the negative aspects of aging, and their perception is skewed, because they never consider the positive side. As Jones pointed out, injuries can be "depressing," or they "can be an inducement to develop." Jones, like Trisha Brown, is seeking other ways to train and move. He is looking at age as "an opportunity to reinvent." Douglas Dunn's admiration of jumping is partially due to the fact that's it's more difficult with age because the legs "aren't as fleet," but, with the "diminution of vitality and extension," his reinvention has been to increase playfulness of character as well as to focus more on the ability of the upper body.

All of the choreographers agreed that, as Kenneth King said, "Although the technical prowess wanes, the more mature body exudes incomparable experience." Solomons, commented, "One nice thing about getting older is the wisdom that comes with aging. You outgrow vanity and all those things that stand in the way—that made dancing difficult." Dunn admitted,

> Movement has become softer because age has talked me out of the compulsion to overdance; because strength, agility, physical power in general, no longer outline the limits of my identity; and because I now sense that a more generous impulse gives the moves a value previously I was blind to.

Many of these choreographers actually find beauty in aging dancers. Nancy Meehan said, "There is more background to draw upon and I understand things that I didn't even think about or couldn't have understood before." Molissa Fenley pointed out how age is more revered in Japan. She loves to watch more mature dancers because of "the sense of longevity: how many times that leg has been lifted or how many times that body has done a plié." To her, "the sense of experience within the body is so beautiful," and "with an older dancer there is the sense of an understood world." Meehan commented that older dancers have more "nuance, texture and richness in their movement," while Newman said, "older dancers have great wisdom in their bodies" and "know how movement behaves."

Aging as a choreographer necessarily means not being able to execute all of the moves on one's own body. Newman brought up the idea that "the degree of being able to dance and the vision changes," but the question remains, "How do you take yourself out of the physicality of the work and still make it have vitality, life, and a physical presence?" How long does a dancer-choreographer continue?

Meredith Monk's answer was to figure out what to do with the ability she has now, because "to try to fight it doesn't make any sense. You have to give in to it and then you'll find something else." She strives to work with what she has rather than wishing for something she doesn't have. Kenneth King wants to keep going for another forty years. Dan Wagoner "listens to his own heart and returns to his own passion and delight in order to offset physical loss." Rennie Harris suggested that the question is "how long can your body go?" He said, "As far as hip-hop, there's no real age to stop. They change the way they approach it." He thinks, "Seasoning is a good thing." A little seasoning enlivens the palate, and we all need seasoning to spice up life.

For Molissa Fenley, dancing and choreographing continue "as long as I'm interested in it, it doesn't go on as long as my body can do it. If my body can't do it, like when I had the accident, I find another way." As Fenley said, "our culture thinks age is a bad thing. It reinforces the belief that as you get older you get more annoying, or more debilitated . . . that's just our culture, that's what we do to our older people."

Countering this idea by celebrating the virtues of maturity, Gus Solomons jr established his company, PARADIGM, comprised of older dancers, the youngest of whom is forty-seven. Solomons offered, "Since 1996 we've been demonstrating how older dancers can still be eloquent movers. I made PARADIGM into a company because I perceived the demand for what we were doing would be great." Without tricks and with plenty of stillness, these accomplished dancers are showing all generations that movement performed by a masterful dancer can be riveting, regardless of age. PARADIGM is an illustration of increasing the appreciation for and the value of a dancer's life.

"Very old trees have a presence about them, a gravity, that draws you in, makes you quiet, and fills you with awe and respect" (Weil 2005: 113). "Old trees, like old whiskey and wine, certainly have more character than young trees, but that is not the main reason that we venerate them, consider them sacred, and make pilgrimages to see them. We honor them because they are survivors" (Weil 2005: 115). The dancers in PARADIGM are seasoned performers, survivors in the field, who have a wealth of experience to delight audiences.

It is also unusual for dance companies to exist for a long period of time. Only a handful stay around. Producers are looking for what's new and innovative, the latest trick to sell and interest an audience so more money can be made on tickets. Where does that leave midlife artists who have had their careers launched and then plateaued? Often they are passed over for the younger, upcoming star, who is fresher for the Fresh Tracks performing series. Few choreographers become a Mark Morris, touring the world, with his own building in Brooklyn, and few are able to have the breadth and length of a performing career like Paul Taylor's.

The third situation concerning age and dance is the actual age of the company performers themselves. It is one thing for the public to see an aging well-known choreographer on stage but quite another to see aging bodies of "regular" dancers. Is society ready for this? How many companies have "older dancers"? Nancy Meehan thought "people are much more tolerant of seeing an older dancer on stage than twenty years ago." Right now, a dancer is generally assumed to be "older" when she is past thirty. In November 2005, in a *New York*

Times article about Karole Armitage, one of her dancers, Theresa Howard, commented that she was, at thirty-four, an "older dancer" (Hohenadel 2005: 8).

It's true that most dancers quit dancing by thirty if they are unable to support themselves and haven't made it into a professional company. Those who have entered the professional dance world and are lucky enough to make a living at their profession still face the challenge that after thirty they are assumed to be getting "old." This idea is a self-perpetuating cycle: The audience sees young dancers. Because most professional dancers are under forty, they think of themselves as "old" if they are over forty and generally stop performing, so the audience rarely see dancing bodies over forty, and think (and expect) dance is supposed to be for the young.

Not only is this arbitrary age limit a perception for the audience and dancers, it is also a perception for most choreographers. Many of the choreographers didn't seem to get it that there should or could be a possibility of other dancers over forty onstage beside themselves. Most of them spoke only about themselves aging and dancing. However, Rennie Harris said that many of the hip-hop dancers are fifty and can still "bring it." Then he said that his own dancers didn't look older, except when they "started to get bellies on them"—as if bellies and gaining weight are necessarily connected with age. What are the 2008 statistics about today's youth being overweight?

Doug Varone said he had a reputation for "not hiring young dancers." He prefers to have dancers with "a lot of life behind them," who can add their life experience to his work. He actually prefers dancers in their thirties and forties. Lucinda Childs commented that technique and musicality are what matters to her when dancers audition. She didn't think someone would audition who was fifty but didn't seem to care if they were fifty, as long as the technique was there. Is it possible for technique to remain as brilliant at fifty?

Most of the choreographers referred to forty as the outer age limit for dancers, and I got the impression that most of them didn't consider having anyone much older than forty dance with them in their company. It's acceptable for the choreographer to be onstage at fifty or more, but rarely is anyone else of that age seen performing with them.

Realizing that many people love to see what older dancers have to offer, Gus Solomons jr is definitely the exception to this rule. Another is Liz Lerman, who has created a company of dancers of cross-generational performance. Yet another exception is Meredith Monk, who experimented with the concept of age when she was twenty-six and who has always had all ages, races, and sizes on stage. She, of course, falls between the cracks, because she is not doing "dancey dance," that demands speed and technical physicality, which usually requires more youthful dancers. As a singer, she wants to share "what a ninety-year-old voice sounds like." In our youth-obsessed, young-body-oriented culture, is it more acceptable to perform and present age through the voice than the body?

In conjunction with the unavoidable fact of aging comes the inevitable end of life. Since *Further Steps* was first published, three of the choreographers (Wagoner, Jones, and Monk) have lost partners. Monk commented that by losing her partner, death "also brought life into perspective." Louis Falco was fifty when he died on March 26, 1993. Arnie Zane died at thirty-nine on March 30, 1988. Both men died of AIDS. Mel Wong died July 17, 2003, of a heart attack at the age of sixty-four. Bill T. Jones, who is HIV positive, has had to carry on, knowing "what's at stake with my life as an artist. Now, though I am aware of the passage of time, I am not so much burdened by it." Death, like aging, is part of the life process. "Growing old should increase, not decrease, the value of human life" (Weil 2005: 103).

Would that the above statement were true. As I was running my daily 4 miles on the paved cliffs by the ocean in Santa Cruz, a sudden gruff voice shouting from out of a Ford truck window startled me by yelling, "Yeah! Grandma, do it, go!" My first response, after the surprise of having someone yell at me, was to be stung by the "Grandma" nomenclature. I immediately felt sad, and bad about myself, until I kept running and, a minute later, realized that I run for myself and for how it feels. I don't run to try to look younger.

I realized it was my own ego, conforming to society's idea of beauty as youthful, that let me feel the sting of those words. The reason I run is because it feels good, I like the endorphins, and it lets me concentrate on my body in a different way, by being present in every breath. Whereas I don't run to stay young, one benefit of running is that it keeps me in shape. Mostly I run so that I'm feeling my body from the inside, feeling my breath, feeling my bones, contacting muscles that I don't otherwise engage with the same vigor. And for the same reasons, I dance.

So many dancers throughout history have referred to dancing from the inside out. Isadora Duncan wanted to express from her soul. Doris Humphrey wanted to dance from the inside out. Certainly Erick Hawkins developed a technique based on feeling the bones, contacting the pelvis, releasing the muscles and letting the flesh hang off of the bones. Nancy Meehan continued his explorations, finding even more possibilities to express strength with the above metaphors while expressing a state of being. Even Graham used metaphors of feeling from the inside by telling students to move from the vagina (Graham 1991: 211.)

Jawole Zollar has also come forth and talked about dancing from the inside, "expressing truth to speak that truth to power," or "finding that quality inside yourself and then developing that outward." Mel Wong always tapped into his inner being, as he let his intuition guide his choreography. He would sit still, eyes closed, and go into a meditation to clear his mind in order to tap into his creative well. Then he would get up and begin dancing, dance a phrase or two, then walk away and let the dancers repeat the phrase to make it their own. If he liked it, he'd keep it, but he always said that he "let the movement pour out of his subconscious, from the inside."

"Yes, our bodies will decline and decay, but aging, if accepted and not resisted, can lead to maturity and all of the promise implied in the colors of sunset and fall foliage, in the perfection of ripe fruit and the pleasure of expertly aged cheese" (Weil 2005: 109).

Besides aging, another major question posed to each choreographer was about gender in relation to dance. I asked whether their thinking about gender had changed over the years, and, if it had, how it had affected their choreography. I wanted to know if, during the past twenty to thirty years, they were more conscious of the choreographic lens of such issues as who initiates the movement, who is manipulating whom, who is lifting whom?

Kenneth King readily voiced his opinion with, "the issue isn't manipulation but giving dancers autonomy. The idea that gender parity means women should partner men is laughable for its simplistic counterparity." Rennie Harris indirectly corroborated King's statements when he said that everyone in hip-hop is a choreographer who already has autonomy by creating a unique self-style. King believes choreography requires "the abdication of the choreographer," so, perhaps hip-hop is, as Harris suggested, the direction in which modern dance is headed.

Harris also pointed out that there is a gender disparity in hip-hop for who gets recognized. He said that the males are the ones who "take the spotlight in hip-hop." "Although there are a lot of women who do hip-hop, and who are *amazing*, the media push or highlight women for their sexuality. They don't emphasize the women to show their skill and ability. I think it's wack that there are a lot of women choreographers not *celebrated*. Where are the women?"

Solomons mentioned that gender nonspecificity is a fundamental principle of post-modern dance and that both ballet and modern partnering classes now at New York University are "nongender-specific." Several of the choreographers in this book intentionally try to transcend gender by choreographing asexually. Fenley stated that her dances "present equality" on stage, "whatever the nationality, gender or age." Likewise, Mel Wong choreographed what he considered asexual, spiritual movement, unless he was purposely trying to make a political statement or to emphasize a stereotypical gender role.

Gus Solomons once again went against the flow by admitting that his gender awareness has perhaps changed in the "opposite direction." He indicated that in the 1980s he worked with pure movement that had no gender specifications attached to it, but now he perceives anything Carmen DeLavallade does as being feminine. According to Solomons, who manipulates whom, or who initiates or supports, has more to do with "physical capacity" of the company than it does with gender.

Meredith Monk has long played with the idea of subverting gender roles. Since 1972, with "Paris," she has undermined stereotypical ideas by mixing gender roles together. In "Paris" she wore a mustache, while wearing a skirt, while Ping Chong played a female character with male attributes as well. Now Monk continues to disrupt gender stereotypes in her vocal work by interchanging singing roles so that the females sing below the males, while the males sing in falsetto. By crossing gender lines, she has gone beyond "limitations in thinking," pushing the envelopes of these constructs.

Jones and his partner Arnie Zane were responsible for breaking barriers of same-sex dancing together on stage. As gay men, they danced, partnering and touching each other, demonstrating to the world that homosexuality was part of life. They proclaimed that the image of same-sex dancing together onstage was here to stay, so it was up to viewers to get used to it, thus opening up more possibilities for others. "The message of their work was consistently one of racial and sexual tolerance" (Bellafante 2005).

However, Bill T. Jones candidly admitted that he had a "spotty record around issues of gender" when it came to female dancers. With his "preoccupation with male strength and assertiveness," it took his former teacher, a woman, Lois Welk, to point out that his choreographic roles for women were lacking. Now he "listens more carefully to the women around" him and considers what they have to offer and bring to his choreography.

Whereas Jones and Zane initiated the acceptability of gay men partnering each other onstage, Jones pointed out that he didn't want gay men to have the attitude of "super queens" in his company, and he sometimes had to tell them or give permission for them to be strong. In the same sense, he recognized that he doesn't want to take away female sexuality in his company, just because that is not his preference. He wants his female dancers to be passionate onstage. Valuing each company member for his or her own individuality, he believes every dancer should be themselves onstage, "their whole self," regardless of sexual preference.

Jones and Zane set the stage for other choreographers, such as Doug Varone, who is proud of the vanguard role dance has taken in this forum and thinks "it is essential to show the world as it is, as well as to screw around with both traditional and nontraditional roles." Varone continues gender exploration by presenting dancers who appear as "everyday people from all walks of life."

What about gay women in dance? Lucinda Childs believes "a strong gay male presence has been apparent for a long time, but a female gay presence is finally beginning to emerge." She noted that by the 1960s gay males had achieved "well deserved prestige" in the art world, but gay females were "better off to not be openly gay." Today though, "gay female choreographers who are *out* are not necessarily just drawing attention to that." She thinks "it is a good sign that we can think that there are female choreographers who happen to be gay, not female gays who happen to be choreographers."

Zollar brought up the idea that people view her company as being predominantly gay. Are people jumping to conclusions just because it's an all-female company? Zollar says she doesn't ask sexual preference during auditions, nor does she care about it. Do people make similar assumptions that all male dancers are gay?

Zollar suggested that only in America is there the perception that all male dancers are gay. She didn't believe the same perception necessarily existed in Europe or in other countries. Both Zollar and Harris highlighted the fact that male hip-hop dancers are not necessarily gay. As Harris said, hip-hop is "a dance form where the men are not afraid to dance [. . .] Hip-hop is just another extension of Black African-American culture in this country." Culturally, it's acceptable for heterosexual men to dance.

Harris pointed out that the public doesn't see many straight men in concert dance, but in hip-hop you can "wear whatever you want to wear," suggesting that the costumes or unitards male modern dancers have been known to wear are off-putting to a straight male viewer. Harris thought that "the way men are depicted in concert dance just doesn't come off as something masculine enough for men," but when males see other males do hip-hop, it makes them want to dance.

It's not possible to discuss changes in attitudes about gender in dance since the 1980s without mentioning the AIDS crisis that literally wiped out a generation of gay male artists. More than 80,000 New Yorkers died of AIDS, destroying "the collective memory of an audience—the seasoned gay audience, perhaps the most culturally receptive group any city has ever seen" (Muschamp 2006). While the city has registered the cultural impact of this loss, the effect produced by the loss of the gay audience is "more insidious" (Muschamp 2006). Although the AIDS crisis may have started with gay males predominantly, the disease itself has no gender specificity.

Likewise, the universal scope of dance "transcends" both race and gender. So think Varone, Fenley, Meehan, and Wong. Similar to these artists but one step beyond is Kenneth King, who has delved into explorations outside the construct of gender by presenting the fusion of the sexes in the form of the hermaphrodite. As Judith Butler asserted, gender exceeds being either male or female, and futuristic King points us toward that possibility in both his writings and performance.

Although this may not be true now, at the turn of the twentieth century, modern dance was about the woman. Women founded it and continue to outnumber males in the profession. And yet the tables have turned so that it seems males now rule the dance world, get most of the funding, grants, tours, and college jobs. Rosalind Newman brought up the issue of gender inequality in dance. She said there are about nine females to every one male in dance, but women are viewed and treated as the "other," when they are actually the majority. She wondered why women, who historically founded the college dance departments, seek out males and give them the college teaching jobs. Are women perpetuating the patriarchy?

Lucinda Childs disagreed with this idea. Since colleagues such as Trisha Brown, Laura Dean, and Twyla Tharp have achieved success in the modern dance world, Childs thought there was actually more opportunity for women choreographers within the modern dance community than in the ballet world. As King stated, "sexism is endemic to ballet—ballet is women—Balanchine's twisted credo is also political and set the field back decades." For the most part, ballet has remained entrenched in the patriarchy, the Balanchinian model of carrying on a tradition of maintaining a puerile mentality by referring to dancers as "girls and boys." As Childs pointed out, women in ballet generally still are overlooked as choreographers and rarely considered as a potential "emerging choreographer."

On the other hand, Childs adamantly denied any possibility of gay males controlling the dance world. "Absolutely not." Even if more males get funding and touring than women (which is a gender issue), Childs thought it had nothing to do with "the gay issue." Others referred to a "gay mafia" but didn't want to be quoted as using that terminology. Is this a homophobic thought? Is there any truth to the idea that gay males, or males, control the dance world in the USA? Does it have to do with sexual preference, or is it just a fact of life that males still dominate the culture in the United States of America?

Statistically, on average, women still only make 76 cents to the dollar of every man. Inequality in the USA still predominates. The World Economic Forum's Global Gender Gap Report 2006 ranked the USA twenty-ninth according to economic participation and opportunity, education, political empowerment and health and survival, of gender equality. The USA "lags behind many European nations" and also falls behind Canada" (Bonoguore 2006).

Women choreographers are not the only ones who think males have the power in the dance world. Ann Murphy wrote in *Dance Magazine*, November 2005:

> A great deal more work needs to be done to make such equality for women a reality. In findings published last year (2004) by the NYSCA, the evidence indicates that men are on top—even in dance where women are numerically stronger. The rosters of large presenting organizations are dominated by male performers, directors of large dance companies are predominantly male, and funders bequeath a larger portion of their dwindling pool of resources to men. Though this field was shaped by women, women are finding fewer mainstream opportunities today.
>
> (Murphy 2005: 54)

Does the perception, if there is one, that men dominate the dance world have to do with more males, gay or not, being on the panels that grant funding so that more males are given awards? Does this reflect Zollar's theory about those in power protecting their own power base? Does it have to do with patriarchy in general? Solomons didn't think there was inequality in dance. "Since women's liberation, women have been making more waves about issues of exclusion of women from getting grants, and being presented. I think some women make it more of an issue than it really is. I don't think there's overt discrimination against women in dance."

Douglas Dunn was also aware that there was a perception of gender discrepancy. "The gender issue has seemed hotter, people openly complaining about men having opportunity out of keeping with their proportion of the field." Although this may be the perception, what can be done about dissolving or dispelling it?

Zollar's solution was

to do all I can to support young, emerging choreographers. Rather than complaining about it, let me try to get the playing field a little more level by what I can do. I can't go out and change the whole dance world, but I can have an impact in this corner that will hopefully ripple out. And I think that's what we can do.

Regardless of either numbers or power dominating gender in dance, it is still perceived as a feminine art. As Susan Foster asserted in "Closets Full of Dances," the founding women of modern dance strove to "bring women and a female presence into the public sphere" (Foster 2001: 160). While they succeeded in "deflecting the objectifying force of the male gaze and ennobling" female dancers, they did nothing to challenge the conceptual idea that dancing was feminine or to assuage the prejudice against men dancing (Foster 2001: 160).

Ted Shawn set out to revive the respectability of male dancing by creating an "almost hypermasculinity," using virile movements which resembled men working in the fields, athletic motions, or other male forms of labor. As Foster pointed out, both the early female pioneers, as well as Shawn, referred back to the classical Greek dancing for respectability (Foster 2001: 162). Reinforcing racism and colonialist nationalism to propel the acceptance of their own dancing, Duncan, St. Denis, and Shawn distanced themselves from primitive, savage, and sexual gyrations while ennobling their dance as high art. The women cultivated an air of independence, chastity, and spirituality, while Shawn promoted masculinity by reinforcing an antisexual platform that deflected the lens of homosexuality from him and his company of male dancers.

Ironically, Shawn had homosexual relationships, as did the first female modern dancer, Loie Fuller, and Isadora Duncan allegedly had a long-time liaison with Mercedes de Acosta. Since homosexuality in the USA has historically been so closeted, history still does not reveal the true sexual preferences of many noted modern dance choreographers. Among dancers there is an "inside dirt," or word-of-mouth knowledge about various affairs and experimentations of different choreographers, but publicly, up until Bill T. Jones and Arnie Zane, most choreographers were very discrete about exposing their sexual preferences.

Many of the second or 1950s generation of choreographers and male dancers— Cunningham, Nikolais-Louis, Taylor, and Hawkins—deflected homosexuality or bisexuality from themselves and their choreography by creating abstract dances without emotional content. Cunningham concentrated on time, space, and movement, while maintaining a balletic posture and heterosexist mode of movement initiation.

Although it appeared that Cunningham "cultivated the body as a neutral field" (Desmond 2001: 175), his choreography up until the 1990s conformed to traditional heterosexist modes. The men did most of the initiation, lifting, turning, and supporting of women. Women were the ones primarily manipulated, turned, lifted, and supported, but since the movement was executed without emotion, the bodies appeared neutral toward each other, thereby deflecting sexuality and disguising the choreographer's sexual preference. With the above emphases, which conformed to the balletic conventions of choreography, Cunningham was able to maintain a heterosexual sensibility, while removing its implied sexuality in the dance.

Nikolais-Louis used theatrical lighting and costuming, which often hid the body, thus averting gender scenarios. Taylor, like Cunningham, retained the heterosexist norm in his choreography but simultaneously introduced androgyny while often highlighting masculine dance as well. Hawkins frequently used masks, ritual, and metaphor to portray humankind's harmonious relationship to nature. His dances were sensual, not sexual, and they conveyed a serenity, refinement, and grace with a poetic presentation of the human experience.

The postmodernists' openness about sexuality may have radically changed theatrical presentation onstage since the 1960s, as Childs remarked, but total transformation comes slowly. Closely linked to gender, with perspectives equally slow to change, are the subjects of "family" and "the body" in dance. How have attitudes towards these topics evolved over the past several decades?

Rosalind Newman brought up that having a baby affected every aspect of her life and put things into perspective for her, since it "was the most ongoing creative activity." Rennie Harris brought up the point that female company members left because they were having a family, but men who have a family continue to "do their thing."

Although Isadora Duncan, Doris Humphrey, and Twyla Tharp had children, how many other female dancer-choreographers have had families and continued to dance? How many male dancer-choreographers have had children? Douglas Dunn and Mel Wong both had children. David Gordon and Valda Setterfield, Art Bridgman and Myrna Packer, Eiko and Koma, and David Dorfman and Lisa Race are dancing couples with families that come to mind, but aren't these the exception rather than the rule?

Perhaps they are the minority representing the attitudinal change since the 1960s, but, generally speaking, dancers don't create families and continue with dance as their profession. Traditionally, dance has been a vocation where dancers seem to be more wedded to their career than to family, and it's especially difficult for dancers trying to raise one to be taken seriously as artists.

When I was fourteen, dancing outside of Philadelphia in a local ballet company called the Devon Festival Ballet, a man came up to me after a performance one day and introduced himself. He told me he thought I had talent and wanted to make me into a ballerina. He asked to meet my mother and then explained to her that he was on the Board of Directors of the Pennsylvania Ballet, which at the time was just forming. He wanted me to commute into the city every day to take class.

My mother's reaction was, "Who is this fifty-five-year-old man, interested in my daughter?" And, "You don't want to be a professional dancer!" Her reasons were loud and clear: "You won't be able to have a 'normal' life. You won't be able to be popular in school and concentrate on your studies because you'll spend all your time commuting and dancing. You'll be associating with weird theatrical types. You won't be able to have a family, and you won't have any money." And you know what? She was right about all those things!

As a dutiful daughter, I had no choice but to follow her wishes, and I didn't study at the Pennsylvania Ballet at that time. What my mother didn't realize, though, was that the passion I had for dance would magnetically draw me to dance anyway.

However, by delaying my pursuit of dance, she indirectly spared me the pain of learning that my body was not suited for ballet. Although my proportions were fine, my legs are curved and shaped so that the line is not long or straight enough for ballet, and even when my feet are fully pointed and legs fully extended, it appears that my knees are somewhat bent. Ultimately, this "defect" would have prevented a successful career in ballet.

The body's appearance is of utmost importance for professional dancers. Along with a demand for youth, dance has a long tradition of requiring a long, lean body. Has anything changed about this aesthetic presentation in the past three decades?

Most choreographers agreed that body type mattered to their work, in the sense that they wanted their dancers to have facility of movement, flexibility, and to be able to embody the choreography in the way it was intended. They emphasized their decisions were not necessarily about having the thinnest dancer, but that *how* they danced was most important. Bill T. Jones, who actually used a 300-pound dancer onstage, admitted that he isn't doing that now, because he wants a certain look.

As Zollar stated,

> The body types; short, tall, larger, skinny, don't matter. They have never really mattered to me, but I think it's mattered to other people who have seen the work. Sometimes it was disturbing to people, and sometimes it still is disturbing to people. The aesthetic of the "thin is in" is still out in the dance world in full force.

Many choreographers said that they had "varied" body types in their companies, but in some cases the idea of variety is within a narrow range of thin and thinner. Perhaps tall and short, or bodies with curves versus no hips are included within that range, but, for the most part, the thin aesthetic remains. A few, like Bill T. Jones, Meredith Monk, Nancy Meehan, Jawole Zollar, and Doug Varone, have included more diverse body types, but it's usually the exception rather than the rule.

However, as Jones pointed out, if funding allowed for more company members, perhaps companies could be larger and encompass more diversity. When a company focuses on fleetness and facility of technique, the requirements for a one-dimensional body aesthetic, by necessity, prevail.

Although Meredith Monk used diverse body types early on, such as a 250-pound man in *Juice* (1969), she has gravitated away from the dance world into more of the opera/music/theater world. Is that world more accepting of varied body types than the dance world?

"'The dancing body reads as a complex site of cultural and political enactment, imbricated in a complex interaction of social constructions and manipulations of the same" (Chatterjea 2004: 89). Dancers, models, and Hollywood stars seem to share an anorexic or near-anorexic requirement for their performative skills. This extreme emphasis on being thin also comes at a time when Americans are more overweight than ever. What are the implications of this for our society?

As part of society, dance is intricately and indelibly connected with politics, economics, and social change, and it can be viewed as a cultural mirror, reflecting the state of its country. Although I don't remember who said it, I remember hearing in my first dance-history class with Professor Andrea Watkins, in 1973 at the University of Massachusetts, Amherst that one way of judging the health of a culture could be to look at how many people in the society dance. I remember thinking, even back then, that our society had gotten away from dancing. It was something ritualistically performed either for courtship, at weddings, or at the inaugural ball (where more emphasis seemed to be placed on who was in attendance and what people were wearing than with the steps they were dancing). Happily, there does seem to be a recent resurgence in social dancing. People are taking ballroom classes, dancing samba, salsa, tango, swing, line dance, and more.

The 1970s and 1980s were perhaps the golden age of modern/postmodern dance. People nationwide were imitating Twyla Tharp's hairstyle and leg warmers, and modern dance classes throughout the country sprang up as popular art forms for exercise. Many people took modern classes to get in shape. Then came the introduction and popularization of aerobics, step-aerobics, jazzercise, and sports training fitness centers. Suddenly people started migrating to those classes, and the emphasis switched from art/exercise to toning muscles, trimming weight, and getting the heart rate up. So went the art of dance.

The political environment changed in the past thirty years as well. When asked what that change was, there was an array of responses and emphases, but, without a doubt, all the artists agreed that these are very dark times for the arts and for our country. At the time of their interviews, most of the artists were saddened, disappointed, angry, and skeptical about the political environment.

Meredith Monk expressed her feelings boldly and succinctly when she said,

> As a Buddhist practitioner it's daunting to wake up in the morning and realize that our leaders are the embodiment of the three poisons, which are grasping, aggression, and ignorance [. . .] The whole society is being hypnotized by fear [. . .] The media is pouring on the fear. I believe it started in the 1980s, when there was a concerted effort to take money out of the educational system and put it into weapons, because a mass of ignorant people is a lot easier to manipulate. This is a plan that's been ongoing.

Rennie Harris indicated beliefs similar to Monk's by suggesting that when the arts are taken away from the culture, the people can be controlled. Dan Wagoner commented, "These are backward times for art and dance. The arts cannot flourish because of fear and conservatism." Nancy Meehan added, "I believe that we are moving through one of, if not the most agonizing, critical periods in human history, and for the globe itself." Doug Varone corroborated these sentiments with, "I think it is a very sad state of affairs we are in at the moment."

Almost everyone mentioned the events of 9/11 and how that had changed them and our world. Lucinda Childs noted,

> We are dealing with the fact that our lives have changed, and that we think differently about just about everything. But before Katrina, many of us assumed that progress had been made on how to deal with a major catastrophe – natural, or otherwise – to a major city, but unfortunately it seems we're really not as far along as we need to be in addressing this kind of problem, and that's very disturbing.

Kenneth King added his thoughts by supplying us with suggested reading material about 9/11 and the Bush Administration, while Bill T. Jones mourned that the generational revolution he thought he was a part of, was in fact, "a lie [. . .] And it is frightening, and it's infuriating." He further commented that "everything I and many of my generation took for granted is in question now."

As Wagoner postulated, the pendulum swings back and forth, but right now, "we are swinging so deeply into obesity of both body and mind, how can we get back? [. . .] I wish our culture were more insightful."

The political climate has very deeply affected the dance world. As many of the choreo-graphers discussed, in the 1980s there was a huge feeling of prosperity. There was a lot of funding, and numerous dance companies were thriving. By the late 1980s, during the height of Reaganomics, the debacle with the 1989 retrospective of Robert Mapplethorpe's homo-erotic photographs and with another exhibit of Andres Serrano's, *Piss Christ*, a photograph of a crucifix immersed in urine, an atmosphere of mistrust was created among members of Congress for funding the arts.

This resulted in the discontinuation of funding for individual artists by both the NEA and NYSCA (New York State Council for the Arts), causing a major blow to choreographers, who had grown dependent on funding for themselves and for general operating expenses for their companies. It hurried the dissolution of Childs', Wagoner's, and Newman's companies, to name a few. Childs mentioned that she was unable to keep going in the USA, but, ironically, was simultaneously championed in Europe.

As Fenley, King, and Childs complained, expectations were created and decreed that dance companies would start acting like business corporations with boards of directors seeking corporate sponsorship. King lamented that a "political juggernaut" had dance companies "indentured to the corporate oligarchy." Childs mentioned that smaller companies were at a disadvantage, and politicians seemed uninformed about the difficulty in finding private sponsors. Those companies who didn't stiffen up to the business side of life either fell by the wayside or had to reconfigure.

Many of the artists commented about how this spurred dance to become more commercial, by forcing companies to concentrate on getting high attendance numbers. Ticket sales became the main emphasis, not the art itself. In order to reach the masses, dance was commercialized, commodified, and viewed as a product. Monk, a MacArthur Award recipient, said, "We are living in a no-culture culture. How does an artist survive in a culture that doesn't care about art except as a product? [. . .] We are living in a very product oriented society that has definitely quantified everything."

Fenley bewailed the all-pervading commercialization of daily life, of being told what to think, wear, watch, and how the idea of entertainment has so encroached on art that the masses expect to be constantly entertained without having to think when viewing it. She surmised, "If everything is commercial, it's the death of art."

In contrast to this, Bill T. Jones and Arnie Zane initially set out to be "distinct, wild, and successful." Their creation of *Secret Pasture*, in 1984, was touted as commercial because it included a set by graffiti artist Keith Haring, music by popular composer Peter Gordon, and costumes by designer Willi Smith. Although the word "institutionalization" initially may have been taken by Jones and Zane to be a "bad word," the two quickly adapted an infrastructure with an administration for marketing and promotion; they became an exemplary dance company which was run like a business. A decade later, Bill T. Jones received a MacArthur "genius" Award. What is the lesson for today's dance artist? Art must be both entertaining and profitable in today's world.

While funds were drying up in the USA, other countries were beginning to increase support for their artists. Living in Hong Kong, both Wong and Newman witnessed German, French, British, and Australian embassies promoting their dance companies, while the USA lagged behind, sending abroad only the tried and true American companies such as Alvin Ailey, Paul Taylor, and possibly Merce Cunningham.

Today, choreographers from other countries have much more security and stability for their companies than their US counterparts. With more government support, they have more rehearsal time and more access to production possibilities, so it is easier to be more experimental and to use props and sets onstage such as dirt, water, or cutting-edge technology. Choreographers in the USA have to scramble to pay for rehearsal time, with little funds left for production.

Zollar brought some hope into the situation by remembering that there is great wealth within the USA, but it must be found and tapped into. And, "it's a question of figuring out how to do this." Not wanting to go the corporate route, Molissa Fenley has discovered how to get a group of patrons to support her. Rennie Harris, mistrustful of being financially dependent on anyone, is still figuring out the best route for him.

Doug Varone commented that when he was "the new kid on the block," it was an adjustment for him and other companies in the early 1990s to adapt to available funding which was couched in initiatives involving outreach work. Companies were not always equipped to enter prisons, inner-city schools, or at-risk centers, and they had to figure out ways to create skills and "proactively take charge in new ways." He mentioned organizations such as Dance USA and Dance NYC, which are "positive forces to build a network for the community and a solid base for the art form to be seen and heard."

The above economic factors impacted modern dance in other ways as well. With the advent of college physical education departments incorporating modern dance into their programs, the popularity of modern dance increased so much by the 1960s that many colleges created separate dance departments. Those same departments seemed to have reached their height of support and popularity by the end of the 1980s, and now, many departments are being scaled back.

It has been difficult for college and university dance departments to maintain numbers in the twenty-first century, when universities, now acting like corporations, require research grants to bring money to the departments, when funding is scarce, budget cuts for education rampant, and accounting is the most popular major on campuses. Students select majors in terms of getting a job nowadays, and dancing is, as Gus Solomons jr said, "at the bottom of the heap" for financial security. In the 1970s many of us had the luxury or the naivety of being able to follow our dreams. How many have that luxury today? The practicality of paying rent and the high price of fuel have superseded dreams and lives.

Fenley said, "Dance has continued to be the worst paying profession possible." Although it's always been a struggle for aspiring professional dancers, dancers today are confronted with a different situation to that of the 1970s. The job scene is perhaps even more challenging now. Well known for working at multiple jobs of waiting tables, bartending, teaching, or, more recently, word-processing, or making lattes in Starbucks, dancers grab any job with flexible hours in order to take class, rehearse, and tour. Many professional dancers used to be able to support themselves through teaching modern-dance classes within the city and the surrounding environs.

When I danced professionally, I taught alternately at the Modern Dance Studio in Hoboken, NJ, in a private downtown high school, and was Visiting Guest Artist at Trinity College in Hartford, Conn., where I taught almost nonstop for two days, in order to be in New York City the rest of the week. Presumably schools benefited from the professional dance teachers, and enthusiasm for dance was spread.

In the 1970s, choreographers usually taught class in the city, thereby training dancers in their own technique while supplementing personal income. Usually, dancers took their choreographer's classes, three to five times a week. The situation is different now.

With the introduction of aerobics, jazzercise, Pilates, Feldenkrais, Alexander Technique, Rolfing, floor-barre, along with the increased popularity of martial arts, kick-boxing, body-pump, yoga, plus more availability of cultural dance forms (African, salsa, samba, belly-dancing, Indian dance, Balinese dance, hip-hop, swing, contact improvisation, etc.), dancers started drifting away from daily modern dance classes. Lured by other somatic classes, many dancers, even in the early 1980s, began taking a daily ballet class instead of modern dance and supplemented their ballet class with another body class.

As Soho and the East and West Village (where most dancers used to live) became increasingly gentrified, rents rose, the prices of dance classes increased, and dancers were forced to scramble for more jobs and to look elsewhere for housing.

A snowball effect began: As dancers dropped out of modern-dance classes, choreographers found themselves unable to pay studio rent and were forced to stop teaching classes. Since dancers had fewer classes to choose from, increasingly they went to study other body disciplines. Many became trained in Pilates, yoga, or other somatic forms, and they began trying to make a living through those instead of through dance.

Newman elucidated that dancers are not "inside the field" in the way they used to be. Perhaps many still work in a body-related discipline, but they're not working with dance as art. They're not making up phrases, experimenting with movement, thinking about musicality, dancing next to someone and sharing the space, choreographing, or thinking about movement as an expression. They're not even learning how to teach dance. Rather, much of the focus has become about reducing the inner thigh by a quarter of an inch or developing a six-pack. Some would say that the emphasis in dance has become more about tricks and the external appearance, which is about as far away from the beginnings of the art form of modern dance as Isadora Duncan would have ever wanted to imagine.

With time, the corporatization of dance companies pushed dancers to learn multiple movement styles in order to make a living. No longer did dancers concentrate on one modern dance technique. Increasingly, companies who obtained funding opted for dancers who had stellar balletic training. Getting the leg up, pointed feet with high arches, and a long thin body (though this has long been the case) became even more of a requisite for professional modern dancers. In a sense, the look of a dancer became more important than the demonstration of a unique choreographic style.

Along with the disintegration of training in a specific codified modern-dance technique came the interweaving of somatic training and study of dance forms from other cultures, as well as from the aforementioned movement practices. Along with studio closures came an increase in site-specific performances, performance art, and cross-disciplinary devised collaboration. Choreographers began letting dancers have more democratic input into the creation of movement, with the result that today much of the movement has become choreographer-led rather than solely created.

Perhaps this is one of the greatest distinctions between modern and contemporary dance. In the first several generations of modern dance, the movement was almost solely created by the choreographer. Now, so much of the movement is created by the participating dancers, many think that the movement all looks the same; there is no distinctive movement style. Due to somatic study and scientific knowledge of kinesiology, technical ability has skyrocketed. Dancing can be luscious and startling, but, as I heard Hanya Holm say at the Early Pioneers Conference at SUNY Purchase, "They may be technically better, but there's nobody home inside."

Newman affirmed that American dance, with its "brilliant movement invention," took on a homogenous look, "without a distinctive voice inside the movement." She suggested that "physicality for the sake of invention" created "delicious dancing," but other countries questioned its superficiality.

As funds for dance dwindled, presenters increased their desire to have "safe bet" moneymakers in theaters. Rather than risk presenting new, avant-garde companies, often they would look to present those companies that ensured a sold-out house or that drew press and media attention. And, with other governments promoting and funding their companies, the emphasis shifted to larger international companies or exotica outside the regular so-called American realm.

Solomons jr saw the situation as a mixed bag. With programmers and presenters more savvy about drawing an audience, he thought important work remains underexposed. Seeing who gets presented causes young choreographers to think their work must be accessible, so, according to Solomons jr, modern dance has become "more about entertainment than about art, and that's not good." The upside of this is that he thinks more "average citizens" are "seeing work that they wouldn't see otherwise."

Where are these folks seeing dance? One result of the 1970s dance boom was that more theaters across the country booked modern dance. Varone commented that dance was decentralized since the 1970s, and that has been good for the rest of the country as well as for modern dance. Companies are located in more cities throughout the nation now, but within the USA, New York remains the place where the most dance activity happens. Choreographers agreed that New York was previously looked to as the center of the modern-dance world, but now it has lost its reputation as the center for the cutting edge of dance. According to Newman and others, "people don't look to America and New York as the center." There isn't any one center anymore.

How does modern dance from the beginning of the twentieth century relate to concert dance at the beginning of the twenty-first century? What similarities or disparities are there? If she were alive today, would Isadora Duncan like what she saw? Duncan thought dance emanated from the soul, from the solar plexus. She was an atheist, so what did she mean by soul? What would she say today? In the USA in the early twentieth century, the idea of the soul constituted a predominant Christian reference. With the influence of Eastern religions today, is the connotation of the soul necessarily the same?

I think Duncan, as a product of her time and culture, would have found some new-age ideas to be in keeping with what she was trying to express through dance. It's just that today's language is different. Instead of soul and solar plexus, we talk about dancing with "expressive energy," "chi," "*kundalini*," or "coming from the center," which we now know is 1.3 inches below the navel. Isadora Duncan may not have known today's terminology about chakras and chi, but her references to feeling the dance make me think she tapped into the same energy source that audiences perceive as most communicative today.

From what I've read about Duncan's dancing, she had a phenomenal ability to express a feeling of oneness, of wholeness, centeredness, a connection to something greater than herself. She tapped into those universal feelings people yearn for and find so satisfying. She moved audiences in a fresh new way.

Today's contemporary dance spans the entire continuum of what dance can be, from emotional/spiritual to pure movement or entertainment. Along with globalization comes the fusion of many dance forms. Though the state of dance may be in recession within the USA, as Lucinda Childs suggested, there is good dance happening in surprising places. Other countries *are* supporting their choreographers, and though the name may have changed from modern dance to postmodern or contemporary dance, concert dance as an art prevails.

A multifocal universe for dance continues throughout the world, and these fourteen artists remain strong, positive, and passionate about their art. As Wagoner said, the pendulum swings back and forth. Childs revealed that she couldn't imagine that the spirit of dance for which Isadora Duncan fought would ever be put out completely. Childs admonished us to look around and keep our eyes open, for modern dance is happening throughout the world right now. It may be morphing into something we haven't anticipated, but that's the beauty of the art form.

As Claudia La Rocco in the *New York Times* suggested, in today's dance, "boundaries are blurring" with a "fearless do-it-yourself aesthetic," which exists for reasons both artistic and economic, leading to "wonderfully rich, unmediated worlds in which artists' ideas drive new creations" (La Rocco 2007).

> Much of today's best work is re-examining everything about performance. It is a quieter re-evaluation than what occurred during the '60s and '70s, which came complete with manifestoes, but the sense of a restless repositioning against an insular tradition is similarly vibrant [. . .] For performers in their 20s and early 30s, people like Chase Granoff, Ann Liv Young or Levi Gonzalez — are a new generation creating work without having served a long apprenticeship in a dance company, and distinctly uninterested in honing a specific movement technique.
>
> (La Rocco 2007)

These young artists reflect a "prevalent sensibility" of "feeling more kinship with contemporary visual art and film than with conventional dance practices" (La Rocco 2007).

Globalization penetrates almost every aspect of our lives, and, together with the all-pervasive internet, our lives are so drastically impacted that our cultural forms are changing. As Kenneth King said, although "it may initially sound discouraging, it also implies another (imminent?) sea-change. The parameters of our givens and conceptions are shifting"—about the body, time, age, race, gender, art forms, information, space, culture, and about the Earth itself. As these parameters transform, so does the world of concert dance.

There is no doubt that modern dance has morphed many times since its inception at the turn of the twentieth century. Over 100 years later, the dancing in concert dance does not look the same as it did in 1908, nor should we expect it to, but that doesn't mean that the seminal ideas about it have disappeared. Isadora Duncan wanted dance to be viewed as a high art, one that was as inspirational as listening to a symphony or seeing a sculpture.

Maybe it's too much to expect each choreographer to reinvent the choreographic wheel in terms of movement style, so a more democratic, random method of putting movement together has become more reflective of the twenty-first-century web that interconnects us all. One shared commonality is that all people on Earth dance, no matter what the race, gender, age, geographic continent, or economic situation.

Harris suggested that there is an "incubation period of dancers making connections between the movements of other dance forms right now." As technology increases its instrumental influence over us and our world melds into global consciousness, movement in concert dance will continue to register these changes in ways yet unknown.

The physicality of it, the look, may change, but the continuation of a physical expression of art will not. Whatever it's called, and whatever the RAGE, further steps will always continue to dance.

Lucinda Childs (1983). Photo © Thomas Victor.

Lucinda Childs

After graduating from Sarah Lawrence College as a dance major in 1962, and studying with Merce Cunningham, Lucinda Childs began her career as choreographer and performer in 1963 as an original member of the Judson Dance Theater in New York. After forming her own dance company in 1973, Childs collaborated with Robert Wilson and Philip Glass on the opera *Einstein on the Beach*, participating as leading performer and choreographer. The opera premiered in 1976 in Avignon, France, and was revived in 1984 and 1992.

Since 1979, Childs has collaborated with a number of composers and designers, including John Adams and Frank Gehry, on a series of large-scale productions. The first of these was DANCE, choreographed in 1979 with music by Philip Glass and a film/decor by Sol LeWitt, for which Childs was awarded a Guggenheim Fellowship. Since 1981, Childs has received a number of commissions from major ballet companies; these include the Paris Opéra Ballet, Pacific Northwest Ballet, Berlin Opera Ballet, Lyon Opéra Ballet, Les Ballets de Monte-Carlo, Geneva Opera Ballet, Ballet de l'Opéra du Rhin, and the Boston Ballet.

Since 2003, she has choreographed new works for Mikhail Baryshnikov's White Oak Dance Company. In 2005, Childs choreographed *Ten Part Suite* for the Boston Ballet with music by Arcangelo Corelli. She has also choreographed Stravinsky's *Symphony of Psalms* for MaggioDanza in Florence, Italy, May 2007, with the revival of *Daphnis et Chloe* choreographed in 2003. In 2007, she returned to the Ballet de l'Opéra du Rhin to choreograph and direct Stravinsky's *Le Rossignol*, and *Oedipus Rex* for the Opéra du Rhin, which premiered in Strasbourg in March 2007, and she also appeared in Robert Wilson's production of Bach's *Passion of Saint John* at the Théâtre de Chatelet in Paris. In April 2007, *Chamber Symphony*, with music by John Adams, was revived by the Bayerisches Staatsballett in Munich, where it premiered in 1994.

Since 1992, Childs has worked extensively in the domain of opera, in Luc Bondy's production of Richard Strauss's *Salome*, which she choreographed for the Salzburg Festival, and which was revived for La Scala in Milan, Italy, in March 2007. In 2005, she choreographed John Adams' new opera, *Doctor Atomic*, directed by Peter Sellars, which premiered in October 2005 with the San Francisco Opera, and which was revived by the Lyric Opera of Chicago in December 2007.

In March 2007, the French and German Arts television channel ARTE broadcast the film documentary by Patrick Bensard *La Cinémathèque de la Danse*, which features Lucinda Childs in rehearsal with Mikhail Baryshnikov, and the Ballet de l'Opéra du Rhin in New

York, London, and Paris, and includes interviews with Mikhail Baryshnikov, Philip Glass, Anna Kisselgoff, Yvonne Rainer, Susan Sontag, and Robert Wilson.

In 2001, Childs received the Bessie Award for sustained achievement, and in 2004 she was appointed by the French Government to the rank of Commandeur dans l'Ordre des Arts et des Lettres.

Privileged Time in the Moment

During my first interview in 1980, I was still interested in doing dance pieces in collaboration with visual artists and composers, full-scale productions. This period was inspired by the work I had done in 1976, on *Einstein on the Beach* with Robert Wilson and Philip Glass. At that time, I was being presented regularly at the Brooklyn Academy of Music. There was a demand for that kind of work, up to and including *Available Light*, choreographed in 1983, in collaboration with architect Frank Gehry, with music by John Adams. I went on to work with the visual artist Tadashi Kawamata, from Japan, in 1987, and that was wonderful, but then the dance boom started to decline, and suddenly there were difficulties with funding, beginning in 1989.

This was a critical period for me when the whole issue of censorship came up with the National Endowment for the Arts (NEA). Robert Mapplethorpe had been one of the artists with whom I had collaborated, and I followed the course of events leading up to and including the closing of one of his exhibitions at the Corcoran Gallery in Washington DC. I wanted to participate in the protests that were taking place among the artists, but the result was discouraging. In a letter to the then Director of the NEA, John Frohnmayer, I complained about the censorship statement that we were obliged to sign in order to apply for grants. He replied, "If that's how you feel, don't apply for grants, or just don't take the money," so I thought, "Well, that's straightforward."

In any case, in the interest of keeping the company going, it was hard to turn down the invitations we had in Europe from Théâtre de la Ville in Paris or the Festival in Avignon. Also, in 1992 there was a second revival of *Einstein on the Beach*, which involved touring in Europe, as well as in Japan and Australia. So we were doing very well in terms of earned income from foreign invitations, but it was difficult at home, as we had always counted on the NEA for general operating support for the company's administrative expenses. In addition to the troubling censorship issue, at a certain point, we no longer fit into the guidelines for a company grant, because we hadn't appeared in New York on a regular basis. Thus, the smaller independent companies like my own were no longer eligible to apply for general operating through the NEA; we were only eligible to apply for funding for individual projects, which makes all the necessary planning and preparation virtually impossible, as you never really know until the last minute where you stand in terms of budget.

By European standards, what our government was providing us with was very little, but without any state or federal support, I had no guaranteed unearned income for my company. It was very difficult to compensate with income derived from fundraising, even with touring support for rehearsals and performances for an extended period of time. Many European choreographers have much more security and stability for their companies than we do. And, without a doubt, I have received more support as an artist there than here. In 2004, I was appointed by the French Government to the rank of Commandeur dans l'Ordre des Arts et des Lettres. And, in 2007, the French and German Arts television channel Arte broadcast a film documentary by Patrick Bensard, *La Cinémathèque de la Danse*, which features excerpts of my work from the 1960s to the present day in rehearsal with Mikhail Baryshnikov, and a revival with the Ballet de l'Opéra du Rhin of *Dance* (1979), created in collaboration with Sol LeWitt and Philip Glass, along with interviews with Philip Glass, Anna Kisselgoff, Susan Sontag, and Robert Wilson.

The most disturbing thing about the censorship issue, and the thing that I feel is the biggest disadvantage for the American choreographers, is that the politicians seem to me to be uninformed. Some of them have the attitude, "Well, if you are so important why can't you find a private sponsor?" This kind of thing is much easier for the larger companies, who can offer larger exposure to attract the interest of sponsors.

I think that professional dancers should be able to protect their standards and that choreographers should try to help them. I know that the dancers in my company have worked at all kinds of jobs, hopefully teaching jobs, but a lot of times that is not the case. A full-time job for a dancer can be an obstacle, because in order to survive in the community as a professional dancer, you have to be free to train and to take class every day.

Our twenty-fifth anniversary at the Brooklyn Academy of Music (BAM) in 2000 was an important event for me because we had not performed in New York for five years. It was a wonderful invitation, but still, in order to make it feasible financially, it was necessary to raise money, and I found that this was more difficult than ever. I worked very hard in preparation for this twenty-fifth anniversary season. Two years prior to the performance date, I began looking for new support everywhere, working very carefully with a fundraising team, step by step by step, having meetings to re-evaluate the situation every few months, doing everything possible, everything I could think of. But in the end, the presentation at BAM was a huge financial strain. This had happened a number of times in the past—to end a New York season with a large deficit—but this time I was discouraged that even with the prestigious invitation from BAM for the twenty-fifth anniversary season of the company, we were unable to bring the fundraising up to the level that would have been necessary. So, I decided to disband the company.

Since 2000, I have worked on a freelance basis, for other companies in Europe or in the USA, bringing some of my dancers with me when possible to help me set work on other companies. I've worked a lot with ballet companies who are interested in modern work. Many of these companies already have works in their repertory ranging from Balanchine to Forsythe, which is an enormous plus for me as my work is very demanding. What I've always done is to ask the artistic directors to let me come ahead of time to do a workshop with the dancers or to at least watch class.

One of my recent projects was in Geneva, for the Ballet de Genève. They have two works of mine. One of the works was created originally for my company in 1993, titled *Concerto*, with music by Henryk Gorecki, which has also been in the repertory of Baryshnikov's White Oak Dance Company, Les Ballets de Monte-Carlo, and also the Introdans Company in the Netherlands. Geneva Ballet also commissioned me to choreograph Ravel's *Daphnis and Chloe*. I've worked in the domain of opera for a number of years and have been introduced to a number of composers not necessarily associated with my aesthetic, among them Gluck,

Mozart, Strauss, Wagner, and Verdi. Thus, Ravel's score was an interesting challenge but not a territory entirely unknown to me.

Daphnis and Chloe was more of a narrative ballet. After working with Wilson, I've been fascinated with exploring the realm of semi-abstract expression, where the dancers are not necessarily telling a story but are working with the narrative material in a fragmented way, suggesting movement motifs, which can then be associated with the elements of the story. This was also true for *Histoire*, a duet I choreographed for the Martha Graham Dance Company in 1999.

In September 2005, I worked in San Francisco on the premiere of *Doctor Atomic* with music by John Adams, with whom I have collaborated, and whose music I have used on a number of occasions. It was directed by Peter Sellars, whose work I have known and admired for years. He wanted me specifically for this piece, I think primarily because of knowing my work through my involvement with *Einstein*, with Philip Glass, and Robert Wilson.

How has my movement evolved in the past twenty years? It really depends on the music. The movement improvisation that I do in preparation for making a new work is always inspired directly from the music that I work with. All the material that I choreograph builds out of the music, depending upon how it's structured, how it sounds, and, ultimately, what movement material I feel works with the music. Once I've developed the material for each dance through improvisation, I bring it into rehearsal with the dancers and try it out on them.

Up until *Einstein*, in 1976, I didn't work with music at all because I admired so much the "look" of the Cunningham dancers, knowing that the music of John Cage, Morton Feldman, or David Tudor coexists with the dancers who are not relying on its rhythm but are entirely independent of it. They have their own rhythm, which I think is beautiful discipline. They are able to sustain these rhythmical structures among themselves in a collective way, and it doesn't change that much from night to night. So, for a period of time in the 1970s, the dances consisted of dancer's phrases, which were combined in many different ways without any kind of musical accompaniment. When I first began to work with music, I didn't want to go against it, or ignore it, or go with it in such a way that it's illustrated by the movement but to create some sort of dialogue with its rhythmic structure and the structure of the choreography.

My use of the geometric patterns really has not changed much, except that, in the 1970s, given the format of a specific dance, I would work on these structures from an overhead point of view with diagrammatic scores, which are maps of each twenty seconds or so. I sketched out many of the ideas on graph paper even before the dancers came into rehearsal to try to see what patterns can be created with the phrases and to analyze how they can be combined. Now I don't do that, I tend to work more spontaneously but with the same underlying concepts.

What major events have affected my art over the past twenty years? Certainly the situation with the NEA, which hurried the dissolution of my company. For a while, as I mentioned earlier, I did write letters and tried to deal with the problem head-on, but I found that the better way for me personally to devote my time is to do what I know how to do and to focus on ways to continue my career. For example, if a director would call and say, "I need someone to choreograph the *Dance of the Seven Veils*," I would hardly even say, "Well, why exactly do you want me to do this?" I would be happy to just jump on the plane and go, and this has worked out very well for me. I have done quite a lot of work in opera. It is something new,

Lucinda Childs Dance Company, *Concerto* (1993). Photo © Peter Perazio.

and choreographers are being used more and more because of the concerns of the directors in opera nowadays, to bring the visual aspect of the whole project up to a more contemporary level.

Another important thing for me, since I don't work so much in this country, was to be invited by Boston Ballet in 2004 to create a new work. That was an interesting chance for me because I am so used to working not only outside my own company but outside my own country, so this was a very nice welcome experience to have contact with dancers who are also based here in the States, although so many of them all come from other countries. This is true for all companies now—they are all international.

Nine-eleven was a staggering event, and I still feel overwhelmed by this whole situation. I think everyone does. We are dealing with the fact that our lives have changed and that we think differently about just about everything. But before Katrina, many of us assumed that progress had been made on how to deal with a major catastrophe—natural, or otherwise— to a major city, but unfortunately it seems we're really not as far along as we need to be in addressing this kind of problem, and that's very disturbing.

How is that affecting my art? I find that the work I do happens from day to day. So, I try to prepare in advance for each day as much as possible, but the real work can only happen when I am actually there with the dancers. I feel it's a kind of privileged time and that I'm living in the moment, moving as quickly as possible but open to the unexpected.

I don't think I have ever made a political piece. Being part of the Judson was perhaps political. There were some politically active members, and we were criticized for stepping outside of the vocabulary of dance, and some thought that this was a very negative, destructive point of view. I don't think so, but I also don't think of myself as apolitical; I want to do the right thing, and I feel that the best way for me to do the right thing is to not try to latch on to some big political agenda but just to deal with what is going on around me and what is affecting my dancers and to figure out how I can establish the best possible environment for them.

How has the question of race changed over the past twenty years? Being in New York, I think everyone is sincerely welcome into the dance community. I never had any sense of discrimination of any kind. The only thing that would make a case for racism is with the economic situation, since you need to start when you're young. Children from underprivileged backgrounds do not have access to the kind of training that I had growing up as a child. So, this is perhaps an issue in terms of who can then consider the possibility of a professional career in dance.

I had a lot of difficulty dealing with the equal-opportunity pressures that came up in the 1990s because I felt, "since when was my company *not* an equal opportunity employer?" I found it very difficult to abide by these guidelines. I objected to the idea that it was necessary to put a clause in advertisements for our auditions. I was sympathetic to the idea that it was put there *in case* someone would think we weren't equal opportunity, but still, it was a difficult time for me.

Gender, well, that's a difficult one. But there is the issue of gay male, as opposed to gay female. A strong gay male presence has been apparent for a long time, but a female gay presence is finally beginning to emerge. Gay female choreographers, who are *out*, are not necessarily just drawing attention to that. I think it is a good sign that we can think that there are female choreographers who happen to be gay, not female gays who happen to be choreographers.

Attitudes have changed radically since the 1960s. In the 1960s, the male gay community would embrace some women in a certain very limited way, but not always gay women. I think that this is why we have the peculiar terminology always referring to the "gay" and "lesbian" community, and I think it came about because the women felt so excluded, and were afraid that the term "gay" just meant just *male* "gay." By the time of the 1960s, gay males had achieved a level of prestige, which was extraordinary and well deserved, and they didn't want it diminished. I mean, that's what I would assume. Many people wanted to be part of their community because of their position in the art world and to be involved with the fascinating personalities. But for a gay female in the 1960s, if you had any choice in the matter, I feel you were better off to not be openly gay.

Do I think gay men control the dance world in terms of funding and touring? No, absolutely not.

Why aren't there more female choreographers recognized? Women choreographers actually have had more success in the modern dance community than in the ballet community. Many of my colleagues are female. But if there are more male choreographers sustained by funding and touring, I don't think it has anything to do with the gay issue.

Age in relation to dance? Many opportunities have come my way, and I have been busy and involved doing the projects I want to do. Age is conceivably a factor, but I find that the way people work is the important thing. Going into the room and doing what I do, people aren't going to think, "Is she fifty-five or sixty-five?" Age isn't so much of an issue for me right now.

I stopped performing as an ensemble member in the company a long time ago in the 1980s, because I wanted to be able to be outside the ensembles. As a soloist, of course, I can make work that I feel I can still do, and I don't envision performing so much anymore as a dancer, but I continue to perform in Robert Wilson's works, as he continues to want to use me as a performer.

Is an audience receptive to seeing older dancers on stage? Well, I was extremely happy to notice, reading the *New York Times*, about Beverly Schmidt performing a solo program recently. Beverly came to Sarah Lawrence when she was still part of the Nikolais' company and was already at that point—beginning to make her own programs. We all went down to Henry Street to see her, and we all loved her so much. She's a genius as far as I am concerned. I don't know what has happened over all these years, but I just was thrilled to see that Beverly had come back and had done an evening, so I think that that is hopeful.

For me, what you see is what you see, and the age is not the issue. If the technique is there, the will is there, the spirit is there, I wouldn't question age. If I auditioned dancers and someone turns out to be thirty-five or forty, it doesn't make any difference to me. At fifty, I don't imagine they would be at the audition, but it depends; it's possible, I suppose.

I don't look at age as an issue. I am looking at the technique, at the musicality, at the individual, how they are going to commit to a project, how they are responding to the material. That's really all I care about, and sometimes it's very nice to have mature people in a company.

In terms of body types, I have always had a wide variety of very tall, very short, some very thin, some not so thin dancers. It's not so much of an issue for me. I like the individuality. In the ballet companies, certainly dancers are slim; they are not heavy. For the workload, the aesthetic, and the pressures of this contemporary time, dancers have to deal with certain restrictions about their appearance.

How has the political environment changed from the 1980s to now, and how has that affected the dance world? In the late 1980s, I was crushed, really depressed, by the whole issue of censorship, the question of AIDS, and the devastation to the community and the feeling of "how do we cope with all of this." What helped was that many personalities in the performing-arts community, such as Laurie Anderson and Philip Glass, were out there in an effort to raise money and to bring greater awareness to the community.

I would agree, in terms of geographic environment, that New York City is no longer the center for dance. I think that New York drew as many dancers as it did because there was such a wide variety of dance companies, small companies, mainstream modern companies, small ballet companies, major ballet companies, but I feel that this has definitely changed. Also, one of the attractions of New York was the quality and variety of teachers available, and I know that now many dancers are disappointed, that many teachers now have difficulty maintaining studios in New York. But I don't think there is another "New York" somewhere else.

I really have no idea what is happening now with dance and funding. I have no contact or knowledge of what is going on at the NEA since it has been over five years since we even qualified to apply for funding.

I think it's true, that modern dance is in a fragile situation now. One of the things that was very hopeful for me at the time, the moment when I was giving up the company, was that the White Oak company of Baryshnikov was in full swing and commissioned a work of mine, the *Past/Forward* program, which included works from all of the choreographers at Judson, as well as a new work. I've also choreographed two solos for Baryshnikov, along with *Concerto*, which, I think, was important and very interesting for people who just read about it or saw pictures and never saw any of the Judson works. It's really too bad that his company folded, because there is nothing else like it, and nothing else like this may ever happen again.

What is the direction of modern dance? Well, I think it depends on the artists. It *is* an art form, and that was what Isadora Duncan was fighting for. One of the most fascinating things for me, growing up and thinking about a career in dance, was to see her struggle. She was determined that dance should be on a level with the other arts; that dancing shouldn't just be at a wedding, or a cocktail party, but should be on a stage with designers, such as Gordon Craig, and great composers. This was an amazing struggle, and so inspiring, when I think of where she came from and where she went. I can't imagine this spirit being put out completely.

It is very important in this day and age to keep eyes open. Things are happening all over the place in modern dance, perhaps in places that you wouldn't imagine. The young company of Kabako Faustin Linyekula was just at the Yerba Buena Center. It was amazing, and very unexpected. When I think about what they have been up against . . . so that was a very helpful (and hopeful) thing to see.

Thursday, September 29, 2005

Douglas Dunn in *Echo* (1980). Photo © Johan Elbers 2008.

Douglas Dunn

In 1971, while a member of Merce Cunningham Dance Company and of Grand Union, Douglas Dunn began presenting work in New York City. In 1976, he formed Douglas Dunn & Dancers and began touring the USA and Europe. In 1980, the Paris Opera and the Autumn Festival invited him to set Stravinsky's *Pulcinella* on the Paris Opera Ballet. He has collaborated on film and video-dances with Charles Atlas and Rudy Burckhardt. He works with artists (Mimi Gross, David Ireland, Uli Gassmann, Jeffrey Schiff), composers (Steve Lacy, Joshua Fried, Bill Cole, Eliane Radigue, Alvin Lucier, Robert Ashley, Linda Fisher, John Driscoll, Ron Kuivila), poets (Anne Waldman, Reed Bye), playwrights (Ruth Margraff, Jim Neu), and lighting designer Carol Mullins to present a multifaceted theatrical image. Dunn has received funds for his work from the New York State Council on the Arts, the National Endowment for the Arts, the John Simon Guggenheim Memorial Foundation, the Foundation for Contemporary Performance Arts, and other sources. In 1998, he received a New York Dance and Performance Award (Bessie) for Sustained Achievement. The year 2007 was the first of Douglas Dunn & Dancers' three-year project *Homestretch*, which included new work, revivals, a kids' program, and salon events at the Douglas Dunn Studio. The company's website is at <http://www.douglasdunndance.com>.

Interview with Connie Kreemer

CK: How do you think your work has evolved, how has it changed, or what has effected any change?

DD: I found dancing as my calling at twenty-six. What a relief: an activity neatly combining my physical prowess and artistic interests; a slap in the face of those expecting me to be a doctor or businessman; an arena in which males, by their scarcity, were favored, but in which macho was not *de rigueur*; a pursuit through which, by virtue of its marginal status, I might indirectly fulfill anti-establishment leanings; an enterprise that could replace my dissatisfaction (at being dissatisfied) with the goal of moving toward something better. Beauty, for example.

I'm now sixty-two. Every category mentioned, save the first, has shifted, gradually, but by now rather fully. If art-dance, then, fed a rebellious desire to be different, I now no longer need to disdain others and other forms of work to know my place. If I was running, then, away from the role of a conventional male, I now aim to balance "feminine" and "masculine" impulses and to unlock an assertiveness I was incorrect in imagining I could do without. If I thought, then, that my commitment to a progressive social agenda could be advanced through performance, I now see maximum challenge and enrichment for each in respectful separation of the art-dance and the political spheres. If discontent ignited, then, a passion for secular, structurally rigorous, hard-to-read human display and a yearning for transcendence, I now see, in such underpinnings, elements of arrogance and avoidance and strive to know a dance that might, without metaphysical expectation, spring from, say, gratefulness, empathy or compassion.

What *hasn't* changed through thirty-five years of organizing humans for viewing is my holding to an initially unconsidered tropism, exploration of form. Form means the shape, rhythm and tempo of the body, the arrangements of bodies in space, and the relations of these to forms we know, the ones we see around us in our daily lives, some made by us, some not. Though always eager to develop a previously untried choreographic procedure that might lead somewhere I haven't been, I find my focus falling consistently on the intuitive trial-and-error decision-making about, "Well, is that the right density there or not," rather than whether I'm fulfilling a theme about death or relationship that might be lurking in the back of my mind. I do sometimes have, what shall we call them, "ideas." They tend to hang around before I go into the studio but usually reverse or become irrelevant as work proceeds. A striking example of this insistent fickleness occurred a few years ago during the making of *The Common Good* (2000). I began with not just an inkling but with a clear and ambitious notion: to reverse the usual flow between audience and artist. I sent letters to people who knew my repertoire asking how to make the next dance. What should be in it? What about my dancing do you like and not like? Quite a few responses arrived, and I began diligently making them the basis of my process. There was everything from grand schemes to specific moves people wanted included.

The more I worked, however, the more the piece began to take on a life of its own that was not directly related to these inputs. A serious, seminarrative line took the upper hand, about a man and a woman, with a chorus attending them and influencing their fate, not something anyone had in the least suggested nor I anticipated. Feelings of nostalgia, pain, and loss began to fill the inner space I'd cleared for witty ambiguity. A solo for myself to a popular piece of music went from near joke to the edge of sentimentality. The pinball process was interesting but tough. I had made a commitment to these people. I wanted to honor their requests and my original idea, but I couldn't follow through completely and ended up with a piece rocking back and forth between competing attitudes. Post performance, a contributor would ask where was her suggestion, and I would verbally fancy-dance to assure her I had been faithful to her choreographic offering.

A concept, an issue, anything I might be thinking about building a dance around usually shrugs and says, "OK, go ahead, ignore me, it's your loss," or something nastier. Meanwhile, the form itself, the forms themselves, the texture of the dance, the overall rhythm, the detailed rhythms, all increasingly exert themselves as necessary and overriding. I've just described a case, *The Common Good*, in which alternative "content" altered the direction. But that's the exception. More typically, what's normally called content is giving way to considerations of weight, temperature, density. Suddenly to arrive at a juxtaposition of limbs or bodies that is unexpected and pleasing (sometimes in an "unpleasing" way) takes my breath (and my ideas) away or allows me to breathe deeper. Stories, if any, are left to less conscious decision-making, their possible recognizable cohesion roughed up by my preference for textural investigation over statement. A viewer extracting an idea or narrative line from my dances is generously adorning me with a horse's mouth.

Presenting art that raises questions because it isn't trying to answer any is hardly new, not to mention submitting the art object as something in itself rather than something to look through. For the spectator whose verbal dominates her visual life, abstraction for the eye can be a puzzle, and there are moments when I think, "Wouldn't it be thrilling if I could make (or see) a dance that had unity of declared theme with form that entranced?" But later, I wonder if such a proposition doesn't offend Terpsichore, if her sense of what dance does best isn't in fact close to mine. A conscious rationale for formal emphasis can, if one wishes, be placed alongside deeply ingrained temperamental persistence. What I want to offer, and prefer as a viewer, I might say, is delight in a honed collection of moves available for immediate sensuous experience, rather than an idea moves are designed to exemplify and support. And one could extend the argument, pointing out, for example, how unsuited human movement is, compared to novels, film, poetry, drama, even to music, to reflect adequately the complexities of inner being. But these matters of sensibility rarely bend to mere reason. Movement without added context, competition in sports, for example, just doesn't make an impression on some. Appreciative watching of human motion as such, arranged by a choreographer or found on the street, is developed through personal experience based on interest. The perennially marginal status of art-dance reflects the rarity of this formal/sensuous bent.

Then too, ideas "about"—I suppose because of the way we are educated, especially in literature, where the author's intent, at least in my day, was to be ferreted out, the "underlying truth" of the story, its meaning, grasped and masticated—can even *add* to confusion when it comes to dancing. In 1997, I made *Riddance* and wrote a program note indicating that the five consecutive solos were "inspired by" the Five Element Theory of Traditional Chinese Medicine. A reviewer took me to task for not being explicit enough in relation to the elements—Fire, Metal, Water, Earth, Wood—as if my goal had been, or should have been, literal representation. Since then, I've reverted to my default position in favor of the oblique if not the opaque, at least when it comes to providing associations as handles for the viewer. For me, what's interesting is what form does *to* "meaning," not what form can do *for* "meaning."

Judgmental talk of nonnarrative dance that addresses its sense instead of asserting lack of it is rare. But a tongue-tied or dismissive response at least leaves the artifact as is, available for appreciation or not, like mountains, one of which, when I extolled its magnificence, was identified by a wrangler I came across in the Sierra as "nothin' but a bunch of fuckin' rocks." Mental life organized to provide reassurance leaves little room for experiences generated from skeptical investigation. My 1980 Broadside included the line, "People go to the theater to change their minds." The irony was gentle and comic, holding lightly between cynicism and hopefulness. Today, I'm less hopeful, but not disturbed in being so. I was inspired, when I arrived in New York City in 1968, to see dances of "just dancing" asserting that they could stand on their own. It was a revelation to be offered movement as art without recourse to literary or musical associations and to theatrical hoo ha. Wonderful: a cleansing of the visual palette in relation to human form. I experiment with ways to add to this simplicity which begets complexity, but dancing per se is still what drives my train.

CK: Are you referring to collaborators?

DD: No. It is because of my focus on dancing as such that I give composers, painters, sculptors, film and video artists, and writers free rein to bring to the situation something substantive based on their own current interests, not something to underline or comment on what's already going on.

CK: What about your own movement? Do you think it has changed over the years?

DD: My first training was ballet. I enjoyed right away the straightforward challenge of attempting to fill shapes and moves already codified and understood. The idealization of the body didn't offend me, and I knew as an experienced athlete the kinds of exercise required and the need to repeat if one wished finally to be able to accomplish a specific feat, to leap into the air, for example, and be still. Carriage was another matter. Having curved inward in protest against the man who divorced my mother, my spine refused a posture of confident display. A prince, just then, I was not prepared to be.

Some years and numerous twists and turns of life later, I saw a man present a flowing vertical without the sternum's added rise. Here was a body trying for the same degree of difficulty, complication, and clarity as the ballet, indeed even greater, without the suggestion of becoming a character: being, rather, while dancing, the person he already was. Performing with Mr. Cunningham in the late 1960s and early 1970s, I also, in the manner of a reluctantly grown-up wild child, sketched and role-played with Grand Union. But it was the body studied in classical proportion making extra-balletic moves that appealed: stylized, worker-like, sensitive, daring in finesse without falling into manner, restrained in blatant show of what the dancing might narratively or imagistically mean, full of mixing feelings that were not required to become determinative of a staged persona, covering horizontal space fleet as a cheetah, grabbing and letting go of gravity bouncy as a springbok.

Lightness is what catches my eye as I watch dancers nowadays. Not an ever-upward-seeking body; not a foot-flexing, abdomen-slapping body; not a shape-forgetting, rough and tumble, feel-up-against-another-body body; not a thick-muscled, trick-gymnastic body; not a casual, just-like-everyone-else body; not an overly precisely controlled, loose, limb-swinging body. A body, rather, male or female, that when standing, evinces without strain a physical readiness, an equal valence upward and downward and, in action, is able to fulfill that vertical range, strength of well-trained bended knee providing, when called on, forceful lift-off, sustained flight, carefree landing.

But travel by air is only half of how *lightness* adds to my enjoyment when watching dancing. Despite many interesting twentieth-century strategies to obviate the fact, art represents. Re-presents. No matter how much "life" an artist leverages, we are beholden to a dividing line between what has been chosen to be invited into the aesthetic arena and what has not. Everything can be seen as art, but only to certain objects and actions is our attention asked specially to be drawn. In the ring of the circus designated to dance, the body (so far) must be there. If a choreographer wants to use acted character and narrative devices to depict ranges of human events and emotions, training of the body can be of one kind or another. But for dancing that is less behaviorally literal, the fibrous makeup of the flesh matters, makes a statement even before the first step is taken. Muscular tone and muscular shape, counterpoint of strength and flexibility (some high-jumpers are stiff, some pliable extenders earthbound), these carnal features are in themselves part of the representation; in the design of the instrument, one senses the extent of the dancer's territory and how far and with what degree of aplomb she will lead you through it.

That's the windup, here's the pitch. The plié that makes possible access to "up" does so by saying "down." This gamut from low to high may be just that for the dancer, a physical challenge, a thrill, a cause for pride as prowess increases, deepening bend promoting increasingly wondrous soaring. But for a viewer, the up-down line inside the dancer, one end of which looks to the center of the Earth, the other to the sky, may connote metaphoric forces as well: historically derived and culturally specific, yes, but not thereby, for those willing to embrace a given legacy, any less salient. Seeing patterns in the weave of the many-threaded fabric of imagination woven by artists of a con-tinuous tradition over centuries is an immense pleasure. And for an eye with the agility to associate form across cultural time and space, and no compunction not to do so, yet another cornucopia of riches offers itself up to a sensible perceiver's delectation.

Going on so, I feel in danger of implanting the impression that I see jumping itself as the essence of dancing. Not so. (I better not. I still perform, ascension out of the question.) But without it, without its possibility, one of the few bones of expressiveness Terpsichore throws our way is lost. And its disuse leads to atrophy of others as well. To learn to elevate assuredly requires centering the body. Once the stance knows its nonmoving, neutral place, and the legs have learned not to quibble but to collaborate, not only the earth beneath and air above but also the surrounding space open to explo-ration and definition. Feet ready to go without counting on initiatory momentum of the torso/arms/head, quickness of the entire frame becomes possible. Rapid change of direction, of facing, of "expected" gestural path, which for the viewer equal revisions of intent, makes *surprise*, too, feasible as part of the dance. Not the surprise of slapstick, or of dramatized change of psychological mind, nor of quick, decorative laciness of head, torso, and arms, but the full-bodied thrust one sees in nature, its reason and mechanism not always evident, as when numberless fish turn suddenly in unison.

CK: You've wandered into talking about dancing you see rather than what you do.

DD: Yes, it's difficult to see oneself clearly. Another aspect of form that occupies me daily is invention. "*Invention.*" Everything's already been invented. Watching late-night television I see bits, by the Marx Brothers, for example, that are so close to modern dance passages I've witnessed that I can't believe the influence isn't direct. But each person gets to make what he or she has never made before, so, in personal terms, it's invention, no matter the inspiration. I include versions of what I notice when I sense value in doing so. But more basic for me is to lock and to walk away from the bank vault of eye-recorded images of the street, television, movies, and books, and to explore what the body can do, going with or against its momentums, finding shapes I didn't

Stucco Moon (1994). Choreography: Douglas Dunn. Photo © Tom Brazil.

think it could make, juxtaposing differing scales (big, small), rhythms, tempos, choosing and shaping from what happens as these gamuts cross one another.

By now, of course, I can no longer do as much, not by a long shot. I've stopped jumping, as I said, not because I can't take off, but because landing is treacherous. I have to *remember* not to jump. I can do a version and then transfer it to somebody else, or I get more . . . imaginative (is that the right word?), make up movement in my mind, my mind's body, and then talk the dancer into it; various ways of trying to keep the full spectrum in the work. I do like to maintain a palette with as wide a range as possible, up and down, sideways, quick and slow, and all those things.

Diminution of vitality and extension has led me, in my own performance, to be a bit more playful about the characters I become. Whoever they are, I'm more inclined to make faces, as it were. Also, activity tends more and more to rise; the legs tire quickly, but the arms still play, so attention to the upper body increases. But even for younger dancers, the body is not infinitely malleable. The joints, as evolved, have definite limits. If one wants to develop strength of the kind I want in my work, sufficient to keep shape alive to the eye at a distance, ways of counterposing limbs are further reduced. Within this visually articulate range, the body offers a kind of logic, an order of possible relations between the various movable parts. Having arrived at the opportunity of setting the next unit of movement (putting aside for the moment the matter of overall interconnectedness, formal or otherwise, in the particular dance), *invention* means finding a continuation that is within this physical order, but not the only or most likely, most "logical" one, and not one used in another work. This attitude leads to, thrives on, *variety*. Variety, diversity of movement, its shapes, rhythms, tempos. It's difficult to imagine bodies with little extension and power fulfilling the visual and kinaesthetic appetite of the viewer when movement itself is the main course. The dynamic oppositions of torso and limbs, along with spatial vectoring in the dance's structure, may become an oblique, perhaps for some subliminal, substitute for the psychological conflict of storied dancing. Anything less than a gamut from stillness to highly activated maximum stretch (including jumping) risks leaving unquenched the viewer's thirst for an alternative to the "realistic" behavior available on the street and to live entertainment's usual analogues for human feeling.

CK: Compared to the 1970s, I'd say your movement now is softer and less linear.

DD: At Princeton, I wrote my thesis on the diversity of critical approaches to the sculpture of Henry Moore and called it *Form and Feeling*, a sign that though it appeared first intellectually, this spring of two waters was bubbling from the beginning. Later, when I found the dance, feeling was the sensation of moving, of covering space, of changing tempo, of investigating rhythm; and form was the organization of these actions into adventurous, open-ended kinds of coherence I already understood from looking at art and life in terms of shape, color, and pattern. It was enough to dance staying with feelings related to the steps themselves and to the choice to be watched. My sense of task was to deliver a moving picture, not a diagram of inner states. In a first encounter with modern, a two-week course at the Graham school, I was bothered by the use of tension greater than necessary for the movement. A closer correlation between motion and required expenditure was more in line with my pre-dance experience of manual labor and athletics, nor did exposure to various styles of dramatized dance tempt me from this inclination.

I like talk that distinguishes not degrees but kinds of expressivity. Both acted dancing and "plain dancing" are expressive, a shy person's disclosure not less than, but different from, that of a show-off. Restraint improperly employed can be a means of keeping emotion not just modulated at its point of emergence but inwardly at bay. A plain dancer working to keep certain feelings in the cellar might well evince an overly tensile stretch, an impulsiveness that jumps the rhythm, or other symptoms; or the entire enterprise might be based on needing approval or control before giving back—any and all of which might in fact be interesting to watch. In contrast, I remember Suzanne Farrell's ability to convince me that her leg had gone as far as it could go, but softly, without strain or hurry, without preciousness, no matter the tempo, the way I imagined a leg would extend in Heaven.

To answer your question directly: Yes, my work can now, when the dance calls for it, be softer and curvier: because time has talked me out of the compulsion to overdance; because strength and agility no longer outline the limits of my identity; and because I now sense that a more generous impulse gives moves values previously I was blind to.

CK: There are different categories of awareness that have changed over the past twenty to twenty-five years, one of them being race. Can you make any comment about this?

DD: Perhaps *Cocca Mocca* (1998) provides an example of what sometimes goes on when I'm working. I decided on a large cast and held an audition. I chose eleven dancers on the basis of their dancerly capability in relation to the needs of my use of the body, and on my sense, looking at them, of character. I mean character in the way that every person and every thing has it if you look for it. Everyone walks differently; calling that difference a difference of character is what I mean here. I ended up with one Vietnamese, two Hispanic, three black, and six white (some, not all, American) dancers. When I work, I don't talk much. It was not part of my process to get to know these people and their backgrounds. They come to me to dance, I make a dance. OK. So, one day, I'm working on a trio, and I step back to watch and see a white woman sitting on a black man's shoulders and a black woman circling them wildly. I become aware of the configuration as readable in terms of skin color as representative of different cultural postures. I realize at that moment that I have the opportunity to maintain that kind of attention and work with it. But I don't. I go on making the trio in the formal/intuitive terms I've begun it, space, rhythm, tempo, shape, similarity, and contrast with the other three trios to which it will be juxtaposed, and let the possible narrative play itself out without conscious manipulation on my part.

CK: Can you say more about the dancers you hire?

DD: Working with European ballet dancers, I discovered in what ways American modern dancers galvanize my interest. The former (not all of them), when not portraying a character, dance a persona not unlike one they present when conversing. The latter (not all of them), when not portraying a character, dance task-like on top of a reservoir of emotion. If the dam is not to break, runoff of controlled quantities and timings must occur. For Americans, choreography can offer specified structures for graduated release of feeling. You can read on a face (and body) that's not trained to put on an acted presence a negotiation between the individual's own drive and the forms shaped by the artist. Most often, this American person with no add-on character, who steps on stage with a sign that reads "I'm just dancing," glows, faintly or strongly, with an intriguing passion stoked by primal vigor.

Caracole (1995). Choreography: Douglas Dunn. Photo © Beatriz Schiller 2008.

Logically, the dancer most enjoyable to watch as escapee from social presence is one unaware of being so. A dancer instructed in nothing but the shape, rhythm, and tempo of the movement is left in the dark about a significant portion of what will be seen on stage. Her demeanor is not neutral, but neither is it calculated. It is innocent, clear water with creatures swimming beneath. This species of deadpan, arrived at through underdirection, touches that much praised and blamed strain of American character that yearns for Eden, Nature as a nonthreatening cradle of bliss.

CK: So, your interest is not at all topical. What would you say? "Generic"?

DD: In dance, you have, as given, artifice and live presence combusting together, an alchemical ready-mix. Why dilute it?

CK: Dance as already something before it attempts to communicate?

DD: I fall away from the idea of performance as a kind of high-five interaction with the audience, as if sincerity on stage could be the same as sincerity off.

CK: Would that refute Isadora Duncan's idea of her art as an evocation of an inner spirit of the soul?

DD: It can be that, but it's a character of that, not that itself. The dancer has to convince me of the character even if for her it's the real thing. When I see a dance beholden to a literary theme, or to music it's visualizing, or to a structural concept, I feel "hanging on." Or I feel I'm being instructed. I prefer moves that look as if they've snuck beyond the control of the choreographer. Sometimes a dance aimed like an arrow hits my heart and wow. But mostly, I want to be fooled, not know what I'm looking at, nor how it came to be. Likewise, in my work, I want to get out of it. I don't want to dance in my personal self. I want to become generic self, generic person, generic being, and I want to relate to . . . the audience . . . I want to relate to my dance the same way the audience does. I want it to be separate from both of us, and we're both looking at it and we're both relating through it to our existence, our momentary existence, with our sense of future and sense of past, yes, what we bring to it, but mostly with our vitality of awakening to the moment through paying close attention to a fabrication.

CK: So we're somewhat together in being separate from—?

DD: The question is which aspects of consciousness to hold on to and which to relinquish when dancing and watching dancing. Perhaps an image is more telling: say, all of us jumping into the same ocean at the same moment. We're all in the "same water," but each feels it differently, and, despite being buoyed more than on land, each has to remember to swim to stay afloat. I danced *Haole* (1988), a forty-minute solo, at Drew University in New Jersey in 1990 and was having trouble balancing. I tried harder, adding attention to that aspect of the moves, but teetered all the more. Then it occurred to me to use the audience as support, to imagine them helping me, and immediately found my legs.

CK: What in your view does dance do best?

DD: Dance disappears. One might say that it's supposed to disappear, that its gossamer existence is one of its special features, an inherent quality that goes some way to distinguish it from other forms of art. I dance because I have a penchant for immediate sharing with another every minute's possibility of fresh perception. Willy-nilly, I maintain an active relation to that potential. It's the flipside of form, *how* we see what we see. If I look at it long enough, a leaf will turn brown and fall off. But before that happens, I myself will change. This fluctuating interaction between what we think of as what's out there and what's in here is the field on which my dances materialize.

It's already something to see performance as doer and viewer activating each other's senses and sensibilities, but what makes one dance different from another? A manageable answer is, the specific sequence and organization of moves enacted by specific dancers at a given time, and the proportions, moment to moment and overall, as the dance completes itself. Obvious? Seems so until one hears viewers recount their experience. Only recently have I acknowledged that most spectators don't see the elements of dance to which I pay most attention. Years ago, I had the thought, "What about evolving one piece for life?" But such work would be easy to label. I have an unconscious intention to avoid a label. I haven't wanted to make a style, certainly not a signature. It's hard to get away from yourself, and it's vain to think you could come up with infinite variety even if you don't consider turning out dances as a constant refinement of consistent inner vision. Even admitting it's artifice that gives art-dance half its purchase, I still want to say no to "style," anybody's or my own. I want to get down to the raw thing. I want a constant reopening in relation to space and what's seen in it, vision as unmediated as possible. I don't mean some abstract visual world. I mean the close-at-hand world we see and that waits to be seen, the one by means of which our feelings, if we look, are turned over and reorganized through the progression of each day's dawning, heightening, waning, darkening.

CK: How much coordination is there for you between what you do outside the studio and what you do inside?

DD: Outside, there are two ways I pull veils away, if there are veils—hey, there might not be veils. One is to look at something for a good while. You start noticing your pen, and you get past "I need my pen, that's my pen." You get past the usefulness of it, and it starts to come alive differently. The other is to notice change. We just had our sidewalk rebuilt, and for two months there was a structure of 2×4s and planks; you came to the building and you walked over a wooden bridge, and there was blue canvas on either side covering this or that. A pretty little theatrical set in front of the building. A pleasing variation. A different sense of arriving and entering. "Where am I living? What am I? One of the seven dwarfs?" Then one day, they take it away, and it's shocking, shocking and refreshing. So, attention to change and attention to stillness, or thingness, help reopen my sense of being awake in the world. In the studio, the principal means of refreshment is to alter kinaesthetic habit. New muscle patterns foster new mental and emotional patterns, then these elements play back and forth with one another begetting, at times, dizzying unfamiliarity.

When Chiara sits on the windowsill overlooking Broadway I wonder what she sees. Surely not "buses," not "buildings," not "people in the street." Those are *our* categories. Motion? Size? Color? It's at such a less verbalized level of visual experience that I find myself drawn to work. And even if I can't make the dance she would make with her four paws and twenty-some-odd whiskers, I'm constantly surprised how little what I consciously know, what I've studied and thought about, asserts itself as I work.

CK: Do you watch dancing in terms of your own preferences of body type, degree of stylization, and classical bent?

DD: If people are organizing things, and you sense their desire to do so, there can be a birth of attention. Even things that don't come off for you personally—they don't enrich you because you've seen them before or . . . whatever—still there's always the enticing fact that somebody did this, and in its own way, just because she made it, it's perfect. At that moment, that is what she put out, what she gave you. Even let's say it's too obviously ego-driven, or heart-string exploitative, well, then she gave you a chance to see that, and now you can feel more deeply work that is less manipulative. If you look without a good/bad lens, the dance has a chance to become what it is, including for you, for your experience. It's a thing. It's a form, and as with this pencil, which wasn't invented to be looked at, it can become interesting, can become an enlivening source for contemplation.

CK: Are choreographing and dancing for you a pleasure?

DD: In these activities, my resources come into play at maximum strength and focus. Is that pleasure? The most interesting moments are those where resistance is greatest, when I don't know what to do. I either fight through or wait, or both. Whatever the obstacle, the higher or thicker it is, the more interesting will be, if I get there, what's on the other side. "To move is to love," says Frank O'Hara. I continue to work toward that ideal, toward the statement's implicit victory over a freighted heretofore.

Douglas thanks Joan Benham, Jim Paul, and Anne Waldman for advice and encouragement in editing the interview.

November 22, 2004

Molissa Fenley, *Desert Sea*. Front: Molissa Fenley; Back: Wanjiru Kamuyu. Photo © Paula Court.

Molissa Fenley

Born in Las Vegas in 1954, Molissa Fenley was six years old when her family moved to Nigeria where her father worked with USAID (the United States Agency for International Development). She attended high school in Spain and then returned to the USA to attend and graduate from Mills College in Oakland, Calif., with a BA in dance in 1975. That same year, she moved to New York City.

She formed Molissa Fenley and Dancers in 1977. Early works were commissioned by the Kitchen (1979), Dance Theater Workshop (1980, 1982) and the American Dance Festival (1981). The company began to tour nationally and internationally in 1980.

In 1983, the Brooklyn Academy of Music commissioned *Hemispheres*, with music by Anthony Davis and decor by Francesco Clemente. *Hemispheres* toured for two years in the USA, Europe, Japan, and Australia.

In 1985, Jacob's Pillow Dance Festival commissioned *Cenotaph*, music by Jamaaladeen Tacuma and text by Eric Bogosian, a work which was awarded a Bessie for Choreography in 1986.

The Brooklyn Academy of Music's Next Wave Festival again commissioned a work in 1986, *Geologic Moments*, with music by both Philip Glass and Julius Eastman. Fenley has also choreographed for the Australian Dance Theatre, the Ohio Ballet, the Deutsche Oper Berlin, for Peter Boal, for the Korea/Japan Performing Arts Exchange, and the Pacific Northwest Ballet.

In 1988, the American Dance Festival again commissioned Fenley. She created *State of Darkness*, a solo set to Stravinsky's *The Rite of Spring*. She performed this work fifty times in many venues around the world. The Brisbane Biennial featured this work with live orchestra, one of Molissa Fenley's most memorable performances. A Bessie was awarded to *State of Darkness*. Five dancers have danced this work to date: Molissa Fenley, until 1994, Peter Boal from 1999 to 2000, and Jonathan Porretta, James Moore, and Rachel Foster of the Pacific Northwest Ballet most recently, where, once again, the work was performed with live orchestra.

From 1988 through to 1997, Fenley choreographed solo works in collaboration with contemporary visual artists and composers. A few include: *Witches' Float* (1993), music by Alvin Lucier and set by Kiki Smith; *Nullarbor* (1993), music by Robert Lloyd and set by Richard Long; *Bridge of Dreams* (1994), music by Laurie Anderson and set by Kiki Smith; and *Sita* (1995), music by Philip Glass and photography by Sandi Fellman.

From 1997 through to the present, Fenley has returned to the ensemble form and has choreographed group works with music by Joy Harjo, Bun-Ching Lam, Harry Partch, John Bischoff, and Philip Glass. Performances have taken place at the Joyce Theater, Central Park's Summerstage, the Kitchen, City Center, Alice Tully Hall, Lincoln Center Out of Doors, and many others. The year 2007 marks the thirtieth anniversary of the company.

Fenley has been on the dance faculty of Mills College since 1999, in residence every spring semester. Since 2003, she has also taught choreography at the Experimental Theater Wing of New York University. She was awarded a Prix de Rome for a residency at the American Academy in Rome, February–July 2008.

Molissa Fenley and Dancers was one of twenty-five dance companies commissioned by the Joyce Theater in celebration of its twenty-fifth anniversary and presented a week-long season at the Joyce, December 11–16, 2007.

Personal Honesty

My work relates to the spirit of the human mind, and that human mind is a very large thing. I'm interested in spatial concerns, the individual in space, and its poignancy and what that means. When you look at the stage area, you see the person in space and the space surrounding that person, and what does that suggest? Who are we as individuals in our spaces? That is what my work is about, where you stand in space. I'm interested in having a distinctive voice. I'm interested in working with people who come from different backgrounds, intellectual as well as cultural. Paz Tanjuaquio is from the Philippines, Nora Chipaumire is from Zimbabwe—she and I share a lot of childhood memories; I grew up in Nigeria, and there is a different sense of the world that one has having grown up in Africa.

Going back into trio form seems to be the form I like. Over the years, I've always returned to that as a form that works. If you were to think of three women like me and Nora and Paz, it's a very lovely thing to visually see three women from different cultures coming together and finding their commonality and differences. The choreography becomes the commonality, but I'm very interested in the individual differences of style of dance, of execution. I don't want everyone to look like me. Paz and I look very different, and yet, she is close to the form, true to its nature, and yet keeping it unto herself. That's important for me. I like that feeling of individuality.

Form and structure are another strong interest of mine, and they're what is visible in my work, and yet there is a very strong kinaesthetic feel in my work, a very strong emotional dance feeling in it. Its premise is perhaps from a very abstract stage. I don't think we live in a very abstract-thinking world. The world in the past twenty-five years has become really concrete, and I say that not just as a metaphor; we are concreting the world.

Over twenty years ago, in 1983, I was working with my dance company. Some major works were made at that time: *Hemispheres, Esperanto, Geologic Moments, Cenotaph*. These were large—well, large for me—company works of five dancers. A trio was my main company for many years, and I sometimes added a couple of people more. From there, I made large works for ballet companies in 1986, 1987, and 1988. In 1988, it became very clear that I had to change my whole sense of what I was doing and how I presented my work to the world. I decided to disband my dance company and to work as a soloist, which is a huge thing to do because at that time it was considered a giving-up of something. Solo form was considered a diminutive state of the ensemble form, so there were a lot of prejudices to work against.

My dance company consisted of myself, Silvia Martins, and Scottie Mirviss, two women I had worked with for a number of years. We were all coming into our thirties and things were changing. Scottie wanted to be a lawyer, and Silvia wanted a chance to work with other choreographers and to start choreographing more of her own work. I tried to replace them in the company and find other dancers. I found that with every step forward there were about ten back. There was a lot of dealing with the past, of trying to get the older work taught, as well as trying to build a new repertory for a new bunch of people, and it just wasn't working. I had had a very solid career up to that point, and then things began wavering. In the mid-1980s there had been a great feeling of prosperity in the dance world, with many dance companies coming into existence with a lot of funding and support. For me, and some other dance companies, for whatever reason, that prosperity was starting to wane.

In order to reinstate myself, to create a feeling of renewal, I said, "Okay, I'm not going to try to continue in the method I've been in. This model is not working for me. Small dance company America is not working." So I did disband and started working as a soloist. Luckily, the first major piece I did in 1988 was my version of *Rite of Spring*, titled *State of Darkness*. The idea of *State of Darkness* was to use the beautiful Stravinsky score. It had always been a huge ensemble work of forty dancers, and I had seen and was very moved by the wonderful reconstruction of the Nijinsky original the Joffrey did, so I decided to choreograph the thread of the feeling of that dance, its essence rather than the scenario. It was in that piece that I did in fact renew myself, and it was taken very seriously by the dance world, considered a real rite of passage by some critics. It toured everywhere and put me on a whole different track of how to explore my work.

During the next ten years, I did a lot of collaborations with visual artists and contemporary composers, and it was a wonderful time of exploration. I worked with many visual artists, sculptors, with the idea that this was a totally new form of solo: dancer, sculpture in space, contemporary music. It was a new form for me.

I was starting to find a different audience, much more from the visual arts world. It has been that art world that has continued to support my work, and I think the reason is not only was I working with visual artists, but the dances were being created from a more abstract and intellectual premise.

My work has developed in two different veins. One vein is very contemplative and meditative, and the other is more "dancey," big movement in space. The solo dance period lasted until 1997, and then I started thinking I needed another resurgence or renewal of myself. These renewals in my career happen because things are waning, interest is being lost, I'm not getting as many bookings, maybe I'm losing interest in it as well. I was starting to feel lonely in the studio, whereas in the beginning of that exploration it was absolutely wondrous to work that way, and I really learned a lot from spending so much time alone. But it had come to an end for me, and I wanted to have a dance company again and realized that's not necessarily a viable situation, but I could work from project to project.

I've been working with Paz Tanjuaquio since 1996. She does her own work as well, so when I know far in advance when I'm doing a project she's someone I always call upon, and there are other women and other male dancers I've worked with in this project period I'm still in. Another thing that happened during this period is that the New York City Ballet principal Peter Boal and I have worked together quite a bit. In 1995, I had a very bad accident and was out of dance for a year and a half. I asked Peter if he was interested in doing one of my dances. I also worked with Peggy Baker at that time. Both of these people are very accomplished dancers and accomplished minds of our time, interested in things outside of themselves. Peter was interested in the idea of dancing a lengthy solo because in the ballet world he wasn't necessarily able to do that. A typical ballet solo would be three to four minutes. So, I've made several works with him, and it's been a wonderful collaboration, and we continue to work together. And I did the same thing with Peggy. I've made several pieces for her. Those two dancers gave me a way to continue working while being injured, and I continue to have a very strong relationship with both of them.

While I was injured, I made a dance called *Chair*, trying to continue to choreograph through that long time of recovery. Both with Peter and Peggy I was able to get up and show movement phrases, although without much technical clarity but with enough information that they would be able to extrapolate what I was doing.

Working project to project is how I'm continuing with my company now. I'm also making a very large piece for a dance company in Asia, made up of three Japanese dancers, three Korean dancers, and three Hong Kong dancers, and that project will be touring in August. I'm going over there to make it, and then it premieres in each place.

Another thing that has been very important to my work in the past twenty years is going to Asia. I've been to Japan eleven times. I have a strong following there, and I feel that wherever your work has a following that's where you want to work because you have support!

It's been important for me to find my own model for how to keep a dance company going, to keep myself interested in how to work. Now I'm in a really nice situation at Mills College where every year I come for one semester and I'm salaried over the year, so one semester's salary is given incrementally over the academic year, and it's very, very helpful. Being an independent artist in this culture is not viable anymore, and the stability of being involved in a university has helped tremendously. I have a studio to work in while I'm here, which is amazing.

Twenty-five years ago, there was a lot more support from the National Endowment for the Arts. There were individual grants, and now they don't have that any more. New York State Council on the Arts also offered individual grants. I don't even know what the grant bodies are interested in now. Over the years, I've developed a very solid support system of a small group of patrons. That's how I keep alive, between a small group of patrons and my teaching. The performances are coming here and there, but they are not enough to pay for my upkeep like they were at one time. My work in Asia has kept me going. I've had wonderful residencies there. I was at the University of Tokyo for three months this past year.

Recently, I've just been thinking, how do I keep all this going? I know that I am really committed to the art form of choreography. I am very committed to what I do. I'm committed to seeing it continue, not only for me but for others as well. I love teaching choreography. I'm finding that to be a very wonderful involvement. I like being involved with the Masters candidates here at Mills College, helping with their concerts, the writings of their theses, and their thinking about dance. I'd like to get my ideas down and write a book about choreography because I think there is a lot to be said. I'm very interested in visual art, and I have been able to incorporate that into my teaching. There is a lot for me to continue to do. I feel I'm continuing to perform very well right now.

One criterion for success in today's art world is to adapt to the change in the culture's interest. Some changes of that interest are brought about by true artistic experimentation in media and technology; other changes are forged through a commercialism that is all-pervading, impossible to ignore. The marketing, the advertising, the spin—we are surrounded by a commercial world telling us what to think, how to dress, what to watch. And the corporate backing for the arts, of course, has all of this in mind as choices are made to decide who does what. I feel that when serious work is presented, it's appreciated, and yet this idea (entertainment—don't think) is so deeply entrenched in our culture, it's insidious. Have I adapted? It's hard for me to say. I think I'm pursuing a kind of dance whose subject matter is about time and space, my interest in the work comes from the making of the work itself, in a dialogue with itself and with my perceptions of the world. It's a thread of meaning that I want to follow through the making of many works of dance. I remember back in the 1980s I was told that I could be the "Jane Fonda of dance," that I could cash in on my training techniques (all in the gym, running long distances) and sell exercise videos, but the idea bored me. I wasn't interested in sharing the means of a physical training, I wanted to share the artistic result of taking that training into a different time frame of dance making, into speed and continuity. I can control myself, and my own inner sphere, and try to present work that illustrates my world viewpoint that is optimistic. If everything is commercial, it's the death of art.

I feel it is very important for our culture right now to ensure that people of all races are able to have the opportunities white culture in this country has had. If that means that I have to step aside for this person or that person, I am very willing to do that, because I feel in order for anything to change, somebody has to step aside and say, "Yes to affirmative action." The white culture has to agree that is the case because we have to get on equal ground, and we never will if everyone is angry and can't budge. Equal ground means that, yes, people who have not had the opportunities have to be given more opportunity because white culture always has opportunity. Now, women in the white culture don't always have opportunity, but that's another issue.

In terms of gender, I choreograph asexually. There isn't a male role versus a female role. I've never done any kind of partnering when someone lifts someone else. I've done things where you're actually attached, maybe hand-holding or holding someone's shoulder or leg, but I've never worked with the idea of a couple, doing a *pas de deux* as such. Even when Peter and I dance, there is never a sense of him partnering me; we are partnering each other. It's a very equal situation. That's what I want to present on stage: equality; equality of everybody, whatever the nationality or gender, and whatever the age.

I will be forty-nine this next year, and I feel I'm dancing pretty well. I think of how age is more revered in Japan. Age is a wonderful thing. I love to watch more mature dancers because the sense of experience within the body is so beautiful, the sense of longevity, how many times that leg has been lifted or how many times that body has done a plié. I think it's a very profound experience watching an older dancer. I love young dancers too, but what I sense from them is very different. There is a feeling of the new world, and with an older dancer there is the sense of an understood world.

Age and the body: there's a neurosis about the body that's been cultivated by all the advertising about beauty and slimness. We have a huge obsession about food and weight, and, as a nation, should be embarrassed: lack of exercise, sedentary lives . . . car society, it's shocking. The culture is led to believe that the cheap food being sold is nutritious; physical education

Molissa Fenley, *Lava Field*. Left to right: Cassie Mey, Wanjiru Kamuyu, Molissa Fenley, Ashley Brunning. Photo © Paula Court.

is being taken out of the schools; and long hours of sitting in front of computers . . . television. Here we are in this beautiful world, and people are inside. These are very, very large issues.

The body ages, and what a great thing it does. This is a great form that changes through time from one thing into another, and I really embrace that. I like that. Yes, there is a sense of, "Oh I can't leap as high." After a weekend of dance at ODC, where we were dancing at an intense level, I felt that it really took me a couple of days to bounce back. But that's because I could bounce back. I could take the time off. If I had a performance the next day, it would not be a problem. I think as an older dancer, you know how to train your mind. A lot of it is mind training. What kind of inner work do you do? It's not necessarily spiritual work, it's discipline and commitment and passion for the work, which is just inherent for most performers. There is a reservoir you tie into. But yes, it's harder on the body, it takes a little longer to come back after a big push.

Do I see myself dancing forever? Someone was asking me that the other day: How long does this go on? I don't think that's a question I can really answer, because I could get run over by a bus tomorrow, so I need to say it goes on as long as I'm interested in it, it doesn't go on as long as my body can do it. If my body can't do it, like when I had the accident, I find another way, like when I did that chair dance. Or I find someone else who can do it that is as close to me as possible, as close to the meaning as possible.

I fell pretty badly on an opening night at the Joyce (1995) and tore my anterior cruciate ligament, the old "blow out the knee" thing, so I had to have surgery and get physical therapy. It was about a year and a half before I felt that I was back in shape. This happened when I was forty. The body is enormously restorative. The more energy you use, the more energy you have. The more you ask of yourself, the more you can give of yourself. For me, age is a wonderful thing, to watch the body and to watch what the mind is interested in. If I were to look over my expanse of work, from 1977 to now, things have changed as to what is of interest. Now I'm interested in reconstructing all of *Hemispheres*, which was from 1983. I'm interested in seeing the whole thing again and physically reembodying it.

Definitely, our culture thinks age is a bad thing. It reinforces the belief that as you get older, you get more annoying, or more debilitated . . . that's just our culture, that's what we do to our older people. It's not like that in Asia. Kazuo Ohno is dancing at the age of ninety-four. I think Merce Cunningham has been very instrumental in making people realize that age doesn't necessarily mean that you're decrepit and should be put to pasture. It is changing. I think that prejudice comes from another world, like the gymnastics world where you're over the hill by the age of eighteen, or in sports. I remember when Jimmy Connors was forty and people thought he had better retire. He really pushed the envelope about age. I would say our culture believes there are prime years for an athlete and then you just have to quit or go off to something else; in dance, modern ballet and contemporary choreographers use age in their interest.

Dance has continued to be the worst paying profession possible. Why is that? Perhaps if dancers demanded a livable sort of pay there would not be a dance form. The only reason there is a dance form is that dancers have been willing to forgo having a retirement fund or health insurance. How many dancers have health insurance? I only have it because I'm teaching at Mills now, and I have it for half a year. So, if I get sick, I have to make sure I do it while I'm teaching!

In terms of the environment of making work, right now I have to make it a mental environment. It has to be about my own inspiration, my personal dedication to work; when that's there, I continue to make work. Few choreographers have dancers always there to work with every day of the year.

I have a group of patrons that support my work because we, as a group, have said this is an interesting thing to do. It's interesting to work creatively. It's not interesting to go the corporate route. I don't want a big school. I've never had a big board of directors. Maybe that was a mistake on my part way back, but my foundation is composed of three people and it's small and they agree with what I want to do, so I have control. I think that you pay for that kind of freedom.

In the middle of the night you wake up and have to deal with yourself. That's when a person has to say, "Yes, I'm leading my life in a good way," or "No, I'm not." It's about personal honesty.

From the late 1990s through 2001, I was working in a trio form. Then in 2002, I was invited by a consortium of women artists in Korea and Japan to make an intergenerational dance. The eldest dancer was sixty, and the youngest was turning thirty. It was a fascinating experience. I made a work called *Kuro Shio*, which means "black salt" in Japanese, named after the ocean current that travels south down the Japanese coast and along Korea. The current could be thought of as creating a commonality between the Korean and Japanese women from the effects of weather and, thus, temperament. After I made that piece, I wanted to set it on dancers in New York, so I decided to expand my company to six.

In 2004, I decided to reconstruct *Hemispheres*, which is a work I made in 1983; the original had three dancers: myself, Scottie Mirviss, and Silvia Martins, with music by Anthony Davis and his band, Episteme. I thought that it would be interesting to use all six dancers in the company for the reconstruction. There are four parts to the work; each dancer would perform two parts, giving everyone a chance to be in it. I danced Part I and Part IV; someone else would do II and III, etc., so it was always a threesome, but the threesome was constantly shifting. It was really marvelous to reconstruct that work. Anthony flew in from San Diego and rehearsed with musicians from here for a week; then we performed it at The Kitchen. It was a huge undertaking. We performed it a few times outside of New York as well as a performance at Bucknell University in February 2006. I had been in Oakland, Calif. (every spring semester I teach at Mills College), so I went back to New York for a couple of days to rehearse with everybody before traveling to Bucknell (in Lewisberg, Pa).

I have a group of dancers, so that even though I'm not in New York all year long, I can be assured that they will keep up the repertory. Everyone does their own work as well, but they're also very mature, loyal, and dedicated to mine. I come in the week before, and everybody's already rehearsed and ready to go. It's a very nice group of people, and I feel lucky and very happy about that. Of the six dancers, two have said they really only want to do the *Hemispheres* reconstruction because they're moving on to different things. So now, it's four of us working together. Ashley Brunning, Wanjiru Kamuyu, and Cassie Mey came to Mills in April to perform *Patterns and Expectations* with me. This was for a faculty concert; they came in and rehearsed for a week. I then set the work on Mills dancers for a subsequent performance at Sonoma State three weeks later. I set it on two graduate students, Margaret Cromwell and lola a. katie, and they danced it with me.

Twenty years ago, I would always have set rehearsal times because there was always so much more work and we would be traveling. In between travel would be the time to make a new work. Now the traveling is quite diminished, certainly nothing like it was in those days, so I work from commission to commission. I'm always rehearsing myself, and, in terms

Molissa Fenley, *Lava Field*. Wanjiru Kamuyu and Molissa Fenley. Photo © Paula Court.

of the dancers, rehearsal depends upon a performance coming up. We work project to project. I'll assume that I need a six-week period to work, or maybe a four-week period, depending on how long the piece is and how much time everyone can give me. I tend to work in bursts like that. It may be every day for a month, and then we do the show, and then that dance becomes something that again becomes intact, and the dancers rehearse by themselves when I'm not around.

Turning fifty was not a problem. It wasn't a shock. I started referring to myself as fifty when I was forty-nine, so by the time it happened it didn't matter anymore. I'm nearly fifty-two now. It's lovely to stay in the art over a lifetime . . . a lot of aging is really just in the mind. We have a very strange way of dealing with age in our culture. Certainly one thing that's clear is that, with age, if you get injured, it takes longer to come back. That's just reality, but I feel like I'm dancing well, with minor problems. I'm very disciplined to keep all this going. I'm careful to warm up as much as I need to and try not to stint on anything because that's really when injuries happen. It is hard to give yourself the time you need for constant care when teaching. If I walk into a rehearsal and haven't warmed up, that's no good. Do that a couple of times, and something's going to go, and what can you do? You just have to be really conscious of that and give yourself time. So here I am, giving myself time. [This interview is being conducted while Molissa is in the studio warming up.]

Surprising, but who knows what things become interesting at different points in life? What's fascinating about continuing art over a lifetime is that the pursuits or the interests are constantly shifting. They have a lot to do with experience and maturation. They also have a lot to do with what's going on around you and your response to it. Experiential changes.

What are the major world events that have affected my work and art? I think we're all affected by global warming, and, for me, that's one of the major issues I'm constantly thinking about. I'm not sure if it's changed my art in any distinctive way. I just think it's something that I'm constantly aware of. Women's placement in the world is another topic. I just saw a work by Nora Chipaumire built on the idea of what's going on in Darfur. That's certainly something that's part of my thinking. As an artist, if you're alive and awake in the world, what's happening around you is definitely affecting, and it can affect the way you work and the way you perform. It's very important to me that my work is altruistic, and that it has to do with inviting the mind to enter into its own inner poetry. I'd like to think that the art experience allows or gives an opening for a person's quieter thoughts and poetic moments. That's what I'm thinking and like to be doing as a contribution. There's something poetic, in the discipline, fruition of the work, and in the way it's performed, that to me is a real sharing of experience. Something that I've worked on for a long time is shown. Teachers and people who are in the arts help the continuation of the world in a good way. That's what is meaningful to me.

My economic environment has remained the same for a long time now. It's patron-oriented. This year, I got a nice grant from the Jerome Robbins Foundation, but basically it's individuals who like my work that support my company.

My community is the community of humanity. I love to perform free outside per-formances because then you're assured that people are going to be able to come. On the other hand, what I do also resides perhaps most eloquently inside a theatrical situation. Unfortunately, that means ticket prices and other expenses. Thankfully there are more and more outdoor free concerts presented by the city.

My work is about dance. It is movement-oriented, space-oriented, time-oriented, which, to me, is the ultimate poetry. In watching, one has to be able to focus to see the work structurally unfold; the meaning comes from the unfolding of that structure. I don't think my work is meant to be seen by everybody. I'm clear in being committed to the work, and it continues within whatever form I can manage at the time. The work is seen best by a receptive audience, of course, but even in unreceptive ones, something is going to transpire. It could be that they like the music or that they don't like the music, that they like the dancers or they don't like the dancers. You just never know what people are going to be affected by, so I would prefer not to worry about that, and just make work that has a continuing dialog with the work I've made for thirty years.

Recently, I premiered a new work called *Dreaming Awake* (music by Philip Glass) in Rovereto, Italy at a big week-long music festival. The festival focused on the range of Philip Glass's music from very early works like *Music in Twelve Parts* to the premier we just did. It was a very nice evening, he playing piano and me dancing. We also performed a work from 1989 called *Provenance Unknown*, a work in five parts that is danced by me and Cassie Mey. It's a work that we've performed over the years for a lot of benefits—things like Amnesty International or Tibet House.

Right now, I'm working on another evening with Philip Glass and Jon Gibson. It's an evening of duets, Philip and Jon, Philip and me, Jon and me. We will be performing the evening on October 6 in Allentown, Pa. as a benefit concert for the New Arts Program in Kutztown. I'm also making a piece to Harry Partch's early work, a work from 1952 called *Castor and Pollux*, and that'll be done at Mills next year. I'm going to make that on my dancers first, and then set it on the dancers at Mills when I come next spring (2007).

Another very exciting project coming up is that the Pacific Northwest Ballet has asked me to reconstruct *State of Darkness*, my solo to *The Rite of Spring*. It's only been danced by me, between 1988 and 1994, and by Peter Boal from the New York City Ballet (in 1999). Peter is now the Director of the Pacific Northwest Ballet. *State of Darkness* will be set on three casts: two women and one man, and will premiere on May 31, 2007; I'll be setting it this fall 2006.

I just finished a work that was really different from anything I've ever made. The music is by Fred Frith, and it's composed for Joan Jeanrenaud (cello) and William Winant (percussion). Some of the instructions to the musicians are things like "tear a piece of paper," "throw a ping-pong ball across the floor," and "throw a can." I thought it would be really funny if the dancers did that as well, in the midst of doing their steps. The piece is titled *Patterns and Expectations*; patterns get set up, and then something shifts. You see something evolving, and you expect it to go a certain way, and then it goes some other way. The newspapers come out of a collar in our shirts, and suddenly they're torn, and the ping-pong balls are hidden in a little pouch on the side of the costume. Then, there's a whole hammering part. I've never done a work like that before. It's sort of Dadaesque. I really enjoyed it.

I go day by day, month by month. I really don't have a five-year plan. I'm not a corporate entity. I just don't think that way. I've mentioned the plan for the fall and the plan for next spring is my teaching at Mills. I've got that much figured out. For me the thing is to keep experimenting.

May 10, 2003

Rennie Harris-Eichenbaum (1999). Philadephia Museum of Art. Photo © Rose Eichenbaum.

Rennie Harris

Lorenzo (Rennie) Harris was born and raised in an African-American community in North Philadelphia. Since the age of fifteen, Harris has been teaching workshops and classes at universities around the country and is a powerful spokesperson for the significance of "street" origins in any dance style. In 1992, Harris founded Rennie Harris Puremovement, a hip-hop dance company dedicated to preserving and disseminating hip-hop culture based on the belief that hip-hop is the most important original expression of a new generation. Harris's work encompasses the diverse and rich African-American/Latino traditions of the past, while simultaneously presenting the voice of a new generation through its ever-evolving interpretations of dance. Harris is committed to providing audiences with a sincere view of the essence and spirit of hip-hop rather than the commercially exploited stereotypes portrayed by the media.

Harris has performed for the Queen of England and the Princess of Monaco. Nominated for a Lawrence Olivier Award (UK) for best choreography (*Rome and Jewels*), at the turn of the century, he was voted one of the most influential people in the past 100 years of Philadelphia history. He has been compared to Basquiat and twentieth-century dance legends Alvin Ailey and Bob Fosse. He has been awarded three Bessies, two Alvin Ailey Black Choreographers Awards, two Ethnic Dance Awards, a Pew Fellowship Award in Choreography, a Herb Alpert Award in the Arts for choreography, a Philadelphia Rocky Award, and, recently, he was the recipient of the Pennsylvania Governors Artist of the Year Award. Harris continues his vision for hip-hop via commissions to create work on companies other than Rennie Harris Puremovement. To his credit, he has created works for Alvin Ailey, Dayton Contemporary Dance Company, Philadelphia Dance Company, Colorado Ballet, Memphis Ballet, Pennsylvania Ballet, and Complexions Desmond Richardson, to name a few. At forty-four, Lorenzo "Rennie" Harris is atop the hip-hop heap—its leading ambassador.

Movin' like a Soundwave

Dance is a part of my culture; it hasn't ever been extracurricular for me. I don't remember it having a beginning really, although I remember dancing. I danced at home, in front of my door, in my house, if someone had a birthday party, or even at church. I never heard a voice that told me I needed to dance or anything. It was just regular stuff to me. I think people forget that dance is a way we worship a higher being. It's always been a part of our society; from death to birth, from wartime and in peacetime, dance has always been a part of everything.

I like to say that movement is the last manifestation of one's reality; it's what you do that defines you, the action that you take. Moving is the way we stay alive. If we all stopped moving today, tomorrow we would die. We wouldn't die instantly, but our organs would shut down because they need to move. The world is on the axis, and it moves, the planets rotate, everything in the universe moves—without movement, you die.

Dancers are historians, priests and priestesses. Every generation retains information in their bodies, and when they're expressing, they connect to a higher self, a higher being. I think it holds true for anyone who expresses, however they express, and whomever their most high may be. This is how we worship. At those moments of expressing, those are the moments we feel the best. Our spirit is at peace, and we're connected, even if we're just doing aerobics. The body is released, and in tune, so all the physicality we do throughout the day is a way of staying alive and worshipping.

What has happened though is that society has convinced us that dance is something extra. It's an extracurricular activity outside of us that has a structure. Then we are supposed to follow particular patterns in order to dance, or in order to express ourselves. What happens in the schools, as well as in the dance world, is that we buy into this and begin to think that this structure is a *godline* and not a *guideline*. In a guideline, we're allowed to move off the path, have our experience and, hopefully, get back on the path. But we've been convinced that in order to dance, here are the steps: "one, two, three, and four." No. There's an internal rhythm always present in dance, and it inspires the external rhythm to come out and to become manifest physically.

Movement is powerful, and that's why it's the last of all the arts to be supported. There are so many reasons why we, as dancers and choreographers, are in the place we are financially. I think the reasons are all political. The common senses, or our common sense "ability" has been numbed, neutralized. If we could just understand our history, we would know that when it comes to the arts, one of the first things during war is to either destroy or steal the art. It is taken from the people because if the culture is taken away, you have them. The culture embodies expression, movement, visual arts, voice—all of the things needed to express, but if that is taken from a people, they can be controlled.

We can march on Washington, but to march on Washington, we need people to move. When there is war, music and drums are played, and people are moved. If you can get people to be proud of themselves and want to exercise and do right, and feel good, then their minds will be clear. And when their minds are clear, people want to hold others accountable for their actions. In movement and expression, we acknowledge these things, and we get there quicker, and we move people in a way that the controlled arts don't. They just kind of make people numb. "This is to make you happy"—that's it, and that breeds a false sense of happiness.

I first got paid for dancing when I was about fourteen or fifteen in 1978. It was at the Philadelphia Folklife Center, which did a program through the Smithsonian Institution. They were documenting hip-hop dance as folklore, and somehow got in contact with us and began to pay us to go into schools to talk about what we were doing. Before that, I actually don't know why I was doing it, but when I started getting paid, then I realized why: to get paid. I feel the same way today; anytime I come outside of my community, then it's work. When I'm in my community, I don't think about the things I do for free. That's my culture. If someone wants to have a piece of that, then it becomes work. Eventually you create a community, a national or global community, but even then that community is still small, because everyone you meet you don't necessarily bond with. My national and global family still adheres to my community in that all they have to do is call. Anything else outside of that is a way for me to survive and take care of my family.

Through the work, I realized I was beginning to deal with my issues of molestation, family, and religion, and I began to deal and "own up" to them, to be responsible for those issues as part of becoming "the man," not *a* man, but becoming *the* man that I'm to be. So, the work brought a very strong sense of rite of passage. As a young man, it's a rite of passage. One, it's a physical showing of strength. Two, it gives a sense of prowess—that sense of "I'm a man," and it's almost like you're calling—you're being sexy, and you're flexing and flirting. In the movement itself, if I'm standing on one hand, I'm saying that I am together in my mind, body, and spirit, and the only way that I can be on one hand that way is because all of this is collectively together.

Hip-hop always honors where life comes from. In this country, we misconstrue what hip-hop is—the winding of the hips and all—it's always been part of traditional dance, and it's gotten tainted because of the media. In its infancy, people thought about hip-hop from a different perspective. They didn't think dancers were anything more than people who just danced for fun. When we'd do the Q&A after the performance, they would ask, "What do you do?" I have dancers who were English teachers, ex-pre-med, accountants, and it was interesting because everyone thought, "It's the hip-hop dancers," and then the dancers would say, "I have my degree in so-and-so." They'd have three degrees, or a Master's in this and that, and people would raise their eyebrows in disbelief. "Yeah, hello, we're more than you think." Even then they were professional cats, who were doing their thing—that's how they made their money, but some cats just continue to do it because they love it as a passion.

Whether it was hip-hop or not, those rites of passage are happening for the youth in this country with their groups of friends. PopMaster Fable (Jorge Pabon was his birth name) said (and I may be quoting him wrong), "We're confusing youth culture with hip-hop culture." They're two different things. Hip-hop is an extension of traditional African dance and culture—the African Diaspora—and it is very much about a rite of passage: learning to think quickly on your feet, from rhyming, to being creative or innovative every day. Having to change pushes the mind to think quicker. Those games that we play, even in dance, when we're "challenging each other," it's not a competition, it's a game of wit. To see if I can catch your rhythm, and throw your rhythm back to you, and then add my thing on it. Or, do your movement, do my movement, and now what? "Can you top that?" It's how can you be smart about it? This is a dance form where someone who flips can lose to a person who has great timing. They might catch the break in the music and come out and do something funky with their torso or their arms—and this other guy just did a flip—but everyone loves how this guy came out. So it's not really that type of competition, it's the idea of, "Can you think?" "Can you think quickly?" "Can you be smart on your feet?" That kind of thing.

To me, it's all very similar to rites of passage in traditional cultures. When the men go in the bush, they come out as men, and they do the dance to show the village that they're fit, body, mind, and soul. And the same thing applies to women.

Today's modern dance is moving towards something different. Prior to this shift, I always thought that modern dance was no longer modern but out of contact. It wasn't moving forward, it wasn't evolving. I think it is evolving now with a new generation of young kids in the universities, colleges, and community centers who have been raised with a hip-hop mindset, whether or not they were in hip-hop movement or dance styles associated with hip-hop. They understand what it is aesthetically and have a sense of something different. They seem to have a different expression, a different movement, which expresses *their* generation. Each generation thinks a certain way, and so it makes sense that the audience of modern dance or ballet is declining, because there's no transition from one generation to another for the younger generations to make it relevant today.

Movement in modern dance is changing because of hip-hop. It's beautiful to watch because now we're in an incubation period of making the connections between the movements of other dance forms such as modern, ballet, and jazz, and the hip-hop movement. What they call a *tour* we call a *tour*, and there is an explorational conversation like, "Oh, this is the same thing right here," "this is release," "this is where the contraction goes, and where the plié is, or where the *tour jété* happens." The youth are making those connections because of living in a hip-hop culture, learning hip-hop in schools, and learning in higher education. It's informing their work on a whole other level, and I find that exciting.

What major events in my life or the world have affected my art? I have had a very dramatic life, and everything about it has informed my expression. I was told that the drama in my life would slow down soon. Having done commercial work prior to fine art or hip-hop dance theater, I realized that this was where I was headed. My mindset in commercial work was that it was my pay. Even though now I feel that idea stays with me, there is an understanding now that I *need* and *have to* express, because this is what has been healing me. That my stories are relevant to someone else, that I'm touching other people's lives means it's important for me to do this.

For a long time, I was thinking about quitting, because I thought there was something else bigger than this. I love choreographing, and I love dancing. It feeds me spiritually, but then, there's something else that I feel is out there for me. Through the work, I also learned that I had to keep on doing it. No matter how tired I get, no matter how much I really want to quit, I keep going because it really *is* touching other people's lives in ways I would have never imagined. During the past few years, I've been coming to grips with and accepting that this is my path, and I must finish it out. "Do what you're supposed to do and stop defeating yourself."

But it's cool. The road's getting clearer; I can see a little bit better down the road. I'm not so willing to jump in blindly as I was before. It might have to do with age. I think, "Okay, what's happening?" "I'm forty-two." Even though that's still young, at the same time, I've probably got fifteen years or so before I really start to think about what I need to do and what's happening with my life. Am I secure? God willing, I'll be healthy at sixty. Am I gonna make it another twenty years? Now I'm in that phase of my life where I'm thinking ahead, although I always think ahead in a lot of other situations, but now I'm caring about what's happening. Before, I didn't really care. I thought, "Whatever: I could die tomorrow and no one will really remember my name." Having this journey has brought me all of these new insights I don't think I ever would have had without dance.

I had two childhood companies: My first one was the Stepmasters, where I was the co-captain, and then my second was the Scanner Boys, which came around in the early 1980s. I was the captain of that crew. That disbanded in 1991 and 1992, so we've been around for a long time. Then Michael Pedretti from Movement Theater International in Philadelphia called me up and offered me 1,500 dollars to create some work without the Scanner Boys. I created work using different dancers, and that's how the company Puremovement was born.

I separated the different dance styles; we did some house movement to jazz, and hip-hop to hip-hip/fusion jazz. Then we did some popping to electronic music and in Philadelphia, it was the first time they saw it all separated. We gave examples like, "Here's hip-hop. This is not hip-hop 'proper'—but it is hip-hop, because it falls under the umbrella of hip-hop." It was the first time Philadelphia had seen these movements separated. I don't know what was going on around the rest of the world or in New York, but for the longest time in Philly, most people always thought of hip-hop as one thing. As far as I'm concerned, and some historians may argue this, hip-hop dance, the *real* hip-hop dance didn't happen until the mid-1980s— that's when it started. And not that it *started* then; it became clear that the term "hip-hop" was specific to social dances of the 1980s and 1990s. And that's what hip-hop dance is. Everything else was pre-hip-hop, was funk. So there was "rocking," which was also done to funk, and then Campbell-locking and popping was done to funk, and even some of breaking was done to funk then breakbeat music, and then electro-funk music, with Afrika Bambaata and those cats. Hip-hop as concert dance didn't begin in 1991. It dates back to the early 1980s as everyone was trying to co-opt it and collaborate with street dancers at the time. These things started to separate, and then it was presented as concert dance: using hip-hop movements to do it. It was the big thing for us in Philadelphia, and it just kind of took off like a snowball rolling downhill.

Hip-hop was going on before 1991 because there was Popmaster Fable and Mr. Wiggles and Crazy Legs, and those guys did a thing at PS 122 called *What Happens Now?*, which was the first hip-hop play. It was being developed at the same time we (Rennie Harris Puremovement) were coming together as a group. So, things were happening, it was just a matter of us coming in and forging hip-hop dance theater versus hip-hop theater. Although it was happening, the issue was that people in America weren't ready for it. They wanted to see it in the street, because they started calling it "street dance," when it was not street dance. Just because we went to a block party and danced in the street didn't make it street dance. This happened in community centers, recreation centers, in the community. When they started calling it "street dance," that kind of pushed everyone to pull out their cardboards and go to the street. I'm not saying that it wasn't, but we never thought of it like, "We are street dancers." I mean, we did, at one point, because we were young; we didn't know. But it happened in my mom's house, and at the little girl's party down the street. The church had a school party, and we went, or in the summer there were always block parties.

I started choreographing when I was thirteen. I was always the designated choreographer as a kid because I knew what I liked when I saw it, and I was pushy. I was a big fan of musicals and still am. I would get *Oklahoma!* or another musical and watch the movement. Then with my friends, when it came time to make something up, I'd say, "No, no, we gotta be like this!" Or "This has to flow like this," and they'd say, "Wow! Alright, cool!" So, I became the person who was always choreographing the most of what we called "routines" at the time, and, by the time I got to the theater, choreographing was like candy.

What was the most difficult for me was dealing with movement in space. I knew how to deal with the space choreographically, but I had to find specific movement in hip-hop that would allow travel across space. That was the hardest, and it made me scratch my head a few times, because some of the movement I used was aggressive. It would take a lot to move from stage-left to center, and, by the time a cat got to center, he'd be worn out. Even still now, when I bring freestyle dancers from the club, or b-boys or b-girls to the work, and they've never performed in the theater, they have a hard time, because suddenly they have to travel their movement and find how to navigate through this aggression versus putting it all out on a level of ten in one spot.

When I choreographed earlier and we had to use space, we didn't use movement individually, we did it as a group. All of my stuff was specific—no one "soloed out." For the theater, I realized that I had to keep the foundation of hip-hop, which was, "There's no such thing as a solo*ist*, because everybody's a soloist" and they had to learn to do choreography together, and move together, while, at the same time, not be exactly alike. If they're exactly alike, then it's really not hip-hop. In television today we can call it hip-hop, it's evolved, but it's more like jazz with isolated movement and some hip-hop, and it's being *called* hip-hop. They're very locked in: Everything's together, tight.

When you see a real hardcore hip-hop dance company doing their thing, whether it's choreographed or not, you will see a person interpreting the choreography for that person's body. They're all going to move the same way, the same direction, and have the same momentum, but my weight may be slightly over to the left, while his or hers is to the right, doing the same movement. And that is kind of like the foundation of hip-hop—it has to have a sense of individuality. You have to contribute "you" to the pot. So, that was the thing that became clear in working in theater. There were some obstacles for me because I was used to moving groups—like, groups together in choreography—but then not adhering— for my style at the time was popping, which was not very group-oriented—but now employing hip-hop, employing house, employing Campbell-locking. I had to go into these things and study them more, because although I knew of them and could do them, I couldn't do them well. I had to practice to find those specific movements that would allow each dancer, at any point, to stay in flow and move across by himself or herself, or as a group, using a hip-hop movement.

In hip-hop, movement vocabulary is looked at as choreography. When I choreograph, 95 percent of the movement is mine, 5 percent belongs to the individual dancer. The dancers are very mine-mine-mine-mine oriented. If you take one of their movements, they say, "Oh that's *my* movement!" In the concert dance world, my understanding is there's a vocabulary of movement that can be used at any given time. In hip-hop, people have movement specific to them, their "signature" movements. They may not want it to be part of my choreographic vocabulary. The hard part when choreographing in hip-hop is that the movement itself has to be invented or created by you. There's no universal tongue that says, "Okay, we're all going to do an X-Y-Z." Then the other part is now they have to learn my movement, which is hard, because they're not used to moving my way. They're used to moving for them; they're not used to moving universally with a universal law of movement and vocabulary. So, those

Don Campbell, Legend of Hip-Hop. Photo © Bob Emmott.

are some of the barriers I've come across in regards to working with hip-hop movement and using the concert stage.

There is a universal tongue happening now, so if there's a foundational house movement, like the Jack rhythm, everyone knows it. "Okay, let's do this Jack rhythm here." And I may give that. That's not necessarily mine, it's just some movement that now is becoming codified. And so, as it's evolving, there are movements that I know but don't know under a specific name, because someone has only just codified them, or a particular region has codified it. I may use a wrist roll, but a wrist roll is not necessarily mine, it's from a Campbell-locking style or something. So, my choreography is a little bit of codified vocabulary that people do know now, and a little bit of my own inspiration, and a little bit, perhaps, of my being inspired by one of the dancer's movements. I may see a move and say, "Oh I like that!" and I may create something off that, or say, "Hey, can we use that in the choreography?" I put a disclaimer about the choreography in the program, that "choreographic phrases and vocabulary are contributed by the dancers," so that it is cohesive and at least acknowledging that some of their movement has been used in the work itself.

As this hip-hop evolves and the movement becomes more codified, I'm interested to see how innovative it becomes, because its foundation is to be innovative: They don't want to do the same thing twice. And it has to be *nice*; it has to be *dope*—off the Richter scale. It just can't be "blah". It has to be, "Aw man, this is hot!" And those are unspoken laws for the movement, so, if it becomes codified, what's that going to do? Will we continue to be innovative? Are we being challenged to be innovative? How is it evolving?

Part of the choreographic structure allows improvisation. It happens on stage all the time. My dancers flip offstage into the dark—they don't care. My rule is, "You can do whatever you want to do, but it'd better be good; you'd better make me look good." It's as simple as that. "Now if it's bad, it's on you." Some cats, my guys, are known for doing it to play with each other because a lot of times, the first time hitting the stage, most hip-hop cats want to project out, because they're used to being in the round. When you're in the round, you can feel everybody, so you're not really thinking about projecting out. But when you hit stage or television, people are taught to project out. For my company, I tell them, "Don't worry about projecting out. Dance for us on stage so we have fun, and in the event that we are connected, it's going to hit like a sound wave and go out to everybody else." And so, these guys play jokes on each other. One guy turns around doing a choreography and faces the other guy and does the choreography backwards towards him, to mess him up—that kind of thing. They're in the wings, yelling and screaming and stuff like that.

The choreography is set, and then they can do what they want to do, as long as it is within the parameters of giving a good show, and the presentation is still connected to the work. Then, once in a while, maybe a year or two later, I come back and reset it. It's normally not on purpose. I do it because I start thinking, "That's not the choreography. What is it?" "Okay, let's go back to the original." So, I just bring them back and let them go again. With something that we were doing for years, I remember the original way it was done, and *why* it was done a certain way. What I do then, as they argue with me, is say, "Let's go get the tape." And there it is. It's in the tape, right there.

As long as the work is allowed to breathe, they can change the work, change the choreography somewhat in terms of the movement vocabulary, but not what the work is about. There needs to be a foundational structure involved in the choreography, so it could be 75 percent choreography and another 15 percent allows for some improvisation and the work to breathe and evolve to something else. Then the other last little percentage will be for the guy who wants to flip into the audience or run into the wings.

In terms of considering race, at first I didn't think too much about racism. When I get inspired to create, I just do it without a thought process. Then, afterwards, I stand back and look at it. I was surprised at what came out. For me, the idea of race always came up because it was a big part of my growing up, but I didn't realize how affected by it I was until I saw it on stage. Then it made more sense, so I decided, I wasn't going to curtail it.

One of the first suites we made was called *Falling Crumbs from the Cake.* I worked in Holmesburg Prison in Pennsylvania for about four or five months. One of the prisoners had given me a poem at the end of their workshop, and it was called, "Falling Crumbs from the Cake." In the workshop, we had asked why they thought they were there, and 99.9 percent of them said "racism." Thinking that was interesting, I decided I was going to dedicate this suite of work to them, so we danced to the last poet's poem, called "Die Nigga".

The first time I heard the poem, it just blew me away; I'd never heard anything like it. I would have the guys get up, come out, and fall to the floor, jump down to the floor every time the word "nigga" was said. Generally, half the audience or everyone would leave in the beginning. At the end of this piece, it said, "Die, nigga, so black folks can stand up." The audience couldn't get through the first three pieces, because it was just too dark, and it was about racism, so we used to call it our "walk-out piece." I realized my pieces weren't about blame, because I was born in 1964, so I wasn't really around before the Civil Rights Movement, but it was about how racism still affects me, and how it still affects us, and why we still don't talk about it. We still have to deal with the issue of racism.

The headlines would be, "Harris Brings Angst Dance to So-and-So." I used to get off on that, actually because I knew I was being made the puppet, as we became known as "the hip-hop dancers." We were being used as the babysitters, the clowns that were going to come and entertain the kids, so I stopped doing commercial work. I stopped doing that kind of stuff a while ago. I'm not going to do that in theater. I'm going to do what matters to me, and what matters to me are the issues that are coming up in my world, that I'm starting to deal with now. And so, people would bring their kids, and kids would leave with the parents and think it was horrible. At that time, people never asked, they just thought, "Oh, you're a hip-hop dance company." They saw maybe one piece we did that was amazing and they would ask us to come do a full night. We would come, and then they'd say, "Oh. Um, um, um . . . could you um, could you maybe not do *that* piece?"

I would want to respond by saying, "I don't know what to tell you, except hip-hop is just another extension of Black African-American culture in this country." There are always those two things with each other, the good and the bad. There's Tupac talking about being a gangster in one rap, and then in the next rap, saying, "Our women need to keep their heads up." This also exists. We can't not acknowledge that it doesn't exist. You can't have the one without the other. If you're going to see the greatness and beauty of what it is, you have to see the death, pain, and suffering, because they both go hand in hand.

I'm going to acknowledge where I'm at, and this is where I am. Race played a major part, especially with hip-hop. When Bambaata brought all of that together as a culture, it was about taking over where the Black Panthers ended. And that was to learn about your people, to be proactive about your culture and be proud about that. And there was peace, unity, and having fun; that was hip-hop. How do we learn about ourselves? We had to study and learn and go back into our culture and learn about the culture at the community centers.

Racism informed my work a lot, especially in the very beginning. Now it's more the idea of what it means to be a human being. Take the word "being." What does that mean? It means "to be," "to exist" without rhyme or reason. This is what we're not doing—we're not existing. We're not just moving, and celebrating, and dealing, we're projecting into a place that we don't belong—into the future. We're not in the future right now. We're right here in this moment. We can't touch tomorrow or anything that's going to happen tomorrow, the food that we're going to eat tomorrow—we can't touch it—and the food that we ate in the past is not real now. The only thing that's real is right now. So, that's where I feel my work is going. How do I acknowledge where I am right now? How do we as humans on this planet acknowledge that we're not evolved as far as we think we are? Technically and technologically, we think we're evolved all the way, but our spirits are not there with it. Our minds are not there with us—we're like children.

How does age play a part in my company? The core company is going into their early to mid-thirties. They've been with me since it was five core members; four are still with me. Some of them were seventeen, eighteen, or in their early twenties when they started with the company. When I hired these guys, I thought they were grown-ass men. I didn't notice some of them were still in high school. They had bodies like men. They looked like men. They were out late, hanging at the club. Eventually, I realized some were just getting out of high school, some were just starting college, and some were *still* in high school. Age wasn't a problem in the very beginning, because I didn't think about it. Now I think about it because we've come to a place where we have to be more responsible. I have a lot of young people who want to dance with me. I say, "If you're in college, stay in college. I won't take you until you finish." If they've already made a decision not to go, I may take them.

As far as hip-hop's concerned, there's no real age to stop, it's just a matter of how long can your body go. And, even then, some people still go and just change the way they approach it. Half the rappers, the old school cats, are reaching their fifties now. For myself, I'm forty-two and still kickin' on the stage a little bit. I don't get up from chairs too quick anymore. The metabolism's slowing down, and I've gained a little weight. As much as I dance, you would think I would be thinner, but I stopped dancing at the level I was dancing, and now I dance when I *feel* like dancing, versus performing with the company in every piece. I've been thin half my life, up until I was thirty-three or thirty-four, and then I started to gain a lot of weight. It's definitely changed by way of settling. I don't think about it much because in my head, I still can move like I'm fifteen. It's funny—I videotaped myself doing a movement, and I was like, "Oh yeah!" I just thought I was moving so fast. I looked back, and thought, "Oh my god, that shit is slllloooow . . ." Oh man—in my head, I was killing this thing, but, as they say, you get a little bit more *seasoned*, and I'm going on a *seasoning* right now.

It's still good, because when I'm dancing, I know I can do an all-nighter, but I'm constantly drinking Red Bull. What's great is that I can still *hang*, and that's all I'm worried about. As long as I can hang in the circle, at the club, without really feeling like I'm out of shape, I'm fine. I think I'm doing great in that way. And a lot of times, it is funny, because somehow it will come up, and I'll be asked, "Man, so how old are you? "FORTY-TWO." "Oh my god! Wow, man, that's amazing! I want to dance like that." And to me, I'm thinking, "Well I'm just kinda getting started." I've got a whole other fifty more years to go, or at least forty to get down. And with my style, I think there's a little bit more longevity, because I don't do a lot of flipping, and that kind of thing, where I'm attacking my body and having to be aware of my space, up and down, with gravity all the time.

Your dancing and flexibility can stay with you if you stay with it every day, into the transition of your age. Then you're going to hear something like, "Wow, man, you can still do that?" It's 'cause this person's constantly doing it every day. And, as life hits you, other things become priority, and the body says, "Oh, you're not using me? Let me pull that back a little bit." But I think it's good because then you start to figure out another way. And that's when it becomes like, "Ohh . . ." It's not about the claps, it's not about the bang. It's not about the six o'clock, or the flip, or the head spin. It's about the *timing* . . . the understanding of timing and feeling the people that are with you and knowing when to go forward a little bit, and when to pull back.

My oldest dancers are thirty-four or thirty-five now. I don't think people see our group and think they're older. Actually, there was one period when I looked up on stage at all the guys—they do this one piece where they all have their shirts off—and I thought, "Wow, I don't remember so-and-so having a belly!" There were all these little bellies forming, and I had to say, "Yo, y'all have to look at this tape, because uh . . ." And they were all like, "Oh, oh my God!" and they straightened it out eventually. So, there was a moment that they did actually look like they were older dancers, until they went back to the drawing board, so to speak.

In regards to the future, I want to see if I can still *bring it* at fifty like Don Campbell, who's about fifty-something, and Boogaloo Sam, Toni Basil, Anna Lollipop, and Greg "Campbel Lock Jr." Pope, who are still dancing. They're bringin' it, and their time was the 1970s and late 1960s. I had them at the festival, and they're still doing their movement. They inspired the kids who saw them. But I thought, "Man, I just hope I have a little bit of that when I get older."

What role does gender play in my dance and choreography? I didn't used to think gender played a role in my choreography, but apparently people got upset that I didn't have women—or they *thought* I didn't have women. I've always had women in the company, but the majority of the work came from a male perspective in the very beginning. Prior to 1992, it was, "We just gonna do some work," and there were about five females and three males in the company. Then it evolved, and by about 1996, it was all male, and then in 1998 it became male and female again. Now it's just a matter of whatever I'm inspired to do. It used to be "get in where you fit in," whether you were male *or* female.

Recently, I decided I wanted to work specifically more with women to challenge myself in the *way* women move as something different than how men distribute weight. What are the movement values that women have, versus the values of men who just like to go, "RAAARR!" What are the subtleties of women, and how does that inform male dance? So as of late 2002, in creating *Facing Mekka*, that was my new interest. Prior to that, I never thought of it as anything separate like male or female; it was just whatever work I was doing. I knew women couldn't do *P-Funk*, because *P-Funk* was about men hanging on the corner. They couldn't do *Asphalt*, because it was about affirming rites of passage for men. But when we did *Pon-logo* or *One Love, Do It*, or *Continuum*, these works encompassed everybody in the company, and I was inspired.

Unfortunately, a lot of the women who were in the company left because they were having a family. It's interesting that men who have a family continue to "do their thing." Then I had a few who decided for professional reasons, "Okay, I need to go to another company," or "I want to experience this," or "I'm going to Hollywood to do this and I'm going to go dance with this person."

Rennie Harris, *Facing Mekka*. Photo © Bob Emmott.

I really liked the business mind of the women, because they wanted to know, "Well what are your intentions?" with everything I did, and "When is rehearsal again?" and "What time am I flying out?" They would call me, and it made me step up my game. When we were predominately male at one point, I didn't have to worry. I didn't have to talk to them, or say anything . . . it was just very male. There were no arguments in rehearsal, no one challenging me—just like, "Mmhm, whatever . . ." Not that the women brought that, but the women did challenge my intentions as a male choreographer, and rightfully so.

If I'm doing movement that *I* think is feminine for me, there was a challenge that it may not necessarily *be* feminine. Because I'm moving my hips, does that make it a female movement? I like the idea of exploring what was feminine for me—and not by way of feminine, like I'm going to be *female*, but just less of how a man would do it. I like that.

If the hip-hop movement was on a scale from one to ten, I want to feel what *one* feels like, and *two* and *three*, and how that works and develops up to *ten*. In doing that, I have to pull back the machismo, the attack of it, and that is interesting to me. When studying with the women, I was able to figure out some of that. It's about distribution. If you know where to distribute your weight, each gender can do the same exact thing. So, for me, one of the turning points in the evolution of the company was getting bored with the machismo, whether it was male or female, coming at you in a straightforward way—that's what I mean by "machismo"—how do I have that same energy . . . get to that energy, and still get to the other energy . . . and explore what that *ten* is on that side too, because there's a ten there. What is that?

My interest was to learn both sides to inform the choreography for hip-hop, because, for whatever reason, the males take the spotlight in hip-hop. Although there are a lot of women who do hip-hop, and who are *amazing*, the media push or highlight women for their sexuality. They don't emphasize the women to show their skill and ability.

The movie *You Got Served* was a perfect example. One of my ex-dancers, by the name of Julie Urich, was in the movie. In one of these scenes, there was a b-girl group against this b-boy group. Jules, as we called her, at the time, was probably *the* number one top b-girl in the country, and she could *bring it*. They were going up against these other cats. They never showed the girls dancing. They showed the girls doing choreography, but when they were battling in a circle, when they're supposed to be: "You throw down, and then the other group throws down," they showed the *guys*. Here they had the chance, and time, to make things right, they had everyone's attention with this movie, and they had some of the top girls . . . these are the top hip-hop cats, and these women who are *bringin' it*, and they didn't get shown doing their thing, spinning on their heads. What's that about? That's media, and that was not right.

I think it's wack that there are a lot of women choreographers not *celebrated*. The first ten or fifteen years of the company, of Rennie Harris, were specifically my issue-issues, which were predominately male. That's just the way it was, but now, even with my last project, it was important to, say, "Okay, now I'm ready to address this and move forward." "Where are the women?"

One good thing about hip-hop, in defense of men is, "Here's a dance form where the men are not afraid to dance. Here's a dance form where straight men are on stage, bringing strong energy as a rite of passage." My argument to people at times is, "Don't stop that."

Of course, there are some gay people in hip-hop. Unfortunately, the external presentation is what people see, and then what they define as masculine and feminine. Men are not used to seeing other straight men do trained concert dance. Even though there are some strong roles for men, the way men are depicted in concert dance just doesn't come off as something masculine enough for men, for regular, general boys, to say, "I want to do that. I want to do that." Hip-hop, says, "You can do this, and it's okay to be you and do your thing, and no one's gonna make you—you're gonna wear whatever you want to wear . . ." Culturally, it's okay for men to dance.

At a certain point, at thirteen, fifteen, the idea of, "Well, when are you going to get a job—a *real* job?" comes up, but, up to that point, for young boys, it's okay to dance. And then, even when you become a man and get a job, it's okay to dance at the party, because the men dance. I've always known men to dance. It's only when I got into the "world of dance" that I started hearing, "Man, we need more men."

The political environment affects my work a lot. Can I call people idiots? They're running the country. I think there's a strategic plan to control the masses, for their benefit. Part of what I realized in doing this work is that I was affecting people on different levels as individuals. That became inspirational because I realized that one person can change a lot of things for a lot of people. And so, even in our prayers prior to hitting the stage, we ask that we are allowed to reach the one person in the audience that we're supposed to touch and hope that that person is inspired to move forward and do what they came here to do. Due to the work, I had a woman walk up to me who said, "You know, I want to thank you because I got my kids back." And I looked at her and said, "Well, what do you mean?" and she said that when she saw me perform or heard me speak, she was so inspired that she got off drugs and was able to get her kids back.

I was on a bus somewhere in Virginia, it wasn't even in Philly, and another person said to me, "Hey Mr. Harris, I just want you to know, I went back to school," and I said, "Well, what do you mean?" and he said, "I just graduated from college. I was a high-school dropout, and I saw your company, and that inspired me to go back." So, those things made me realize that we're touching one person—somehow, somewhere. It's not about touching the masses and making them stand up to clap and yell and scream, but somewhere in that audience, we're affecting somebody, and that person's going to do something that's going to help the generation move forward politically, in this country. I feel happy about having some slight contribution to that, because for 1 million men to march on Washington, it took 1 million individual men to do so.

What we continue to forget is that we are individuals who collectively make the group. We're being bombarded in a massive way with things that are desensitizing us. If we can understand that, then we can begin to block that energy, and say, "We *do* have power." If we wanted to stop war today—we can stop this war. We can stop this war at any time we want to stop this war—that's the crazy part about it. Economically, we just stop buying for one goddamned day, and they'd be like, "Okay, we've got to do something."

Whoever "they" are, they are infiltrating the fiber of what makes up our psyche. It's no longer the fiber of American culture, it's about our psyche, and it's becoming global. Where do we run? We don't have a little spaceship to go to another planet. At one point, we have to stop and go, "Alright . . . I get it. Let's change that," or have the understanding to know the change starts with you and your immediate family. Then it moves out like a sound wave to everybody else. That's what happens. Unfortunately, we have dysfunctional families, including my own, so that's a hard thing to change, but the first step is in *knowing*.

Geographical environment? What makes something the center of something? It's visibility. When something is visible, it attracts more energy, and it attracts more people, and it becomes like, "This is the Rome of so and so—this is it." Let's take hip-hop for instance: People painted the West and the East Coast as the two Meccas of hip-hop culture, even though the West Coast is mostly funk styles and the East Coast is electro-funk and hip-hop. Everybody in between also contributed in some way, but they were never focused on. And eventually, after these two things slowed or dried up, it starts to filter—so the new, the people in the middle, are starting to come up in that way.

There was always a hot dance in Atlanta; since I was a kid, everybody knew there was a dance. Most of it came word of mouth through the family, people traveling back and forth, kids meeting each other, and "Hey, this is what I . . ." "Ooh, you saw that dance he does?" Everybody in Philly might be doing it, and that's how hip-hop movement travels across the country. The same would be true with all the dance styles prior to hip-hop, so I think it's because of the "media god" putting things out there. More people are pushing to hear their own voice in the media. People are starting to want to influence more from their cities. I don't necessarily think that New York was specifically the center. It may have been by way of media, but I think if it was the center, then it was missing a whole lot of other stuff.

It was the center by way of visibility. I used to be one of those who thought, "Philadelphia is right next to New York—they're always looking over Philadelphia. Man, we influence a lot of stuff up there in New York!" Because everyone's related, and they go back and forth between Philly and New York all the time. And so then, I was like, "You know what man? I'm thinking about Philadelphia. What did Philadelphia contribute? How can I blow myself up *in* Philadelphia?" And that's what we focused on in Philly—we didn't focus on going outside of Philly to New York to be validated.

When we go to New York, I still get a little scared and nervous because it's New York, but, in my experience, Philadelphia has always been the hardest audience to please. Even its own people who make it as singers have a hard time selling out. It's a hardcore; they'll boo in five seconds. I think even though it's about visibility, about who's contributing what, it would be naive to think that the whole country wasn't contributing, because there is a collective, and if I'm doing something here, somebody's doing the same thing in LA.

What do I think about the economic environment? Fortunately, my company has been fine. Prior to the company, there was a period of time that I was in my survival mode, and I performed with Butoh dancers to ballerinas, with whomever I could get to do work. I always heard people saying, "Oh, you shouldn't start a company," and "This is not a time for companies—no one has a company now," and I thought, "Oh, okay." And, "You shouldn't call yourself a hip-hop company or you may not ever get booked anywhere," and I was like, "Oh, okay." And I would hear of people not doing programs because they didn't get funded, or they were upset because they didn't get funded, and they didn't know what they were going to do—they were losing their jobs. When I decided to do this company, we became 501(c)(3) [not-for-profit corporation] and, through the work, our mission was to educate. I didn't want to depend on grants. I feel, "I dance, you pay me." Fair exchange is no robbery. I looked at it as, "If we don't get booked, no one wants us." I told everybody, "In three years if the company is not moving, I'm out." And so we basically became 93 percent earned income. We had very little support, grantwise, for projects. For working a big project, we'd get that money, but—no gen op [general operating expenses], no other support.

We would sell T-shirts, and some of the T-shirts proceeds would go to paying the dancers. We'd sell phone cards with our pictures on them, and we sold pictures and made a profit. I sold incense and oils at my shows. We did everything we thought we could do commercially, as far as merchandising, to help support the company. I always thought that way: When someone couldn't afford us, we said, "Well, can we get a percentage of the door?" "Just give us a percentage of the door, and we'll be fine." I would work out weird deals. I still think that way, and I think that's what's saved us.

I look at everyone in my office as bringing in their own money, so they pay for themselves. If you were in promotions, you had to bring in some promotional dollars, to pay for yourself—that's how you got your salary—you got paid on commission. Same thing with booking, same thing with education. Anytime we would go on tour, we'd do add-ons. They would find five or six places we could teach, for 250 dollars a pop. They would get 10 percent of what that was, and we would go out for three months. The person who was doing education was getting a good check. So, we made sure that everybody's job generated money into the company, along with the performance fee. And that is pretty much how we avoided the crunch of monies being dried up.

After fifteen years, we're attempting to change our model because we're no longer the new kids on the block. I'm still a little reluctant, but I formed a for-profit business of my own, and I'm looking into specifically how that can help support my nonprofit business as a model. Now that we're shifting, we're beginning to feel what that crunch is, because we're so used to being on the road. We're having to shift the model so that we have visibility. We want to take advantage of the visibility for private/individual donors to help us get through the next fifteen years. That's where we are now. We're looking to buy a building. We have the same problems everyone else with a company has: Dancers want more money. Everybody wants more money. I don't know which one is better: having a high percentage of earned revenue or having it balanced with contributions, donors, and grants. Either way, the control part of me doesn't like being dependent upon other people for something I need to get done, and that scares me. It makes it hard.

When we did our festival, Legends of Hip-Hop, I said to people, "Listen, you want to do this? Let's do it." I call it "the hip-hop way." We'd never think about it, we'd just do it. Sometimes it's problematic, but sometimes it shows people that we're going to do it regardless, and that it's going to happen. When you think of it as a community, you don't think about whether you are getting paid. You do it because *you* want support when *you're* down. If you help somebody, they're gonna help you back. And that's the way I looked at it. "Oh, okay, you can only afford a couple . . . lalala, okay look: Can you make dinner for us?" And we've danced for dinner; we've danced for crazy stuff with shelters. It's still the community in that way, and that attitude has helped us. It's the hip-hop way.

March 16, 2006

Bill T. Jones at Wexner. Photo © Kevin Fitzsimons.

Bill T. Jones

Mr. Jones began his dance training at the State University of New York at Binghamton. He choreographed and performed worldwide as a soloist and duet company with Arnie Zane (1948–88) before forming the Bill T. Jones/Arnie Zane Dance Company in 1982.

Bill T. Jones has been awarded several New York Dance and Performance (Bessie) Awards (1986, 1989, 2001, and 2007). He was honored with the Dorothy B. Chandler Performing Arts Award for his innovative contributions to performing arts in 1991. In 1993, Jones was presented with the Dance Magazine Award. In 1994, he received a MacArthur Award. In 2000, The Dance Heritage Coalition named him "An Irreplaceable Dance Treasure."

In June 2006, Jones choreographed *Spring Awakening: A New Musical*, for which he received the 2007 Tony and Obie Awards and the 2006 Stage Directors and Choreographers Foundation Callaway Award. In 2006, he received the Lucille Lortel Award for Outstanding Choreography for *The Seven*, the 2005 Wexner Prize, the 2005 Samuel H. Scripps American Dance Festival Award for Lifetime Achievement, the Harlem Renaissance Award, and the 2003 Dorothy and Lillian Gish Prize.

Creating more than 100 works for his own company, Jones has also choreographed for Alvin Ailey American Dance Theater, Axis Dance Company, Boston Ballet, Lyon Opera Ballet, where he was Resident Choreographer from 1994 to 1996, Berlin Opera Ballet, Dayton Contemporary Dance Company, and Diversions Dance Company, among others.

Jones is an experienced collaborator in a variety of media. He has created works with, among others, Jessye Norman, Max Roach, Toni Morrison, Keith Haring, Robert Longo, Robert Wilson, The Orion String Quartet, Daniel Bernard Roumain, and others.

In 1990, Jones choreographed Sir Michael Tippett's *New Year* under the direction of Sir Peter Hall for the Houston Grand Opera and the Glyndebourne Festival Opera. In 1994, he directed Derek Walcott's *Dream on Monkey Mountain* for the Guthrie Theater in Minneapolis, Minn.

Jones's solo performances have taken him to such prestigious venues as the Milan Cathedral (2004) and the Louvre Museum in Paris (2007).

He is the author of *Last Night on Earth* (Pantheon, 1995) and the coauthor of *Body against Body*. He also authored *Dance* (Hyperion, 1999), a children's book with photos by Susan Kuklin.

Television credits include PBS's "Great Performances" Series (*Fever Swamp* and *Last Supper at Uncle Tom's Cabin/The Promised Land*) and "Alive from Off Center" (*Untitled*). *Still/Here* was codirected for television by Bill T. Jones and Gretchen Bender. A PBS documentary on the making of *Still/Here*, by Bill Moyers and David Grubin, *Bill T. Jones*: Still/Here *with Bill Moyers*, premiered in 1997. The 1999 Blackside documentary *I'll Make Me a World: A Century of African-American Arts* profiled Jones's work. *D-Man in the Waters* is included in *Free to Dance*, a 2001 Emmy-winning documentary that chronicles modern dance's African-American roots. In 2004, Arte France and Bel Air Media produced *Bill T. Jones: Solo*s, directed by Don Kent.

Jones lives in Rockland County, NY, with his companion, sculptor Bjorn Amelan.

What's at Stake?

I tend to blend the development of the company with my own development as a person when I speak about the work. Like many in the cliché of the go-go 1980s, we felt the possibilities were endless. In 1981, I had just appeared in the American Dance Festival Emerging Choreographer's program. By April 1983, I had made *Fever Swamp* for the Alvin Ailey Company. It was a large jump from the downtown milieu of the Kitchen, Dance Theater Workshop (DTW), to a mainstream company. The year 1983 also saw the creation of our company's *Secret Pastures*, an ambitious collaboration between Arnie and me, much decried in some quarters as too fashion-conscious, too slick. Deborah Jowitt, writing in the *Village Voice*, said it was the first modern-dance work influenced by MTV, which Arnie and I took as a compliment.

Secret Pastures, following on the heals of *Freedom of Information*, was a large-scale theatrical spectacle created for the Brooklyn Academy of Music's Next Wave festival. Both these works, created in the first few years after the company's founding, were in contrast to the austere duets *Blauvelt Mountain*, *Monkey Run Road*, and *Valley Cottage* that had made Arnie's and my reputations. We were rethinking who we were.

With this rethinking came an intense interest in establishing a dance company. The company had been founded in 1982. Soon thereafter came the question of institutionalization, which, at that time, we felt to be a bad word. In 1984 or 1985, we were encouraged by the advancement grant we received from the NEA, commonly understood to be the step leading to the much-coveted challenge grant. The infrastructure building and the maturation of our administration and, yes of course, our marketing and promotion seemed to be happening in another world from the one of our creation, and, for a while, we could pretend they were separate. But change was inevitable. By 1983, I was still making solos for myself while collaborating with Arnie in making works for our new company. By 1985, Arnie was beginning to doubt not the company, but his relationship to performing. He often told me that he "did not live to dance." He saw himself as an artist first, capable and interested in working in various media of which dance was only one. I felt the need to be in there, sweating with the dancers on a daily basis, trying to prove something to myself and the world, something about craft as opposed to personality, invention as opposed to pure enthusiasm.

In 1986, the company was six dancers, soon to grow to eight, and, at the time of Arnie's death in 1988, we were nine. Larry Goldhuber appeared in 1986 or 1987. Larry is a very large man and, at that time, was certainly more an actor than a dancer. I met Larry when he was in the audience at a workshop showing. He came up to me, offered his card and said, "If you ever need a big man, call me!" For reasons that I don't recall clearly, Arnie was resistant to including Larry in the company though he had no problem with him as a guest. I had collaborated with Larry on a duet for a solo evening as part of our company's season at the Joyce Theater in 1985. It was called *Holzer Duet: Truisms*. Arnie had liked the piece but still had reservations about Larry's joining our ranks.

Somewhere in 1987, I think, Arnie was making a piece called *Lotus Eaters*, and its subtext was Miami Beach. He thought perhaps he could use Larry as a stereotypical Miami Beach denizen as he was always a "character" in Arnie's mind. Arnie was becoming quite ill by this time and, just before he died, Larry was taken as a full company member and was central in my last collaboration with Arnie in a work called *Brief History of Collage* to a Charles Amirkhanian score of the same name. With the inclusion of Larry at 350 pounds, the perception of us as a dance company was radically changed.

Larry's body focused some unexpressed questions we were having about what the company should look like. Racially, there was very little diversity in contemporary modern dance at that time. Now, twenty-odd years later, there are bodies of every hue. At that time, I knew of no people in wheelchairs defining themselves as dancers. They exist now, but are they in the mainstream? Likewise, with the dance world's Larrys—are they in the mainstream now? No, they aren't. They don't even exist in my company right now. Perhaps these things must go in cycles. Larry Goldhuber is making his own work now. Like other nontraditional dancers, performers, he had to create a place for his body. I think we're in a very confused and conflicted era right now around issues like which bodies will be accepted in the dance mainstream. There has been a certain retrenchment. I would like to think of it as a hunkering down before we spring forward again.

If I could afford to have a larger company, I'd be more adventurous in its composition. The repertory I have created and my preoccupation with a style that is about speed and facility exclude certain bodies. As our organization expands and deepens, our output can become freer with the bodies that inhabit our stage.

There was a time when who we were was more important than what we were doing. Perhaps it was a leftover from the 1970s era of the dance collective. We were unconsciously trying to make community, though I don't think we had the words for it yet. For better or for worse, it was a social vision first. Arnie was known to say, "We're making a picture, not of the world as it is, but of the world that we want to live in." This was on the eve of what became by the late 1980s and early 1990s identity politics.

We didn't think of it that way, of course. We thought we were simply extending notions from the counterculture of the late 1960s and 1970s: breaking through social boundaries, redefining body politics, living the sexual revolution, re-examining power dynamics, the relationship of men to women, men to men, etc., and striving for transcendence in every way.

All the while, our tastes were changing and our dancing was striving for more speed, more technical flair. Alvin Ailey was very kind to me, since the day that he showed up unannounced to watch a workshop I was conducting at the Ailey School in 1982. After some gentle banter about the downtown dance, he invited me to make a piece for his company. There are a couple of things I remember him saying at that time. One was that he liked postmodern dance "when they dance." Later, as he watched my roughhousing rehearsal of *Fever Swamp*, he said to me, "Bill, don't hurt my boys!" Very touching to me then and now. I invited him to our company's rehearsal of *Secret Pastures,* and he said, "I like that. You should give it to us, the Ailey Company. My dancers are better than yours." (What?!!!) With the perspective of years, I now know what he meant, but it did cause me to begin thinking more deeply about dancers and what it meant to be a "good dancer." Up to that time, Arnie and I had always prided ourselves in possessing what we called "naturalistic virtuosity" comprised of sand-lot gymnastics, a sensitivity to shared weight and counterbalance gleaned from contact improvisation and arm gestures. We resisted the notion that a good dancer had to have a classical body alignment. What's more, we felt that there was, throughout the dance world, a tyranny rooted in classical dance values. Our heroes were the experimentalists such as Simon Forti, Steve Paxton, Trisha Brown, Yvonne Rainer, Meredith Monk, Lucinda Childs, etc. Still, we wanted the resources that more conventionally trained dancers could provide, and we set out to attract such dancers.

From the early to mid-1980s, I would say the work's concern was art-historical. We were— in our choice of music, in our collaborators, and in our general style of performing—trying to resolve a pervasive concern, which was the relationship of high and low culture. *Freedom of Information, Secret Pasture, How to Walk an Elephant,* and *History of Collage* were all irreverent spectacles designed as a sort of assault on the formal dance-concert format. We were trying to reconcile our own beginnings as two largely self-taught performers inventing our aesthetic and ourselves as we went from piece to piece with greater resources in our dancers' bodies and in our production budgets. We wanted to be distinct, wild, and successful. We were unconcerned about the future, and repertory did not exist or, if it did, only in an offhanded way.

With Arnie's death in 1988, all of this changed. It was, of course, a much-recorded period of grief for me personally, but a profound period of transformation for the company. Recently, I was looking at a documentary made in 1988 or 1989. In it, I speak of the change from being a member of a "celebrated interracial, homosexual dance duet team" to being a black man alone—a bit dramatic, but true . . . A profound change.

Twenty years ago, not wanting to be defined by skin color, I considered myself an artist who happened to be black, a countercultural point of view. After Arnie died, I realized race was an important aspect of my creativity: in the sense of my mother's voice, singing spirituals, the temerity of survival I could literally feel in my bones, in my muscles as being a child of people who were potato-pickers from the South. I was proud of those things, and with it came a belligerence and an attitude of "I will not forget." The white avant-garde didn't quite understand what was going on.

Only after Arnie died was I was suddenly a black man, who had to find out what that meant. I refuse to be in anybody's ghetto, be it an art ghetto, a gay ghetto, or a racial ghetto. It was a tough, though essential realization to come to, that I have a right to have a black voice that could express all that I am.

The issue of race has become more textured for me. My influences and relationships have been broad and oftentimes Western European. Gradually and reluctantly I have allowed myself to be called a black artist because I have come to feel that the world is capable of understanding that black artists are as diverse in their output and approach as *any* other artist. As I accept this, I no longer have to apologize for my particularities.

Arnie's death allowed me to see the "art ghetto" he and I had viewed with disdain as, in fact, a nurturing place. Manhattan's downtown scene: the Kitchen, Dance Theater

Workshop, PS-122, and, later, the Joyce Theater and the Brooklyn Academy of Music, gave us identity and validity. But after he died, I was left with the question who and what was I and what was the company? Works made in the aftermath of Arnie's death and in the early 1990s were evidence of my personal search and an attempt to celebrate what we had been. This required identifying what we actually had stood for or believed in. There had always been a certain belligerence in the work. It came with the sense that we did not truly belong. But there was also this feeling of being on a mission, an act of defiance. In the makeup of our company, in the way in which we handled each other on stage, in the irreverent uses we made of conventions, in our satire and funkiness, we were insisting that we be seen, that the discourse be changed to see us.

A work like *The Last Supper at Uncle Tom's Cabin/The Promised Land* (1990) had to be big, with a public voice. At that time, I was preoccupied with the sense that—though I was bred to be alienated—I refused to be cynical. I had a need to continue one of our company's traditions, and that was to create instant communities with the feeling and depth of the real world. I needed persons of every description conspiring to reaffirm yet again what I took to be the triumph of the counterculture's social experiment. This big shaggy evening was an implicit protest and an affirmation.

As a choreographer, I have a spotty record around issues of gender. I have a male's pre-occupation with strength, assertiveness, and being heard, even though I am much more ambiguous than this might imply. I use my strong body in a way that can be bullying. My important teachers, not only in the dance world, have most often been women. Lois Welk, of the American Dance Asylum, saw the company some years after we had left the Dance Asylum and said, "Why don't you just get rid of the women? They seem irrelevant in your work." I was so offended by that. It stung me, but what she said was important. Women have always been an important part of my worldview. Obviously, I had forgotten something or was not being clear. Julie West, perhaps the first person to join Arnie and me in the early 1980s when we decided to expand our "duet company," was a tough little woman from Ottawa, Canada. She was an assertive, strong woman who extended our experiments in partnering through her fierce intuition and physical fearlessness, informed by a fine knowledge of contact improvisation.

Over the years, as my investigation has moved to other places, I have seldom had a collaborator like Julie. Questions of gender always resurface, and for that I am grateful. I have to listen more carefully to the women around me and ask, "Who are they? What do we share? What do I need from them? What can they bring to this? What do they need to give their best?"

In this way, the company has evolved. I have some very strong women in the company, straight and gay. There's a whole feminist discourse, or post-feminist discourse, that's not lost on them, and they're very much aware when I overstep boundaries or when I make assumptions about gender.

Sometimes a gay man will come in who thinks because the director is gay, he can be a super queen. I'm not interested in super queens. Excuse the military analogy—I suppose that's the male part—but I convey to them, "I want you to be everything that you are, and what I need you to be is a fierce warrior in my army. I want you to stand up so that as I get older I've got somebody strong behind me." *Strong*. Not to say a gay man can't be, but some of them have to be reminded, given permission, that they *can* be serious and they can be strong.

Bill T. Jones, *Blind Date*. Photo © Paul B. Goode.

I don't want any dancer in the company to ever feel that they have to mute any essential part of their personality in order to accommodate some unacknowledged desire on my part. I don't value women less because they are not men, straight men less because they are not gay. I recognize talent or beauty whether it's male or female. I recognize sexual power and potency whether it's male or female. I demand that each dancer bring to the company and to the work their whole self.

In terms of the political and economic environmental question . . . Though the place of the artist has always been suspect in our culture, the last decade has been particularly unstable. The individual and his or her innovation have long been the hallmark of the USA's image in the modern world. In the art world—particularly in the world of dance and perfor- mance—this has become a liability. Sadly, because the NEA got into trouble in the face of a growing tide of conservatism, it no longer funds individual artists, only companies or organizations. I often think, "What a slap in the face it is that our culture doesn't value us artists and will not stand behind our toughest critique, our most singular visions." To be sure, I have received my fair share of support, but the environment is such that there are a handful of us who are able to make a go of it, and even thrive. The vast majority actually flounder.

During the past twenty-five years, AIDS has been a brisk slap in the face, or more benignly, a Zen slap of consciousness. The politicized cultural climate has delivered its own slap, the recognition of which has been absorbed more slowly by some of us, such as myself . . . I thought I was a product of a revolution, that the doors were open, and we could not go back. I've seen that is a lie. And it is frightening and infuriating.

I never wanted to be labeled a polemicist. However, now that I look back on it, Arnie and I had always felt that even our most abstract, formalist offerings were being thrown in the face of a repressive and narrow mainstream. My works of the early 1990s were simply the next step.

It has been said that *Still/Here* (1994) was a significant volley in the "cultural wars." I prefer to think that it simply focused what was at stake. It helped provoke a nasty and necessary confrontation. Those of us in the world of culture and the world of politics are still dealing with the questions raised: What voices will participate in the discourse? What paradigm will reign?

These things had to be talked about, and the human drama had to be lived through. It was painful, but the company and I survived. I came out of it a better choreographer. One of the benefits of this difficult period was that I had to acknowledge that while I was making my social statements and building community, I had grown away from what attracted me to dance in the first place. So, amid all the confusion and disorientation, I decided to back up and rethink what dancing was for me.

The discussion around *Still/Here* and the culture wars was raging. I was thinking that I wanted to leave the dance world. It seemed not the right place to do what I needed to do as a person and as an artist, but before taking this drastic step, I decided to take another approach. I had to get back in touch with my own dancing as a way of reimagining where movement might come from. I asked Trisha Brown, whom I've always had respect for as a formalist and system maker, to create a piece for me. She was too busy to create a new work, but she would teach me the one she was making for herself. It was arduous, nerve-racking for me. I felt too big, too emotional, too male, too expressive. Still, it was exhilarating to participate in her process. She didn't have the cynicism about originality many of my friends in the art world and I did. She truly sees herself as an inventor of movement. Her invention is rooted in problem-solving and a dogged attention to detail that balances formal design and body shape with the recreation of the elemental forces of gravity, suspension, flux, and weight. The solo she was working on was called *If You Couldn't See Me*. In it, she was to dance with her back to the audience. The costume and music were by Robert Rauschenberg. We performed a duet version of it in France in which I was always facing the audience as she faced upstage.

I learned a great deal about her system's method of creating movement, distilling and performing it. Her style, cool, removed from psychology and issues, took me back to my body, answering the question of what makes dance dance? Likewise, as my body was beginning to age, Trisha's system encouraged greater subtlety and careful listening to the way I moved. I was excited again and made the commitment to stay the course—though somewhat altered—in the dance world.

In 1995, as the tour of *Still/Here* was ending, this time with Trisha gave me the necessary link to my next investigation. I would spend hours practicing her moves and creating my own, using her ideas. It was a pleasure to be so rooted in my mind and physical sensations as opposed to my thoughts and feelings. I made a solo called *Power* (1996) that later became a duet titled *New Duet*. This movement, in various permutations, has proved to be a great teaching tool for new dancers coming into the company. And the dancers kept coming, ever more sophisticated technically. And Janet Wong, since 1995, has been there to train them.

Returning to pure movement investigation was a survival technique, first for me personally as a performer and then as the choreographer and Artistic Director of the company. The mid-1990s, following *Still/Here*, was a time when I decided that the company would stand or fall on the shared language of our bodies—in other words, our style of moving. Janet Wong, whom I had met in 1989, when she was a dancer at the Berlin Opera Ballet, has proven to be the lynchpin joining my personal style of movement and an ever-changing community of dancers. Janet, with a solid command of the classical technique, also has the curiosity and intellect of the best of contemporary dance-makers. She observes my personal style and is able to reconcile that with the torque, loose-limbed flowing style of movement that I saw in Trisha Brown. Janet was invited in first as Rehearsal Director and teacher to help me create the dancers we needed and the style that would unite us. She has now become Associate Artistic Director.

In 1994, I received the MacArthur Award. A great honor, but reason to wonder how could I be so rewarded and still have the credential of a bona-fide rebel? How do I keep alive in myself and in each generation of my group of dancers a sense of wildness, excitement, and defiance that is not bitter but more like pepper on the tongue? Our mantra: What is at stake here? That has been our project since the late 1990s.

What's at stake now has to do with what I call the discourse—the ongoing way in which the society attempts to know itself. I was born in 1952; *Brown* v. *The Board of Education* was in 1954; the Civil Rights Act was passed in 1964; Stonewall Riots and Woodstock were in 1969. I've been shaped by all of the above markers, and yet everything I and many of my generation took for granted is in question now. There was a battle for hearts and minds back in the heyday of the counterculture, but we have not won it yet. I have always tried to live as if as an artist I am an important fighter in this struggle the society has with itself. As an artist,

Bill T. Jones, *As I Was Saying*. Photo © Al Zanyk.

I've always felt that we should ask what kind of world do we need to live in and how much are we willing to give in order to have that world?

Rightfully or wrongly, my life in the art world has taught me that there is a constant exchange going on. Artists—particularly those of us in the performing arts—have to deal with how their work will be funded.

In the dance studio, in my process, no matter what the dance phrase might be, I ask the dancers: What is your relation to this material? Do you own it? Do you accept its implications not just in the dance world but also in the culture? I'm sometimes driven to distraction in doubting the relevance of contemporary dance. But if I can answer the above questions, the work will find its relevance, its voice.

Concerning the question of age, I'll say, "Age happens." Shortly after Arnie died, on March 30, 1988, I planted a star magnolia for him in my yard. It unfolds in full bloom in the early spring each year. This blooming is a reminder of the passage of time and, in a way, of what's at stake in my life as an artist. I was thirty-six years old when he died. I remember at Arnie Zane's memorial at the Joyce Theater, saying to Harvey Lichtenstein, "Some of us would love to see our fortieth birthday." Every year that I have lived since, I can feel as if it was stolen or a gift . . .

Now, though I am aware of the passage of time, I am not so much burdened by it.

At the time of this interview, my back hurts, probably as a result of something I've been rehearsing. I've had knee surgery within the past year. These aches and pains are the result of time and wear. This fact can be depressing, or it can be an inducement to develop. Trisha Brown told me that every ten years she has had to change the way she trains. She is a wise woman, and I'm trying to understand her approach. That's what age is: an opportunity to reinvent.

In terms of performing, I perform less. Sometimes in the studio, I think about a time when everybody in that room was within five years of my age, either younger or older, and now they're people who could be my children. That's distressing to the ego of a performer. They jump higher, they have more flexibility, they have more stamina, but it's also a compliment, an encouragement. It says I've survived. What's more, they're here with me. I am able to attract a new generation of them. They keep coming; they see something here. They want to be here. There's no reason for sadness; there's plenty of reason to have faith in the future, to keep going.

October 24, 2006

Kenneth King as Patrick Duncan in *Dancing Wor(l)ds* (1990). Photo © Johan Elbers.

Kenneth King

Kenneth King has been called America's only dancing philosopher because many of his multimedia dances have generated and been performed to texts and essays, spoken and prerecorded, that stand separately as literary works. His book *Writing in Motion: Body—Language—Technology* was published by Wesleyan University Press in 2003, and his writings have appeared in *The Paris Review, The Chicago Review, /nor* (*New Ohio Review*), *Art & Cinema*, the philosophy journal *Topoi, Shantih: The Literature of Soho, Movement Research Performance Journal, PLJ/Performing Arts Journal, Semiotext(e), Film Culture, Gay and Lesbian Journal International, Dance Magazine, File, eddy, Ballet Review, Panache*, and in the anthologies *Footnotes: Six Choreographers Inscribe the Page, Merce Cunningham: Dancing in Space and Time, The Young American Writers, The New American Arts, Text-Sound Texts, Further Steps: Fifteen Choreographers on Modern Dance*, and *The New American Cinema*.

As the former Artistic Director of Kenneth King and Dancers/Company, he presented a wide variety of dance, multimedia dance theater, and text/performance works at such venues as Judson Church and Gallery, Brooklyn Academy of Music, Museum of Modern Art, PS-122, Walker Art Center, American Dance Festival, the Kitchen, Dance Theater Workshop, St. Mark's Danspace Project, and the Poetry Project, and at various international venues including the Autumn Festival (Paris) and New Dance Munich. His work is discussed at length in Sally Banes' *Terpsichore in Sneakers* and *Reinventing Dance in the 1960s: Everything Was Possible*, and he is a featured choreographer in Michael Blackwood's film *Making Dances*, in Robyn Brentano and Andrew Horn's movie *Space City*, and has appeared in the films of Andy Warhol, Jonas Mekas, and Gregory Markopoulos.

King has taught, performed, and mounted dances at numerous colleges and universities including the American Dance Festival at Duke University; Long Beach Summer School of Dance at California State University; University of Wisconsin; University of Maryland Baltimore County; New York University's School of the Arts, School of Continuing Education and Department of Performance Studies; Brown University; Dance Alliance of New Haven/Yale University; University of Minnesota; University of Toledo; Cambridge School; Princeton University; Wesleyan University; SUNY Brockport; Sarah Lawrence University; Bennington College; Antioch College; New School for Social Research; Trinity College; Pratt Institute; C. W. Post College; Queensborough Community College; the Laban Institute; and the MoMing Dance and Art Center in Chicago.

He has received fellowships and grants from the John Simon Guggenheim Memorial Foundation, National Endowment for the Arts, New York State Council on the Arts, New York Foundation for the Arts, and the Creative Artists Public Service Program.

King graduated from Antioch College, where he studied philosophy with Keith McGary. His dance teachers include Merce Cunningham, Paul Sanasardo, and Mia Slavenska. In 2004, he was awarded a New York Dance and Performance Award (Bessie) for Sustained Achievement but declined it in protest of the Iraq War. He recently completed a second novel.

Dancing the digital body

> The body is our general medium for having a world . . .
> Maurice Merleau-Ponty[1]

Information, like the dancing body, travels and configures signals and signs faster than discursive thought and involves deciphering or translating their interconnective links and imports—all movement is informational or potentially so. My last installment, *Transmedia* (1982), looked forward to the day when a computer would be on every desk and as commonplace as any other appliance. We now take PCs, Internet, email, cell phones, and iPods for granted. Ever since cinematography and the radio, the human body has been undergoing unprecedented *digital* transformations that continue to create new corporeal frontiers.

Technology continues to change the entire physical landscape as laser meets psychomimesis and biotechnology releases the capacities of cells and genes, confounding the credulity of science fiction. After multimedia on stage, the kinetic horizon of technology is the *body itself*. Virtual memory presages cybermnemonic capacities—*neurothetics*—possibly pioneered by twoway glasses with telecognitive transference and micro cell phone earpiece adaptors to *textend* the interactive capacities of the Internet and biosystem, surpassing screens and monitors to spatialize displays like a combo fusion of freeform 3D and teleprompting. Imagine dancers channeling choreography *during* performance, but without a choreographer—progress, baby!

Digitality,[2] the telesynchronous velocities of transmissible information—in essence, how we potentially see or know anything at all—involves the kinemimetic flow of motoric

---

1   Maurice Merleau-Ponty (1962), *The Phenomenology of Perception*, London: Routledge & Kegan Paul, translated from the French by Colin Smith, p. 146.
2   Since my writing engages word coinages, editors request a glossary: *digitality*—all the ways that computerized transmission, transmissability and the speed of info and media inform communications and our lives; *cyberthetics*—the synthetic totality of computerized, digital, and software projection and information systems; *cinemimetimatic*—the pixilated, mimetic layers and registers of projected imagery; *ideokinetic*—how imagery is physicalized, actualized, and internalized in and on the body, movement, behavior, and consciousness; *interprecessionary*—interpenetrating and intraleveraged impressions, details, registers and orders of imagery, movement and (re)presentation; *interstices*—the spaces between gestures, movements, frames, etc.; *kinelexical*—how movement and its registers are read; *kinesis*—the perception of movement and motion;

(im)pulses embodied by clusters of data that composite interprecessionary signals and signs in mosaic interface. Movement in passage dissolves, bypasses, or mutates all codes, and semiolexicality—or the readability of the signs of bodies in motion—has been an ongoing preoccupation. (Susan Leigh Foster was the first to articulate such a kinesiolexical practice, or dance semiotics, in *Reading Dancing: Bodies and Subjects in Contemporary American Dance*.)[3] Like movement, all technology externalizes and exemplifies kinetic and mimetic principles already residing within the body.

Marshall McLuhan clued us in to how the media are externalizations of the senses and nervous system; the Internet similarly transforms the brain. Technology began with the alphabet, and media exemplify different languages and signages; information is processed with peripheral vision and kinetic flexions, as dancers can readily testify. The meridians on the dancer's body serve as electromagnetic sensors and antennae. The body is the wor(l)d, and the planet made flesh is the dance of digitality. Just as French logotechnicians have extolled the death of the author and the disappearance of the subject, might we not do the same for the choreographer? There's just the coextensivity of the *textendable*, the Web's unimpeded circulation and distribution of kinetic signs, data, sites, images, texts, and information links that make mind *Mind*—a vibrating, (co)coextensive epic hyperphenomenon, a supraterrestrial neurosphere. McLuhan, media prophet and prognosticator, would have loved the Internet—it's his incarnation of the global village as a free-flowing electronic continuum kinelexically circulating instant information. It inaugurated the domain of the virtual that Susanne Langer identified in her aesthetics: dance as virtual power.

Multimedia prepared us for the digital body, and choreography becomes corporeal systemicity and kinetic geodicity. The digital body's steady-state rhythms are autonomic and automatic. Because our society overproduces and culture consumes by snarfing bytes, trends, and overnight fads, postmodernism is being transformed by cyberthesia into post-art. Dancing animates the cogito incognito. By 1969, I knew there was information in the dancing body, and I trace my preoccupation with the digital body to a high-energy, nonstop dance I presented in May 1971 called *Inadmissleable Evidentdance: The CIA Scandal* at Washington Square Church on West 4th Street, NYC. It was accompanied by a prerecorded channeled

---

kinesiotheric—the virtualized registers of motion perception; *mimetic*—how language, signs, images, and movement project their parts, effects, registers, orders, etc.; *autoprojective*—the spontaneous or autonomous ways body movement emits and broadcasts signals, signs, images, meanings, and effects; *motoric*—the motor capacity of muscles, media, machines, and locomotion; *proprioception*—the internal processing and components of (inter)sensory stimuli that inform kinesthesia and body motion, including and involving organic functioning, motor coordination, and perception; *semiolexicality*—how signs interactive in movement are read and discerned on the (dancing) body, in a text, film, video, or event; *semionostics*—the (interdisciplinary) applications, applied techniques and even diagnostic understanding or deportment of signs, signage, and semiotics; *tactilic*—references the sense of touch as the palpable basis of both the kinesthetic and gestural; *telesynchronous*—the multiple intercoordinations, overlaps, and references that engage or entrain processes, media, and bodies, especially digitally, by computers or periodistic transference; *valences*—though a scientific or mathematical term meaning the combining power of an element or elements, it can be applied to movement's supernumerary or supplemental effects and elemental intentionality; *vectorial*—as the body moves through space, it engages geometrical coordinates and bearings as virtual lines, traces, and traceries, including perceptual sightlines and bioenergetic meridians.

3 Susan Leigh Foster (1986) *Reading Dancing: Bodies and Subjects in Contemporary American Dance*, Middletown, Conn.: Wesleyan University Press, 1986.

text simultaneously broadcast on Pacifica's WBAI Radio. It foreshadowed the Watergate scandal that brought down the first US president and foretold the "Master Control Panel"—what is now the personal computer and Internet. Dancing could be digital, and I was "programming" movement and cybersthesia.

The dance was composed of long sustained passages of intense whirling (rope dancing) that sprung open and released chains of propulsive spatial volleys and high-speed phrases with sharp, cookie-cutter punctuation, churning and contracting torso, jabbing and flecking semaphoric arms, and gestural feints like kinetic stutters packed in lots of microkinetic detail. The steady-state intensity and nonstop motoric permutability altered body frequency and induced a telepathic state. Excerpts were published in two madcap articles under the alias of Zora A. Zash[4] (Zoroaster and Zarathustra via Nietzsche) in *eddy*, a 1970s dance periodical. It began:

> Everybody loves a s-c-a-n-d-a-l. And in America everything IS a scandal. Instead of epics and allegories, scandals have become our national mainstay [. . .] The New Folklore. "Politics begin in the bedroom; diplomacy: in the KITCH-shun (get it)?" [. . .] Instead of a New Deal, we have the NEW Conspiracy. Everyone is forced to act on, or under, double sets of contradictory orders.

The fact that body movement contained information that could be tapped, translated, and deciphered seemed to me a given. But when I tried explaining this to some of the Judsonites, I received blank stares—their pedestrianism was still in revolt against the expressionist fallout of Martha Graham's symbolic *Sturm und Drang* style; her alienist father had counseled her: "The body doesn't lie." Dance at the time seemed at loggerheads, preoccupied either with fairy tales, angst, or the regime of everyday tasks.

I was aware that big changes were afoot and that computers would alter all the parameters of our society, experience, and bodies. The year 1971 was more than a decade before the proliferation of the personal computer. Who would have guessed that Marshall McLuhan's 1960s idea of the global village would be realized electronically by digitally fusing typewriter, television, and transistorized circuitries to create cyberspace that would make words, movement, and images reciprocally hyperdimensional and open doorways to artificial intelligence (after Alan Turing, infrared cameras and surveillance aircraft), and become embodied in the 1990s as the Internet? In 1971, I said this secret invention

COULD EVENTUALLY BE A DOMESTIC, DECENTRALIZED, SYNTHETIC COMPENDIUM OF *ALL* HERETOFORE SEPARATE COMMUNICATIONS MEDIA, WHICH COULD BE MARKETED AS A KIND OF PORTABLE APPLIANCE—COMBINING EQUIPMENT AND SERVICE INTERFACE OPTIONS CONSOLI-DATING TELEVISION, COMPUTER, RADIO, MAIL SYSTEM, TELEPHONE COMPANIES, DATA BANK INDUSTRIES, NEWSPAPERS, WIRE PHOTO BUREAUS, EXCHANGES, MAGAZINES, BANKS AND LIBRARIES . . . WILL FACILITATE MANY MORE USES, FUNCTIONS AND A GREATER RANGE OF AVAILABLE TYPES OF PROGRAMS, ALSO NEW RANGE OF STATIONS, STATION INTERFACE

---

4   "Pardon My Leak" (winter 1975–6, No. 7) and "Don't Blow my C-o-v-e-r" (winter 1977, No. 9).

SELECTIONS FOR EXCHANGE OF SERVICES . . . ELECTRIC MAGAZINE FORMATS . . . PSYCHOTECHNICAL SOFTWARE OPTIONS TO EXPAND EDUCATION INTO UNIVERSITIES WITHOUT WALLS . . .

It must have seemed like science fiction, but it wasn't! The boundaries were breaking down between the arts—one of the formidable breakthroughs of the 1960s—so why shouldn't the media also fuse and open up cultural parameters? *Inadmissleable Evidentdance* also began my romance with *essence*spionage, shades, disguises, black trenchcoats, contraband, and transvestite spies—Mater Harry spilling the beans in a dead giveaway wig and cheap 14th Street pink nightie! It also catalyzed my fascination with *semiotic* surveillance of the kinetic interstices of movement where I scouted for hidden signs and clues generated by, or embedded in, body impulses that emitted *seer*cret information. (I had been reading Gurdjieff and Husserl, a potent cocktail.) Deborah Jowitt and Anna Kisselgoff reviewed this dance in 1973; the latter deemed me a romantic!

The dance also revealed our government was keeping secret a new laser energy resource code named "Mesmex" that could make wireless communication possible and do away with wall plugs and Con Ed. We don't have it yet because our government decided to blow untold billions on the Iraq War, investing in oil hegemony rather than the more auspiciously beneficial enterprise of alternative energy. What did and does this have to do with dance? Everything—free energy—body workers know all about it!

Movement and motion connect everything we see, feel, and know. After ideokinesis, cyberthetics, and semionostics, how the body processes information and what information is—kinetically and *kinelexically*—makes a fascinating investigation. Information might be nothing less than the interconnectivity and transmissivity of all and everything! Movement encodes experiences and ideas; it also kinetically encrypts and kinelexically deciphers—Lucian, the Greek philosopher of antiquity, maintained the Mysteries could only be *danced out*. The activation and extendibility of our bioenergetic meridians and the synergy of their interprecessionary interactions ideokinetically projected activate vectorial networks of signal and sign constellations—kinesiotheric inscriptions.

Movement also resembles radar—kinaesthesia is not simply a passive-receptive sense but an active proprioception constituted by an intentionality that emits probes and trajectories and thereby acts on and activates a tactile perceptivity; the voice too and vocal soundings produce an autoprojective capacity, like the wave-detection principle of sonar. Movement is integral to the functioning of memory; muscular flexions activate modes of mnemonic recall whose mimetic enchainment of motoric associations can be as cryptic or as fleeting as dreams. Susanne K. Langer on the origins of the dance:

> The effect of this communal art was certainly enhanced by another motive, perhaps older (there is no telling) that was emphasized by the formed bodily movement: the corresponding mobility of the visual ambient. The Dance, above all else, animated the dancer's world at the command of his own voluntary movements, and may have been a magical activity from its beginning.[5]

---

5   Susanne K. Langer (1982) *Mind: An Essay on Human Feeling*, Vol. III, Baltimore, Md.: The Johns Hopkins University Press, p. 210.

John Cage's injunction "syntax is the military" also applies to choreography—rote, mechanically repeatable structures enforce a predetermined authoritarian precinct mentality, like generals to keep everyone in line. Movement is more likely to be transparent to information when involuntary impulses and automatic internal decision-making are allowed to inform the emerging weaves that open up the kinetic interstices and coordinate a freer-wielding assemblage of steps and junctures. More information and connections erupt in improvisation and when a dance's form, structures, and rules remain open-ended.

Movement is also *cinemimetimatic*—micronarratives and cognitive valences are embedded in the cadences and rhythmic convolutions and could be likened to a holographic labyrinth that engages active transferences between oscillating fields filtered prismatically through the kinetic cogito. Dancing outdoes any teleprompter—words, sentences, and ideas pop into one's field or inner screen, materialize in the air, brain, or somewhere in between. There's information in movement, and its textings too can coordinate a choreography of ideas. Motion currencies (printing press, steam engine, locomotive, galvanic cell, telegraph, etc.) inaugurated the need, speed, capacity, and contexts to *read* and deliver volumetric flows of movement, data, and information in all their various modes, codes, orders, contexts, and extensions. The currency of movement also dissolves, morphs, and mutates the shapes and bound energy of all codes in kinetic interface—the body is constantly telegraphing information to itself and others. Modern dance of necessity continually reinvents itself. Choreography is geodicity.

Dance and language have always been at the core of my explorations of body and technology and have been nurtured by the writer's challenge. A conflict or double life was brewing. A European tour in 1984 made me realize globetrotting and the Gypsy life would impede what I really wanted to do. I needed more time for reading and researching. The essays such as *The Si(g)ns of the Wor(l)d* (1987), poetic collages such as *Scream at Me Tomorrow* (1982), word salads such as *Moose on the Loose* (1984), and character monologues such as *The Tallulah Deconstruction* (1990), written to accompany my dances, were always meant to stand as independent literary works. Mallarmé's right: everything happens to end up in a book!

During the 1980s, I turned to the essay—it's the most challenging and formidable of forms. During the 1990s, I turned to fiction and am working on another novel. Narrative let me open up the rigorous density of style that the essay requires. Sometimes I feel that in spite of the abundance of videos and films, the essence of dance will be just as well distilled and transmitted through the written word. A collection of the many texts written for my dances was published in 2003: *Writing in Motion: Body—Language—Technology* by Wesleyan University Press.

What really interests me about dance—about *Being* being in motion—is the interconnectivity of vectors and ideas, links and virtual circuits. The group process dancemaking I explored between 1975 and 1991 increasingly decentralized the role of the choreographer and generated modes of composition larger than any single brain could originate. The dancers' input and decision-making require intelligent structural responses within a collective continuum at every moment, and this involves a kinetic semiotics for the audience as well—how we read signs while in the act of responding to and fielding signals. Semiotics offers the best model for a dance aesthetics—how signals, signs, configurations and structures interpenetrate and create mosaics of correspondences, images, qualities, meanings, analogs, etc. Movement in process involves the rapid response to flexions, and the assemblage of involuntary movements requires peripheral vision and physiognomic seeing to coordinate how eyes, feet, flow, and passage intercept and align multiple tracks of kinetic information. The exploration of automatic processes was inspired by William James, Gertrude Stein, William Burroughs' cut-up and fold-in methods, John Cage's use of chance, and French theorists such as Michel Foucault and Roland Barthes—the death of the author and zero-degree interference. Learning to dance involves a lot of linguistic feedback. My dance is anchored to a fixed base but is continually permuting—like Heraclitus' river—different every day.

The economic downtown of 1980s Reaganomics proved less and less supportive. I took some out-of-state university jobs but realized I needed to be in New York City, free to dance, read, and write. By 1991, the economic erosion forced me to disband my company, and I moved on to collaborative duets and solos. I made a solo evening *Dancing Wor(l)ds* that combined dance, characters, monologues, music, and text. Having started out as an actor, the otherness of voices moving through my dancing body really intrigued me.

Gender is an altogether different puzzle. One of the most liberating aspects of dance is becoming both sexes, combining force and flow while undergoing the plastic trans-formations of being in motion. Preoccupied with the fusion of the sexes, I researched hermaphrodites trying to find out if there really was an ontological coup—someone who was genuinely both genders. My monologue *The Tallulah Deconstruction* (1990), quite outrageous, celebrated the deep luscious overproduced wit of Tallulah Bankhead: "Darling, when has being dead ever stopped *anyone*?" Her voice was deeper than a truck driver's with an indelible arch, and a thrilling challenge to pull off—with white feather boa, wig, gown, and combat boots! In 1993, I made a solo dance accompanied by a prerecorded essay, *Dancing and Writing* (*On Hermaphrodites*). Hermaphrodites are more mysterious than transsexuals. Sexuality is more complex than gender, and gender exceeds being male or female. The androgyne is archetypal, the hermaphrodite corporeal. Artists too have to be kind of hermaphroditic—transparent to both polarities of their psyche while embracing empathic gender (or ontological) transformations—the ultimate sexual cipher! Hermaphrodites are going to be the gendernauts of the twenty-first century.

Sexism is endemic to ballet—ballet is women—Balanchine's twisted credo is also political and set the field back decades. Anyone want to deconstruct dance politics? And the idea that gender parity means women should partner men is laughable for its simplistic counter-parity. The issue isn't manipulation but giving dancers autonomy. If choreography can require the abdication of the choreographer, then the French theorists' death of the author seems the ideal paradigm. Until the body moves rhythmically and produces isomorphs, there's no form, fission, or fusion. Isomorphs reveal the relationship between shapes and structures and are the building blocks that connect passage and association.

Age, you ask? Don't get *poisonal*! I practice the New Math—subtract twenty-nine from whatever year it is to revise my birth date. D'Nile is more than a river in Spain, Baby—ballet dancers are required to retire at forty, but I want to dance *another* forty! Besides, 1971 already feels like a past life. And what's a little more dissimulation in this geriphobiciatric society? Sure, like everyone else, I'd like some of Ponce de Léon's Magic Fountain of Youth Formula too, wouldn't *you*? Technical dancers always dazzle, but watching a mature body *move* is especially fulfilling because then the dancing body becomes transparent to a lifetime's experience. Unfortunately, there's scant literature to inform dancers how to keep going. Studs Terkel's and Simone de Beauvoir's books, both titled *Coming of Age*, are excellent sources.

Kenneth King as Tallulah Bankhead in *Who's Kidding Whom?* Photo © Johan Elbers.

Kenneth King as Mr. Pontease Tyak in *The Tallulah Deconstruction*. Photo © Johan Elbers.

My mentor has been Frances Alenikoff; even into her eighties she could kick her leg over her head and remains indefatigable—she chants, sings, writes, and paints and has taught me a *lot* about how to sustain myself through nutrition and herbal supplements. Start with coenzyme Q10.

Dancers can be terribly naive about politics and often have very lopsided ideas about history. Where is the sociologist or critic capable of exposing the hidden politics of the arts? The most recent defining political moment? 9/11 of course, our new folklore. To begin resolving the pile of discrepancies in the official version read Jim Marrs' *Inside Job: Unmasking the 9/11 Conspiracies* and David R. Griffin's *The New Pearl Harbor: Disturbing Questions about the Bush Administration and 9/11* (or <http://www.whatreallyhappened. com>, <http://www.copvcia.com>, and <http://www.globalresearch.ca>).

Another political juggernaut: The biggest government con job was making arts organizations and dance companies become nonprofit corporations in order to receive mostly poverty-level funding. Since the 1960s, the arts have been burdened by, and indentured to, the corporate oligarchy—having boards of directors and administrators miring their efforts in more red tape than anyone could want. Then there's fundraising for drubbing one's final illusions. Modern dance got boring—too many practitioners, formulas, and institutionalization and too little money and opportunities, plus the insufferable schmoozing at all those airhead cocktail parties. Why didn't anyone think up an arts lottery, it could have been a billion-dollar windfall!

During the past decade, dance jams have helped sustain my exploration of movement. During the 1990s, they were called Open Dancing at PS-122 and regrouped and became Contact Jam at Judson Church in 2000 but open to all forms of improvisation. Since 9/11, the Jam meets at the Children's Aid Society (219 Sullivan Street, bet. West 3rd and Houston Sts., NYC, 8:15p.m.–11:15p.m., 5 dollars). Moving through an interactive field of dancing bodies zooming by and coordinating in a hairsbreadth with split-second timing very much mirrors process-generated dancemaking. The body can move faster than the brain. It's kind of a paradox, feels inexplicable while it's happening and while watching it occur! You can't beat that expansive euphoria and ecstatic connection. Dancing bodies coordinating with split-second smarts in rough-and-tumble traffic exchange volleys of information that emit fleeting images while ideas pop out of the blue. It's not unlike the cyberthetic thrill of surfing and flipping between windows and websites whose kinetic zap scopes out unexpected connections and vistas that push against the invisible and unknown.

November 1, 2005

Nancy Meehan. Photo © Nan Melville.

Nancy Meehan

Nancy Meehan began her career in San Francisco performing with the Anna Halprin–Welland Lathrop Dance Company and presented her first works there. In New York City she studied with Martha Graham, Andre Bernard, and was a principal dancer with the Erick Hawkins Dance Company. In 1970, she established her own company and school. Since its inception, the Nancy Meehan Dance Company (NMDC) has participated in many festivals, including the New York Festival at the Delacorte Theater, six summers at the American Dance Festival in Connecticut and North Carolina, and it has performed throughout the USA and in Japan.

Meehan has received a Guggenheim Fellowship for choreography, numerous National Endowment for the Arts (NEA) Choreography Fellowships, as well as grants from the New York State Council on the Arts, the Creative Artists Public Service (CAPS), and the Mary Flagler Cary Trust Live Music for Dance Program. In the years following the publication of *Further Steps* (1987), the NMDC has continued to have yearly New York City performances and is starting work on its thirty-seventh season, to be held in 2008.

Dance Mind

What has always interested me is dance that frees the mind and body, opening up new possibilities and dormant perceptions without relying on technology and its effects. I want to invent body language and structures that will evoke states of mind and body that are moving to the audience, dancers, and to myself. From my earliest dances, I've used nature images as metaphors for the mind and have had a fascination with what I call undefinable reality, that state of mind and body reflected through dance movements which is always present and sustaining.

My work is affected by world and current events, the light and motion on the Hudson river outside my studio, people and relationships, the weather, nature, reading, art, music, and animals. All of these influence my work in ways I do not always consciously know. I read about and hear of tragedies, catastrophes occurring all over the world, the condition of the planet and the threats to its survival; all have a very deep and profound effect on what I do in my dances but not in a descriptive or polemic way. I believe that we are moving through one of, if not the most agonizing, critical periods in human history, and for the globe, the Earth itself. The optimism of other periods seems hard to maintain, and this makes the arts more vital than ever for the survival and continuance of a sane human existence. I believe that art can help to counterbalance some of the hideous destructive violence visited upon all creatures and the environment by giving some balance and perspective to the horrors, or at least a brief respite in which to regain some ground lost to despair. Art can also strengthen the will to continue in the midst of an increasingly mechanized, dumbed-down culture. It can deeply refresh the mind and body to find new solutions and the resolve to do something about them.

Dare I say I am trying to make beautiful dance movement, beautiful moments, beautiful dances? Perhaps the word "beautiful" has to be redefined? Today, the word has become a pejorative, and it is contentious and passé to talk about anything being beautiful. I'm talking about art, and much of what I see and hear called "art" does not strike me as art. The definition of beauty can change with different periods of history, and it does keep changing as people perceive things differently, but it can still be sought after. What is this intangible beauty? I don't know, I only know when I see or feel it. It can't be pinned down to any subject, emotion, or dramatic situation, or lack of dramatic situation. It is something that communicates an undefinable experience. One way one can experience this is from art. I don't believe we have a word to define or to describe this. It is an ineffable experience.

Today, there is a constant barrage of images and flux, and I feel the need to slow down to allow for other kinds of experience that take time and space to exist as a respite from the constant overstimulation and frenetic activity and give a breathing space, an opportunity to not have to rush, so that the mind can dilate and clear itself for the choreographic process.

How do I start a new dance? The process brings back a vivid childhood experience. My parents and I were driving down the California coast on Highway 1, which runs along the edge of the continent from San Francisco to Santa Cruz and beyond, in the night time in a very dense coastal fog. My mother had to get on the running board of the car with a flashlight to guide us so my father could see the center line and not go off a cliff into the Pacific Ocean. That's how I often feel when I start choreographing a new dance. It is going into the unknown. It is very hard to give up and let it be what it is going to be. It's painful and frightening and almost impossible to resist self-judgments and to tolerate everything that appears. How or what will dancers and others think of it? I have to learn not to care. The final problem is what do I think of it. But judgment and critical thinking have to be suspended, and I have to tolerate and entertain whatever comes to mind and turns into movement. Movements occur, and again, one may feel deserted and ready to give up. I look at them over and over and see how each dancer does them differently and use the interpretation that seems to be right for each dancer. When juxtaposed, certain movements have to change. I am constantly thinking of how to help dancers repeat something they unconsciously did wonderfully. To recapture the instant, the tiniest movement or shift makes a huge difference. When dancers give themselves over to movement, such complete "surrender" sometimes makes it difficult to repeat. The body is poised differently each day, elusive and crucial. A whole passage can depend on such a thing, i.e. keeping it fresh without freezing it. This is a great challenge to me and to the dancers. It's what gives dancing its validity and vitality and makes the difference between holding a dance together and causing it to lose its essence.

Concentration/focus is key and is intensely compelling to the audience. Its magnetism brings dance to life. There is something tremendously compelling in watching true concentration. It is revealing and lets essence come through the mind and body of the dancer. When you watch and hear a very great pianist, the concentration demanded is astonishing. The same thing happens for dancers. Anyone who is doing anything with undivided complete concentration is very magnetic.

Dance, especially the nonliteral kind, is evanescent and open to many interpretations, which is simultaneously an advantage and a disadvantage. First of all, there is a live person there, who is making very few sounds and is responsible for conveying the choreographer's vision and movement qualities. Whatever the dance and dancers emanate consciously or unconsciously comes through and is reinterpreted and experienced in the mind and body of the viewer, through his or her own layers of experience. How much the viewer lets the movement be itself and does not get bogged down in figuring it out is almost exactly what a choreographer does in inventing a movement. The more judgment can be suspended, both in the time of choreographing as well as in the viewing, the more indecision tolerated and cultivated, the more possibility for fresh things to emerge. The suspension of judgment is crucial for the choreographer, dancers, and audience.

Of course, the choreographer ultimately makes many decisions, as do the dancers, but the audience can be open. There is a saying, "many people see dance through their ears," that they come to a concert with all kinds of preconceptions they've heard either in the art world and/or dance world, don't relax their preconceptions, and are not present to the actual performance experience. The point of all this is that I keep learning to be less critical at the time material is emerging than I used to be, to tolerate things that at first seem highly unlikely and dismissible. On the next day, or weeks or months later, they may appear in a different light or turn out to work in the most unlikely parts of the dance, or they can be finally discarded. But the point is to stay open and ready like an animal. I have to relearn this each time I start to work on a dance but it occurs to me more quickly than in the past; that is, I realize to stop judging more quickly.

I am constantly learning and fascinated by the whole process of choreography, working with dancers, composers, and costume and lighting designers. I keep seeing it from different perspectives, but my deepest interests and instincts remain the same. They are revealed unexpectedly and give a grounding that is sustaining and refreshing for me. It is always from a new angle. Sometimes it takes quite a while into the process of working before I catch a glimpse of where it might be going. It becomes recognizable in new forms and relationships that sometimes I do not perceive until months after the dance has been performed. It is an amazing, exhilarating process which can be painful, and discouraging.

How has my choreography changed? I asked my husband, Anthony Candido, who is a painter and architect and designs our costumes. He thinks it's become "more eccentric, visually different without losing formal structure, more personal but still has universal anchor, loosened up, less predictable, has a more exaggerated and distorted use of space, and abrupt transitions with the disconnect somehow having continuity." There is more gesture included, the movement vocabulary is broader, and spatial arrangements are more developed. Perhaps it is simplified and stripped in terms of structure and more complex in other ways. There is a lot of stillness and use of very slow and suspended periods to give the timeline a sense of expansion. I am using more stillness at a time when so much in the world is speeding up, because I feel a need for that.

I have always worked with live music and commissioned all of the music for each dance. The composer Eleanor Hovda and I have collaborated on many dances and have developed new ways for us to work together and with the dancers. The dancers do not cue their timing from the music. Over the years, I have taken an ever-increasing interest in timing, and we are using counts less than when I was choreographing twenty or thirty years ago, although some movements are counted. The dancers cue visually, so having to be aware of other people around them in this additional way is critical. They are not improvising the timing; they start sensing each other like one big animal. Some phrases are not counted at all. It takes a lot of rehearsal time to work this way. I use a stopwatch in rehearsals, not to be confined to a rigid sense of time but rather to find how long something takes to do fully, well, and that works. It is fascinating to see a phrase or a group of phrases find their own best timings rather than confining them to a preset, arbitrary time frame.

The way I teach dancers the movement is very similar to what I used to do. I give them a movement I have either counted or not. They learn the counts for the movements that I want counted. Then I keep watching them do it and I start to see where they warp things slightly or not, and if I like it, I leave it. Then we don't use counting anymore. This has made a breakthrough in the nature of certain things I'm doing. It's a liberation. I used to count movements, to set a pulse. Now there is often no pulse so as to get to the phrasings and needs of the movements. Different dancers may time the same movement differently, which I like.

When dancers are working without counts or musical cues, they unconsciously observe changes in the bodies of other dancers, much more closely than they normally would when they are cueing from the music or a pulse set by the music. Enough rehearsal time is necessary so that the dancers have time to open up and absorb this new aspect of dancing together. They also have to know much more specifically where other dancers are within the space. That's how they cue. Sometimes the cue is visual or it may be a movement sound that cues the dancers, but they have to pay attention to each other in a different way than if they were paying attention to the music. Again, I'm not saying that one is better than the other. I'm just saying it makes a big difference. (Much of this is unconscious.)

Over the years of choreographing, I have come to understand how everything affects audiences' perceptions, consciously or unconsciously. For example, how much an audience can identify with a dancer's experiences is a strange and very complicated phenomenon. All of this increasing awareness over the years has affected my choreography. I very rarely know what the dance will be when I start. My dances are now increasingly less logically connected. I am as concerned with transitions as ever but recognize that a complete break can also be a transition. Many phrases are independent and free-floating, excerpt-like, but I am still fascinated with transitions as well. No transition is as much of a transition as anything else if it is a conscious choice and it works.

Our first performance of my company at St. Mark's Church in New York City was in 1984. It opened up many new possibilities in the use of space and sound. It was a different space and sound instrument and demanded new structures of performance techniques. At St. Mark's, where there are no wings, it is a challenge to choreograph without dancers leaving the performance space to either walk to the dressing room or stand on the carpeted space. I like to keep all of them on the dance floor throughout the dance's entire length in order to

Nancy Meehan Dance Company. Photo © Nan Melville.

keep the audience focused on the dance and not on dancers coming or going. This has demanded a new structure and has presented interesting problems in choreography. It has forced me to examine and make new kinds of transitions or none at all. There is no *deus ex machina* possible.

It is a challenge for the dancers to keep their concentration and focus at performance pitch for as much as forty or fifty minutes for the longer dances. All of them are most often in every dance in an evening's performance. They have to constantly maintain their intention and concentration at a very high level. I believe this has helped audiences focus in a special way and experience the performance more directly, second by second, to be drawn into it in a different way than from a proscenium stage. This is also possible because they are very close to the performers and can feel the floor vibrations, hear dancers' feet and movement, and experience the sheer physicality of what's taking place; the breathing, eye expression, body heat, sweat which may fly onto them, all are very apparent.

Advantages and disadvantages of a proscenium stage and other performance spaces are obviously very different, and I would not deny their value. I do like the immediacy and sheer actuality of the space at St. Mark's in the way I use it. The audience in the first few rows is almost in the dance and sees it partially from some dancers' viewpoint.

I have noticed how intensely quiet audiences are at St. Marks. The space helps the audience to take the time necessary to allow a suspension of the usual sense of time's passage. The dances interrupt this by passages or instances of totally different dynamic levels, which are both suspended and direct and very active and very slow. I have always been interested in film in that it can go from one spatial extreme to another almost instantaneously. Film can encompass one sense of place that is totally unpredictable from what proceeds or follows it, with close-ups and distances. I've wanted to capture some of this non-sequitur dominance, which also works in the mind, without technology or mind games being involved. In other words, I'm not trying to do this in a technological way but through the dances' structure, timing, the dancers, and the use of space, music, lighting, and costumes.

I do not rely upon or use any complicated technical equipment other than lighting. The music is always performed live, composed for the dance, or the dances are done in silence. The dance, music, lighting, and costumes will speak for themselves.

Over the thirty-five years of my company's existence, I've had male and female dancers of all races and many cultures, which has enriched and brought a freshness to our performances. I have worked with male dancers when they were available.

I am not going into old age happily, but what I find exciting is that I keep learning so many new things, which never made sense before but now do make sense. It is because there is more background to draw upon and I understand things that I didn't even think about or couldn't have understood before. But aging is difficult, and I think for performing artists it is a problem. Choreographing and working with dancers has meant more to me than it ever has because I want to be around dance and dancers so much. Somehow, it's satisfying to me to be with people who are doing it. It is an amazing phenomenon.

I think people are much more tolerant of seeing an older dancer on stage than twenty years ago. I'm sure there are people who don't like it and would rather see young people who can do a lot of virtuosic things older dancers can't, but, on the other hand, an older dancer can bring a lot more to their performance quality than most younger people. I think it balances out, and I very much enjoy working with different ages. I find the older company members are very valuable to have because they understand certain things the younger

Nancy Meehan Dance Company. Photo © Johan Elbers.

people don't and their movement has more nuance, texture, and richness. It is very crucial to have that balance.

Funding for the arts is a major problem. Our throwaway society is always looking to the new, to the young choreographer. Young dancers should be helped, but it has to be balanced. Our culture does not value experience enough but is obsessed with the new, the technical, the flashy. There is less awareness of what older people have to offer and less value placed on it. One of the big issues for dance of all kinds is that the Government is no longer funding the way it could and should. There have been periods when I had no funding for dancers. For the past four years, we have received grants from a private fund to pay dancers and some expenses, which has been a great help and support. When I was a younger dancer, I never expected to be paid and rarely was. However, when I began dancing with Erick Hawkins in the early 1960s, the NEA was starting to fund touring, and we were all paid, but we had to quit our jobs and find new ones upon return. Much of the funding the NEA was granting has been cut back.

Another major change I have noticed in the dance world over the past twenty-five years is that many young dancers no longer take daily technique classes. They tend to take three technique classes a week and then practice and study body-work forms, such as yoga and Pilates. These are all beneficial to dancing but they are not substitutes for daily dance-technique classes. A dance class is a different state of mind and body and is crucial to forming a well-rounded grounding. The other "body-work" classes are very valuable but only in addition to at least five dance classes a week. Economics is a serious problem, and classes are expensive, but it never has been easy for dancers.

Dancers are also starting to choreograph at a much younger age. They are more open to movement that is unusual, whereas dancers in the past would often question certain approaches if they didn't fit into formulas they were used to. Dancers today are generally more open, freer in improvising and less tied to a technique.

I feel dance is often confused with performance art. I believe they are different and that it is important to distinguish between the two. The state of mind of a dancer is different from that of a performance artist. Their roots are different. Dance has its own language and deals with content in terms of that language. In a sense, the content of dance is dance. For me, dance is an art form with extraordinary possibilities and a life and existence all its own, which at its best can bring forth a reality which is undefinable and ineffable.

May 21, 2003

Meredith Monk in concert (1995). Photo © Massimo Agus.

Meredith Monk

Meredith Monk is a composer, singer, director/choreographer, and creator of new opera, music-theater works, films, and installations. A pioneer in what is now called "extended vocal technique" and "interdisciplinary performance," Monk creates works that thrive at the inter-section of music and movement, image and object, light and sound in an effort to discover and weave together new modes of perception. Her groundbreaking exploration of the voice as an instrument, as an eloquent language in and of itself, expands the boundaries of musical composition, creating landscapes of sound that unearth feelings, energies, and memories for which we have no words. During a career that spans more than forty years, she has been acclaimed by audiences and critics as a major creative force in the performing arts.

Since graduating Sarah Lawrence College in 1964, Monk has received numerous awards, including the prestigious MacArthur "Genius" Award in 1995, two Guggenheim Fellowships, three "Obies," two Bessie Awards for Sustained Creative Achievement, the 1992 Dance Magazine Award, and a 2005 ASCAP Concert Music Award. In 2006, she was inducted into the American Academy of Arts and Sciences and named a United States Artists Fellow. She holds honorary Doctor of Arts degrees from Bard College, the University of the Arts, the Julliard School, the San Francisco Art Institute, and the Boston Conservatory.

In 1968, Monk founded the House, a company dedicated to an interdisciplinary approach to performance. In 1978, she formed Meredith Monk and Vocal Ensemble to expand her musical textures and forms. She has made more than a dozen recordings, most of which are on the ECM New Series label. Her music has also been heard in many films, including *La Nouvelle Vague* by Jean-Luc Godard and *The Big Lebowski* by Joel and Ethan Coen. Monk's publishing relationship with Boosey & Hawkes, begun in 2000, has helped make her scores available to a wider public.

Monk is a pioneer in site-specific performance, creating works such as *Juice: A Theater Cantata in 3 Installments* (1969) and *American Archeology #1: Roosevelt Island* (1994). She is also an accomplished filmmaker who has made a series of award-winning films including *Ellis Island* (1981) and her first feature, *Book of Days* (1988). Both films were released on DVD in spring 2007. A retrospective art exhibition, *Meredith Monk: Archeology of an Artist*, opened at the New York Public Library for the Performing Arts at Lincoln Center in 1996. Other recent art exhibits include a major installation, *Art Performs Life*, at the Walker Art Center. A monograph, *Meredith Monk*, edited by Deborah Jowitt, was released by Johns Hopkins University Press in 1997.

In October 1999, Monk performed *A Vocal Offering* for His Holiness, the Dalai Lama, as part of the World Festival of Sacred Music in Los Angeles. In July 2000, her music was honored by a three-concert retrospective entitled *Voice Travel* as part of the Lincoln Center Festival. Between November 2004 and November 2005, Monk's fortieth year of performing and creating new work was celebrated with such events as *Dance to Monk: Choreographers Celebrate the Music of Meredith Monk* and *Making Music: Meredith Monk*, a four-and-a-half-hour marathon at Zankel Hall performed by an array of world-renowned musicians and ensembles.

Cracks and Cliffs

The first thing that comes to mind in terms of major events affecting my art is the death of my partner, Mieke van Hoek, in 2002. We had been together for twenty-two years. When you lose someone that close to you, nothing is ever the same again. My world turned upside down, and everything, including being an artist, was put into perspective.

Ultimately, it seems that life comes down to how much love have you left behind and how have you manifested that love. Things that were so important to me didn't seem so much like life and death anymore. It's not that I'm less deeply involved in my work; in some ways, I am even more committed and thankful to be engaged in something that I love. It's just that the ephemerality of any action seems more obvious.

What is more important now is appreciating the moment, the nowness of a blue sky, but without a concept of a blue sky. Perception has changed. It's more about being aware and grateful for every day, every color, every moment of clarity or confusion, every time I wake up and realize I am not just in this little world that I have constructed but reality is pushing in on me in a great way, waking me up. I work on that a lot.

Contemplation is actually one aspect of making artwork, so each project I work on is not only just a piece of art, it's actually something I am pondering. What I realized at some point is that this way of thinking has a lot of power because it goes back to the very beginnings of art that had to do with transformation or transmutation of nature or reality. Then the act of creating art and performing it makes a change, makes something actually happen, so it's not just like a show and then its over, but something actually happens to the energy in the world.

We're living in quite a dark, fragmented time. To try for an alternative is not a goody-goody thing at all. I think that our work has to be very honest and rigorous, but the ultimate aspiration is some sense of upliftedness, an affirmation of life.

There are artists whose work is about reflecting the culture or reflecting the contemporary reality we are living in, and that work is very much of its time, and it's very important, like holding up a mirror to the society. There was a certain time in the late 1970s to early 1980s when I was working with that idea.

I made a few very apocalyptic pieces, but then realized that my deeper nature is a poet, but a nonverbal one. At that time, I began to feel that the most useful thing I could do instead of stating the problem was to really offer an alternative: to create a performance situation, which becomes a template of behavior, the generosity and radiance of the performers being a powerful aspect of the work. It's more like offering some kind of antidote. I've always been very interested in timeless or cyclical aspects of human nature and nature itself, so that is much more the kind of work I try to do now.

I don't think anybody could have been unaffected by 9/11. I happened not to have been in New York. I was in New Mexico, but I live ten blocks away from Ground Zero. There I was in Cañones, New Mexico, in the middle of nowhere, realizing that nothing would ever be the same after that. That event had an overwhelming quality to it, and when I got back to New York in the beginning of October, I walked out of my loft, turned right and looked towards those towers, but there was nothing but smoke. It was as if the island had tipped, as if the anchor wasn't there. It had such a strange feeling. Of course, we went right down to pay our respects. Then there was the anthrax situation: Which post office was I going to go to, to pay my rent? Did I have to wear gloves and a mask to open my mail? All of that was just overwhelming. I know I'll never forget it. I just knew that nothing would ever be the same again.

Then I went to Ireland to perform, and then I went up to the McDowell Colony in November 2001. The McDowell Colony was allowing artists from New York to come up even for a week, because people were having asthma and couldn't breathe. It was just incredible. I remember trying to work on my first orchestral work, commissioned by Michael Tilson Thomas. I was trying so hard and was working badly and just producing material that was meaningless, and I knew it.

Finally, I was able to settle down a little bit, just breathe into the emptiness and discomfort, and two pieces actually stuck. One of them was called "Last Song," which is the beginning of my new piece *Impermanence*. It has text by James Hillman, who is a friend of mine. He is an American who lived in Europe for a while and worked as the head of the Jungian Institute in Switzerland. I call him a Jungian psychologist/philosopher because he is also a social critic and a social philosopher. He wrote a book called *The Soul's Code*, and he just finished an amazing book, *A Terrible Love of War*. I was reading his book *The Force of Character* when I was up at McDowell that time, about aging and how in earlier days the older a person got, the more character they had and the more respected they were, which is a value that's lost right now in our society. There was also a lot of humor in that book. I read it every day, and, in one chapter, there was a list of words that started with "last;" it was like a litany, and I thought, "This would be very interesting to write a song with."

I usually don't set songs to words, but the way I use them in "Last Song" is more like a chant because repetition is the main organizing element. What I also like is the irony of some of these words: "last inning, last rose of summer, the last laugh, last time." I started working on that song and also on the last movement of the orchestral piece, which became more like a song. I called that last movement "Powder City." It doesn't have words, but it's a melodic figure that the orchestra plays, and, little by little, fewer and fewer people play it.

There's a very violent section with the whole orchestra that happens right before "Powder City," and then the piece becomes almost like a prayer, emptying out little by little until everyone is tapping their instruments like aspen in the wind or raindrops. It's not a very obvious way to end an orchestral work, because it gets quieter and quieter. My idea was about everything dissolving into space rather than have a big climatic ending that seems to be expected for orchestral works. So, from that terrible time at McDowell, those two things evolved.

How has my work evolved or changed over the past twenty years? In the beginning of the 1980s, I started getting tired of theater and became much more interested in the music concert as a format. A music concert starts with simple presence, there's no transformation of time and space; it's very present tense. It was a relief because I had been making all these pieces where you enter another world, but I needed a break from that. What I liked about the concert form was that it had a very honest basis: The audience and the performer are in the same space and time. Then, as a persona, I could start with my simple presence as a singer, and each song could be its own world, so that, throughout an evening, I could actually become twenty-five different personas, rather than one character that evolves in an evening-long work. I felt that continual transformation was really interesting, and I liked the fluidity of it.

At that time, I had made a few albums, but then I started recording for ECM, which is an international label, and that was a big breakthrough for me because "Dolmen Music" became a kind of cult hit, and I was really in the music circuit, which was great. We played as an ensemble during the 1980s, almost like a rock 'n' roll band, particularly in Europe. A lot of people in Europe still don't know my theater work at all, they just know me as a musician, and that's OK.

Then I started thinking, "Well, OK, here is the music concert, and it's very satisfying." I had made "Turtle Dreams (Waltz)" in 1981. After that, the question I asked myself was how could I make a music piece that had simple movement as counterpoint, with the music as the ground base, including extremely intricate and virtuosic vocal parts? So, I created a repetitive side-to-side step, which continually transformed into geometric, layered patterns in space, while the music remained the most complex element. At that time, the concert began with me performing at the piano, singing "Gotham Lullaby," "Traveling," "The Tale," and "Biography," and then we would do "Turtle Dreams (Waltz)" and finally "Dolmen Music."

I started thinking about how to get some other theatrical elements in there and what kind of composition would be between the cracks of art forms that I've always liked to explore. What would the crack between music and theater be if I were really going to take the music-concert format and then add those theatrical elements? What would it be? It would be a cabaret, not in the sense of old cabaret forms, but a new kind of apocalyptic cabaret.

So, we did "Turtle Dreams (Cabaret)," which actually ended up being a very interesting piece. We found a space where we could have tables for the audience to sit at and drink wine. We were exploring also the entertainer–artist relationship, trying to weave together these existing modes in a new way. I loved doing that. It was a very interesting site-specific piece.

After that, my big thrust, other than doing the music concerts, was working on the film *Book of Days*, a feature-length film. I had made *Ellis Island* in 1981, as a half an hour film that held up by itself. I began using film in 1966 as one element in a very complex piece called *16 Millimeter Earrings*. Film has always been interesting to me because, as the great Russian filmmaker Eisenstein said, "All arts meet within the film frame." I've always thought of my work as a tree with two main branches: One is the voice, and the other is various ways of putting all the arts together, or what I would call interdisciplinary work.

As a major piece that took about five years of work, *Book of Days* was a film we shot in France and Germany. The theme was the juxtaposition of the Middle Ages with our time, so the film dealt with historical cycles and the way that certain aspects actually remain the same. It was like a Martian's point of view of culture, so I had television commentators interviewing the medieval characters, the plague as AIDS, the juxtaposition of those two times, and their obvious parallels.

The other very large project in the late 1980s and early 1990s was *Atlas*, which was commissioned by Houston Grand Opera. *Atlas* took a lot of time to make, and it ended up becoming a way of life. Only a few people from the ensemble I had in the 1980s were still around; a number of people had left at that time. Everybody was the same generation in that ensemble: Andrea Goodman, Robert Een, Naaz Hosseini, Ching Gonzalez. People were at the age when their lives were transforming; they were leaving the city, getting married, having children, wanting to be something else and doing all kinds of wonderful things with their lives.

I tried to find people who could project in an opera house, a different emphasis than the other ensemble had. That was quite a large change because I had been working with these people since they were in their early twenties; they grew up with my language of voice. For fifteen years, I had worked with the same people, so, for all of us, there was a sense of grieving. I was lucky though that three members stayed on to be in the cast. I auditioned about 300 singers for *Atlas* and chose fifteen. They had to be excellent singers and musicians and be able to move; they had to be good actors, and they had to be very generous and unique people. There were some funny auditions where divas came in with their black dresses and high heels, and I would loan them my sweat pants.

Atlas was very consciously made so that each person would be a team player and a star at the same time. We were balancing the cast, the way I usually do, with people coming from various ages, sizes, shapes, and racial and ethnic backgrounds. The other aspect I was looking for was a sense of generosity and good spirit so that we would have fun working and touring together. Auditioning and then making the opera was an unbelievable, intense process, and, after that, a few years later, we also performed a concert version of *Atlas*. I'm still working with some of those people.

In the 1990s, after this huge effort of *Atlas*, I needed to pull back and work on a solo piece. That has been a pattern: do something big and then pull back to do a solo or a duet. I worked on *Volcano Songs*, commissioned by Walker Arts, because John Killacky, one of the great, enlightened presenters of all time, invited me to create whatever I wanted. *Volcano Songs* was a piece about one figure moving through a landscape of images, music, and movement, very pure, but visually very rich, like a painting, going back to some of my very early image work.

I had wanted to work on *Volcano Songs* for quite a while. I was interested in volcanic energy as one of the forces at work in the formation of the Earth. I always was curious why anybody would want to live anywhere near a volcano. Why would people farm near a volcano? Then I realized that it's some of the richest earth in the world. I also had just returned from Bali where we had spent one month. I became very interested in the ironic relationship and process of creation and destruction that could exist within the forces of nature. It was a piece about archetypal characters of aging, with a conscious idea of how to make, for want of a better word, "sacred space."

The first conscious "sacred space" piece I made was *Facing North* in 1990, which was a duet with Robert Een and myself. That was a very meditative and quiet piece. The whole space was covered in white, very much like a snowy landscape inhabited by two people. The music was extremely intricate, but the piece was visually spare. That was something I wanted to try with *Volcano Songs*, too. There was a red square on the floor I thought of as similar to the way the Balinese perform something in a little backyard, and, because it has intention, it becomes a sacred space. So, when I stepped onto a little black stripe that formed the perimeter of the red square before I stepped into the red, that was the preparation, and then, once I was on the red, that became the energized space.

There were all kinds of metaphors I was working with. In one section, as an old crone, I put on a black bra filled with beans, and, in another, as a different persona, I put on huge black gloves. It was as if these black breasts or big black hands erupted, as if the body could also erupt. My hair was in many tiny braids, and I used it as a curtain, a mask, and as musical punctuation by hitting the braids on the floor as I did a kind of bow. In another section, I was wearing a hat/wig with braids sticking up in the air like I was a conductor of electricity. It was as if the body itself was the volcano, and a process where everything changes and is moving.

Volcano Songs began with five short a-cappella vocal pieces that were almost like vocal portraits, followed by three short movement sections which had to do with repetitive movement that would keep on going and would transform into another dimension. I called one of those sections "Hips Dance." My movement tendency is always to move with my upper body with a lot of hand and arm gestures, so I wanted to see what would happen if I couldn't do that. Trying to find a new vocabulary for myself, I worked only with my upper leg and pelvis, and that became the movement source.

Another thing about *Volcano Songs* is that I consciously began to think about the act of performing as not projecting, not seducing but just being. This has always been my performing style, but in *Volcano Songs* because of the small space, PS-122, I was more aware of the relationship of energy going back and forth like a figure of eight between me and the audience. In something like the hips dance, what I was trying for was that I was not manipulating the movement. The impulse was allowed to come through so that I was not actually doing it; it was doing me. Nobody else would know the difference, but I knew when the movement was arising honestly, so it was really the idea of a performer as a conduit, in a sense disappearing or becoming completely transparent.

After that, I attempted to try to take some of those principles and put them into a group piece. It was really a kind of gift for the members of my group. I called the piece *The Politics of Quiet*. I knew that I wanted to make a piece for the ensemble and not perform in it, to see what that would be like. So, that piece was really trying to bring some of what I had discovered in *Volcano Songs* to ten singer-movers. Most of the cast had been in *Atlas*, so this was a continuation of the process that began then.

It was not an easy process. I walked into the rehearsals with the music mostly finished, but I kept on trying to find theatrical images or movement images, and the piece kept on resisting them. We tried everything. It was really difficult, a labor-intensive process. I would eliminate images because they weren't working for me, or the piece didn't want them.

The way I feel about making art is that every piece is its own entity and it already exists before I start, so I discover a world that already exists in another dimension, and then I have to figure out what the laws of that world are. I would say to the piece, "Please make yourself known," because I was searching through the dark, letting it unfold, trying to bring it to life. That piece obviously didn't want to have a lot of theatrical imagery superimposed on top of the music or even integrated with the music. It just wanted to be very clean. After I made the piece, and usually I don't even know what a piece is going to be before I make it, I realized that this was kind of a nonverbal theater cantata or oratorio. It was very much about stripping these performers to their essences.

All of the performers were very skilled and brilliant music/theatre performers because a lot of them came from an opera background, so they were good singer-actor-movers. In this situation, what was very challenging for the performers was that there was nothing to hold on to at all. It was like stripping down to bare bones. There were no characters, changes of costume, or specific dramatic situations. *The Politics of Quiet* became more like a ritual, music-driven, with abstract, graphic visual elements. The room or stage was just an open space. I painted the floor gray, had turquoise folding chairs along the sides, and then there were black and white oblong boxes, that almost looked like railroad tracks, stretching across the front. Later, those boxes became a shrine, covered with objects that had been dipped in wax. The piece was very pared down in terms of not having a big set. The music and the light were the landscape.

Atlas was the opposite. There was a world going on backstage of *Atlas*: the costumes were flying, everybody was playing ten different characters, and the whole wall of the set moved. The piece had big production values, but *The Politics of Quiet* was the opposite: no tricks at all, just naked humans, not physically naked, but naked souls. At the beginning, it was hard for some of the performers, but then, as they performed the piece more and more, they started realizing how amazing it was. When they began to get feedback from audience members and friends, they understood how honest and essential their performing was and how much their humanity came through. Then the ensemble won a Bessie Award for its performing, so that was really great. I felt really good about that.

The other aspect that came up at that time may sound ridiculous, but I had gotten a MacArthur Fellowship in 1995, and it was really fantastic, but there was a part of me that was struggling with, "Well now I'm supposed to be Genius! Now what do I do?" It's amazing *The Politics of Quiet* ended up being as good a piece as it was because I felt the weight of the world on my shoulders.

So, after that, I decided, "What is missing here?" I was kind of miserable, and I thought, "What is missing is the joy from the early days of 'Lets do a show'; the spirit of playfulness." One of the great decisions that I made was to have Lanny Harrison come back into the group, because Lanny hadn't been working with me for a while since she is more of an actress, and I had been working with singers and instrumentalists.

Then I had many different ideas for pieces, and one of them ended up being a science-fiction chamber opera, which I named *Magic Frequencies*. In the world of radio teloscopy, scientists are trying to find signals from outer space as a sign of extraterrestrial intelligence. Magic frequencies are radio frequencies or sound vibrations attached to the hydrogen atom. Those frequencies are sent out because scientists think if any life form is going to be able to respond, it would be in those particular frequencies, because hydrogen is the most prevalent element in the universe.

Magic Frequencies was another "between the cracks" exploration. My idea was that there is a dimension that underlies our everyday reality, that's always vibrating and humming and shining. Kent Cullers, the great astronomer who was featured in the movie *Contact*, told me that even as we are speaking, the stars are singing, but we just don't hear them. I loved that idea of invisible or inaudible reality. So, I had little vignettes taking place in ordinary kinds of environments: a dinner table, a shopping mall, a TV studio, the bedside of a dying man. Within each of these vignettes, something unexpected, unusual, or mysterious occurs, revealing the underlying dimension, somewhat like the Buddhist notion of a *bardo*, an in-between world. Each is also unique visually. There are also other sections, which are very

Magic Frequencies (1999). Photo © Clemens Kalischer.

expansive, like the ground base or universe on which the vignettes are mounted. As a contrast to the purity of *The Politics of Quiet*, *Magic Frequencies* was a very theatrical, whimsical piece, with a lot of movement, visually and musically very colorful.

My goal always has been to try to start from zero and keep putting myself at the edge of a cliff, to keep taking risks and to grow by not doing the same thing over and over again. I've always thought about it that way. It's not very comfortable and there's a lot of tolerating fear and discomfort and hanging out in the unknown.

I don't remember exactly how this came to be, but I had been talking for a while with a wonderful visual artist, Ann Hamilton, and I'd always loved and thought her work very beautiful and powerful. I had read somewhere that she was influenced by my work. I didn't really know her, but there was some intuitive link, so we talked about making a piece together.

We started working on *Mercy* in 2000, and it was the first time I had ever collaborated with someone right from the beginning. When you start working conceptually with some-one, as in any collaboration, a lot of it has to do with trying to figure out how to work together. Half of the time was spent on working method and trying to understand each other's vocabulary, realizing that we might be saying the same words but they might mean different things to us. A lot of it was figuring out who was doing what. There is always an element of renunciation in collaboration. What can each person let go of to make room for a new entity? I knew I would be composing the music because Ann is not a musician. Her work is mostly installation art, but she is in charge of every element like the sound and video. I am also usually in charge of all the perceptual modes in my work, thinking of it as a unified vision, but I decided not to work on the video elements because I was very interested in Ann's ideas, and I knew they would be right for the piece. There was a lot of negotiating between us, quite difficult, and very challenging. We were both very strong, stubborn, and determined, and used to having things the way we see them, so we worked through a really interesting process.

Then the process itself suggested the beginning image where the two of us are sitting across from each other at a table. That image became a metaphor not only for our working relationship and our growing friendship but also for the most essential form of mercy. In a sense, the notion of mercy literally begins with being willing to sit or be with someone even though you have gone through something challenging or painful. Ann's beautiful, elegant video elements included tiny video cameras. One was inside my mouth so I would be singing, and you'd see Ann's face on the screen, because my mouth would open as I sang and I was looking at her. In another scene, a tiny camera would be on Katie Geissinger's dress. You'd see people walking towards her on the large screen behind her. The music in *Mercy* was both intricate and primal. I felt like I went back to some of my early vocal rawness, and, yet, the overall forms were very refined and sophisticated.

So, that was one edge of the cliff, and another was that I was commissioned by Michael Tilson Thomas and the New World Symphony to write an orchestral work. Michael wouldn't take no for an answer. It took about five years of me saying no to finally bite the bullet. The reason why I finally said yes was because I realized that I have always wanted to be learning and risking. As I go along, each piece is a learning and growing experience.

I didn't know anything about the orchestra at all. In *Atlas*, I had only used ten instruments, so this ninety-piece orchestra was daunting. In 1999, I started taking some orchestration lessons and really started listening instrumentally, because my work has always been vocally based, and I've always thought of the voice as an instrument. Now, I was going to have to try to figure out a way to consider the instruments as voices and to really hear the colors and not be distrustful.

How could I get past that? What could I really do with an orchestra, which is, by nature, a nineteenth-century institution no matter what I do? How could I subvert that situation with so many givens? That was what I tried to do in this piece, and it took me a lot of learning and listening to understand the vocabulary of the instruments.

Michael started an academy, the New World Symphony, for young people who have already been to conservatory or maybe even to graduate school but who want a little more orchestral experience before they go out into the world to get jobs. Over a two-year period, I went a few times and tried things. I prepared phrases and sections I was working on, which they played back so I could hear. We orchestrated in different ways. I would sing things for them and see if they could get the quality of the voice on their instruments. They would show me various extended techniques on their instruments because that is what I'm interested in vocally. It was very fun to work with them. The young players who were there for two years, who started on it and ended up playing it, found it exciting to see how it evolved and developed.

Then, when Mieke died, I didn't know if I was going to be able to do it. April of 2003 was the premiere, and she died in November 2002. I remember around December, Michael saying, "You don't have to do this, you can cancel it," and I thought, "I really think Mieke would want me to try and do it." I had written a lot of it in New Mexico that last September which was a very happy time for us, so I thought, I'm just going to try to do my best, and so I did. I ended up calling it *Possible Sky*.

At that time, I thought of it as a work in progress, and then I had a chance in May 2006 for the Hamburg Symphony to perform it as a premiere, because I had made some changes since the New World Symphony performance. When you deal with ninety human beings, changes are not that easy. Changing ninety scores is like pushing an elephant up a hill because it's just so daunting to get all those people to understand the changes and be able to fulfill them. That was the next cliff.

The third cliff was writing my first string quartet for Kronos Quartet. We premiered it in February 2005, and it was called *Stringsongs*. It was, again, this idea of how do you make music for instruments that has the quality of the voice? There are four movements, and I think the most successful movement is the last because I literally made the form on my voice and then scored it. When they worked on it in rehearsal, we would play it with me singing so they could actually hear and try to get that slightly different color or quality.

My latest project is *Impermanence*. It is a poetic piece evoking the passages of life. There are two acts or parts to *Impermanence*. Part I is very mysterious and contemplative, very quiet. I realized that trying to make a piece "about" impermanence is an impossible task. How do you create a work about something that is ungraspable, ephemeral? How do you conjure up images or music that imply that everything is constantly changing, that we can't hold on to anything?

One of the ways I thought of working with it was structurally: to make the structure very honest and visible and to contrast Part I with Part II. So, I thought of Part I as a crystal turning in someone's hand, each side or facet having its own integrity or frame. The order was nonlinear so that each section could be experienced purely and then later put together by each member of the audience. For Part II, I decided to go the opposite way, thinking of the metaphor as a stream or river where each aspect flows and becomes part of everything else.

Most of Part I touches upon the feeling of grieving or loss, while in Part II one has the sensation of life going on. Part I is very much about presence and absence; it doesn't refer to death specifically, but it does include a sense of appearance and disappearance as one important element. In the midst of that very quiet continuity, we have a section called "Particular Dance" that is really a celebratory dance about the uniqueness of each person, like a folk dance. Each person's movement vocabulary is very individual, so it becomes the embodiment of his or her being. It's a pure-movement section accompanied by robust instrumental music with changing meters that I composed, inspired by the idea of the dance.

Working on *Impermanence*, exploring notions of mortality, flux, and change, required a lot of patience and courage by the performers and technicians. It ended up being a very affecting piece, which we still love to perform.

How has race entered into my art? My way of working with race has been to make art that is very inclusive both in relation to the performers and the audience; to try to make my work accessible to any human being on the planet. It usually doesn't have particular racial reference points, but hopefully there is a place for anyone to hook into. I was always quite aware of trying to include as performers and colleagues a wide spectrum of people coming from different backgrounds and cultures in my work and was always interested in each person's uniqueness. I would hope that my work leaves space enough to include the diversity of their experience. Some artists' life work consists of delineating the particularities of each culture, but I think what I try to do is to work with fundamental, universal aspects of human nature that all cultures have in common. We all die; we all have families; we all want to be happy.

Gender? My earliest memory of playing with gender was when I worked on *Paris* in 1972. I had just finished a solo, which became Part II of *Education of the Girlchild* in which I start as an old woman and end up a young girl. I remember thinking about how androgynous old people seem, and I used that as inspiration for my persona. Earlier, in *Vessel* and *Juice* I had played with mixing gender aspects: Monica Moseley as the scribe in *Vessel* wore a long beard; Coco Pekelis played Pierre Cauchon, and, in *Juice*, all eighty-five performers wore big, red combat boots.

But with *Paris*, which was a collaboration with Ping Chong, gender play became part of what the piece was about. I've always believed that each of us is a unique combination of male and female characteristics. In *Paris*, I wore a mustache, skirt, and big red boots, and Ping had big, flowing sleeves on his shirt, long hair but also trousers and big workboots, so we were each a composite of male and female. When we were working on the piece, we were trying to find an edge for a tender, delicate duet. Our first idea was that I was going to wear a bear costume, but that seemed unwieldy! When we came up with the mustache, it seemed right, as if we were pasting something onto my character that modified it. There were other little transformational objects that would appear and disappear during the piece. Ping would put on his glasses at one point; in another, we would put on caps and finally coats so that the whole piece became very poetic and mysterious. I found that the mustache gave me a lot of freedom and even though one immediately thinks of Charlie Chaplin, it actually opened up a more metaphysical, dead-pan, Keatonesque humor to my character. We were working against stereotypical ideas of gender, trying to disrupt expectations and open up possibilities.

In *Specimen Days*, I was working with the idea of opposites and dualism in relation to the American Civil War (or any war): black/white, North/South, male/female, adult/child. I played the composer, Louis Moreau Gottschalk; Gale Turner played the photographer

Ping Chong and Meredith Monk in *Paris*. Photo © Beatrice Heyligers.

Matthew Brady; and Paul Langland wore a hoopskirt in the ballroom scene. I was always trying to subvert notions of gender or of any category. Anyone could play anything. *Specimen Days* was about how, when one labels or categorizes someone, then that person turns into the other, which then can easily turn into racism, sexism, war. This theme goes all the way through my work.

Gender play was a deep exploration at a certain point that was very important to me. It's not so important to me now, but it definitely can become part of the palette when a piece demands it. It's like anything else. I worked with the voice as an instrument when I was very young because I needed to explore my voice. People say, "Oh, this or that person has been influenced by you because they are using extended vocal techniques." At the time I started to work, there was not such a label, and it was simply an inner necessity for me to find a language of the voice.

It had to do with my family background, my musical needs, and my psychological needs. It was like I had to do that. My early exploration of the voice was something I was meant to do which changed my life. Those discoveries had to do with expression and being aware of how powerful the voice was as a source, but they never were a means to an end, like how many tricks can I do with my voice? That approach has become a kind of cliché.

I would say the same thing with gender. It's really like these ideas come and they have to do with the world I'm exploring. I've always tried to keep finding new things in my voice. I'm always asking myself, "What is the voice of this song?," and not do things I've done before. And that's a real effort, but it's not an end in itself.

I would say, too, that all these concepts about early site-specific work don't necessarily correspond to what was happening at that time. In the end, all these things have now become codified, and I always get very mistrustful of that. It's like trying to solidify something that really should stay fluid because otherwise the mystery gets lost and it just stays in one place. It's like fixating something.

Another aspect about working with gender and age as well has to do with the voice. Early on, I realized that within my voice were male and female, different ages, characters, and landscapes. I play with that a lot in my music. Sometimes the women are singing way below the men (the men are singing falsetto), so we alter expectations of how music is voiced. Usually, the people that I work with have at least three octaves, so they can take on any role. We don't think of ourselves as sopranos, altos, tenors, or basses. We are going across those timbre and gender lines, and that opens up limitless possibilities.

In terms of age, I think it was strange that at the age of twenty-six I was making a piece about an old woman in *Education of the Girlchild*. How did I know? How did I get that insight at such a young age? It's very interesting that I was concerned with that then, but I think it had a lot to do with understanding human life as a cycle. Now that I am older, I see the process of life more clearly and, as a performer, I have nothing to prove anymore. The wisdom of what I've experienced is what I am giving, and so I feel that my insight as a human being is what I'm giving, and that's it.

In the past five years, a very deep relaxation has set in, and I hope that people can really get something from that. I do have a lot of young people in my audience. It's very sad to see people trying to pretend they haven't lived the years that they have. Honesty is really a great thing to be able to give to a culture so age-terrified, particularly in terms of women. I hope I'll be singing when I'm ninety years old, and I'll be able to share what a ninety-year-old singing voice is like. I think it's moving to see veteran performers.

Have I noticed my voice changing? In the early 1990s, I lost maybe two of my top notes, like my high Ds and Es, but I've gotten more notes on the bottom. I had to get used to that: It's almost like a hormonal change. My voice is in very good shape; I have a healthy instrument; and, since I am my own composer, it doesn't matter what key I'm singing in. There are limitations, and sometimes I do have sadness about them because that is my instrument, but to try to fight it doesn't make any sense, it is just insane. You have to give in to it, and then you'll find something else.

Working on movement is the same situation; you just have to work with what you have. I'm very lucky that I haven't had physical injuries, so I still have the capacity to have a good, varied movement vocabulary. Naturally, as I've gotten older, I've had to be much more conscious of the discipline of caring for my voice and body. I still have a voice teacher and do Pilates three times a week. I don't have the kind of speed as a singer or dancer as I had, but that's something that just happens. You have to figure out "OK, what is this asking me to do now?" There are other qualities that you get, one of which is more depth, both literally and figuratively, and my voice also has gotten a lot more warmth. We are so lucky as creators to be able to work with our material; we can work with what we have rather than wishing for something we don't have.

I haven't ever considered my company a dance company; we are a vocal ensemble with people coming from diverse backgrounds. Some are trained singers who move very well, and some are dancers who are also good singers. My work is very much about unifying the voice and body. I am very lucky because each performer is multitalented and rich with experience. I like seeing and hearing these full, luminous, veteran performers (like drinking a delicious aged wine) on stage. To me, it's beautiful and very satisfying, so I'm not trying to get rid of my company and get twenty-one-year-olds. I also love having younger performers in there; I'm interested in working with a multigenerational group, but I'm lucky enough that my work was never about physicality for its own sake; it was always physicality as an expression. My movement was always gesturally based rather than acrobatically or athletically oriented. If you think about the Native American dances, like in the *pueblos* in northern New Mexico, where grandmothers and grandfathers dance as well as five-year-old kids, it seems much more interesting.

Have my ideas about the body in relationship to my art changed over the years? I've always been interested in diversity of body types. In *Juice*, for example, in 1969, I cast Dick Higgins, who was 250 pounds; Daniel Ira Sverdlik, who was a more normal-size man; Madelyn Lloyd, a six-foot-tall woman; and me, a small person. That was always a kind of subject matter of my work, and I think that I tried very hard to have a diversity of body types, and the movement can be seen as coming through that. That hasn't changed. I'm still interested in the same thing.

In terms of the economic environment of doing my work now versus twenty-five years ago, it's a hard time, and it's a very big struggle. Right now, I'm just trying to get a strategy for continuing. It's really about how do you keep going in this economic climate, which is that no one has any money. It started from the top a number of years ago, and people like me are starting to feel the effects now. I was lucky enough to be able to hang in there for quite a while, but now it's dripping down to me. I think people are very frightened, and the sponsors or presenters are not being given a lot of resources so they don't have what they need. We are living in a no-culture culture.

How does an artist survive in a culture that doesn't care about art except as a product? The visual arts are getting amazing amounts of money. A little watercolor by a twenty-two-year-old artist sells for 75,000 dollars. It's unbelievable, and I ask, "Why is that?" It's because a painting is an object people want to own.

We are living in a very product-oriented society that has definitely quantified everything. How do you become a spokesperson of process by actually doing, by being in the now and not caring about product? How do you do that in a world that has completely commodified everything?

That's one of the things that goads me to continue, because I think this is the time to dig in your heels; it's life or death, you need to affirm what you believe in, your standards, and your values. You have to be more scrappy and imaginative in how you produce your work. You just keep going no matter what, but it's really overwhelming, and I think that it's a constant challenge to not give in to making art into a product that loses its magic. I'm struggling with that right now because the world is definitely going in another direction.

And yet, I feel like I am in demand for what I've got to offer and that people are appreciative and understand my work. We did a fortieth-year anniversary, and it was unbelievable, but that doesn't translate into money. It's not anybody's fault, it's just that nobody has the money to give.

The Government and the powers that be have no idea of the power of art and its healing capacity, even for helping children to learn. It's just being erased. It's a very sad, dark time, and yet, we have a lot of work to do, which is good. The way I think about it is, we just have to survive, and we will endure, and it is just a matter of figuring out how.

There is a Buddhist principle called "the three poisons": grasping or attachment, aggression, and ignorance. It's daunting to wake up in the morning and realize that our leaders are the embodiment of these qualities. What do we do about this? The first step would be to examine those qualities in ourselves and then clarify our aspirations. Part of that is affirming the spirit of inquiry.

I've never been a person who can say, "I'm making a piece about this, and this is what it is going to be" because once I do that, there is no more piece. If you can answer the questions before you have started creating the work, then you might as well not do it. I learned that from my teacher, Bessie Schönberg. So, for me, it's the act of making and allowing myself to remain in the unknown and walk through my fear into interest. The beginning is always so terrifying. I feel like I'm flailing about in the dark, and then once I take one step, I start getting more interested than afraid, so then the interest ends up actually taking over and the fear gets left behind.

You have to walk through the fear, not run away from it but literally move into it, and I think that is a great metaphor for living. If the society could do that, we wouldn't have this war now. The whole society is being hypnotized by fear. That's what all this is about. Being a lifelong student of World War II, I know that Göring said (James Hillman talks about it as well in his book *A Terrible Love of War*), "Oh, it's not hard. All you do is get a common enemy and get everyone in the country completely terrified, and then you can do anything to them that you want." And that's exactly what's happening. The media is pouring on the fear. I believe it started in the 1980s, when there was a concerted effort to take money out of education and put it into weapons, because a mass of ignorant people is a lot easier to manipulate. This is a plan that's been ongoing.

What are the changes in the geographic environment? New York City used to be considered the center of the arts. What are my impressions now, twenty-five years later? I'm not sure if there is a center now. Per square inch, there are still more artists in New York than other places, but in terms of support, European artists are given a lot more for their work than we are. I don't know if there is a particular center in Europe either, but I wouldn't say that New York is the cutting edge anymore. I think that Europeans were very influenced by my generation, maybe even by a generation older than me, and now they've taken the ball and have run with it.

Has the artistic social environment changed in the past twenty-five years? Well, what I miss very much in New York and in the art world is the sense of community I felt when I first came here. Maybe that was because there were fewer people working, but what I first noticed was there was an interchange between all different artists—visual artists, dancers, musicians, and poets—and they were all trying to break down the boundaries of their art forms. There were very interesting combinations of people giving up their root disciplines to find something new, and then maybe going back to the root disciplines with fresh insight. I loved that, and now I don't feel that so much because you can't get your finger on what the New York community is now. It seems very spread out, and it's really a lot of independent constellations, but it's hard to get the feel of what the whole community is, and I miss that.

Audience-wise, we have always been lucky enough to have an audience of different ages, and now I feel really lucky that young people are very interested in my music and work. We did a series of concerts at the Lincoln Center Festival in 2000 called *Voice Travel*. It was three different concerts at three different places, so you could go on three different evenings. I did a solo concert at the Ethical Culture Society; we did a concert at Alice Tully Hall of some material from *Atlas* and other things, and then we did *Turtle Dreams*, and *Dolmen Music*, and some other pieces at the High School for Performing Arts. I found out that about 70 percent of the people in those audiences were under thirty. I'm very interested in that and love these young people.

Some of the pop singers have been doing my music, which is really fascinating. Björk sang a piece of mine, "Gotham Lullaby," that she hasn't recorded as yet but performed in many venues. She has become a friend, and, when I did my fortieth-anniversary concert at Zankel Hall last fall, she performed at it. The idea of that concert was for other people to perform my work. My ensemble and I sang some pieces, but then other groups such as Bang on a Can All-Stars, Alarm Will Sound, John Zorn, DJ Spooky, and the Roches also played my music. What they did was moving and surprising, and it gave me hope that I can pass my work on.

May 1, 2006

Rosalind Newman in *Out of Dreams*. Photo © Johan Elbers.

Rosalind Newman

Rosalind Newman has created a body of over seventy works. She choreographed her first work in 1972, and, after dancing in the companies of Dan Wagoner, Viola Farber, and Mel Wong, formed a company, Rosalind Newman and Dancers, in 1975. The company had major seasons in New York at Dance Theater Workshop and the Joyce Theater, toured the USA, and performed in many international festivals and venues such as Jacob's Pillow Dance Festival, Paris International Dance Festival, Holland Festival, London Dance Umbrella, Sadler's Wells in London, National Arts Centre in Ottawa, and the Akademie der Künste in Berlin. She has set her works on a number of companies, among them London Contemporary Dance Theatre, Pacific Northwest Ballet, and Diversions Dance in Wales. She was also Founding Artistic Director and Choreographer of Dance HK/NY in Hong Kong in 1998; the company had seasons in Hong Kong and toured to international festivals in Taiwan and the USA, including New York.

As a senior lecturer in modern dance at the Hong Kong Academy for Performing Arts (APA), her works choreographed for the APA dance ensembles were performed in Hong Kong and toured to festivals in Korea, India, the Philippines, China, Australia, France, and the USA. She has taught widely as guest artist and teacher at the Western Australia Academy for Performing Arts, Rotterdam Dance Academy, Dance Forum-Taipei, Guangdong Modern Dance company-Guangzhou/China, Beijing Dance Academy, London Contemporary Dance Theatre and School, University of North Carolina at Chapel Hill, and the University of Wisconsin at Madison. She was the course leader in the masters in choreography program at the Laban Centre in London, and now is on the faculty at the Conservatory of Dance, State University of New York at Purchase.

Newman's work has been recognized by a number of distinctive awards, including fellowships from the Guggenheim Foundation, New York Foundation for the Arts, National Endowment for the Arts (NEA), a Gulbenkian Choreographic award in London, and a Hong Kong Dance Alliance award. Her New York company received grants from the NEA, NY State Council on the Arts, Jerome Foundation, and the Foundation for Contemporary Performance Arts. Dance HK/NY was supported with funding for international touring from the Hong Kong Arts Development Council and Asian Cultural Council.

A graduate in dance from the University of Wisconsin at Madison, she received an Alumni Achievement Award in 2006 and was the keynote speaker on global dance at the American Dance Guild conference in 2004.

A Changing Field

Much has changed in my life in the last twenty-five years that is reflected in my work. The first big change was that I had a baby in 1988. Rivka is now eighteen. That experience totally seeps into every part of my life. It made me more thoughtful and made my work appear more reflective as well.

I made a work, *Out of Dreams*, which deals with some feelings about childbearing. It was a solo for myself about giving birth to my daughter. In the piece, I used a giant foam figure, which was like a puppet. I was inside the figure for some sections of the work and outside for other parts. I always thought of the puppet as a woman with maternal encircling feelings. The experience of having a child is so important it puts work into another perspective. That concern is my child and bringing her up, and that concern became most important. It's the most important ongoing creative activity I've ever done in my life.

Her birth affected my whole life, in that I would come home and wasn't able to just think about choreography, or which step goes before another or whether or not I could do a certain gig. You have to invest yourself so totally in children and their upbringing that everything else is secondary for a while, or it takes on another perspective, maybe not secondary, but you think about your work in another way.

It enriched what I did. The amount of time I could spend obsessing about the work got less, but in terms of focusing, and bringing other kinds of emotional richness to what I was doing, that got stronger. In no way did it take away, but actually added to what I was doing. It enriched me as a person, and, therefore, the kind of work I was doing.

Another huge influence was that our family moved to Hong Kong where I taught for ten years. After I had Rivka, we went to Hong Kong for two years, from 1989 to 1991. I was a full-time lecturer at the Hong Kong Academy for Performing Arts. Then we went back in 1994 until 2002, so we were there altogether for ten years, and then I went back for another half year. Hong Kong became a very big experience in my life, in my work, and in the way I think about the world. It gave the work another perspective, another texture. Being outside of America and the New York dance scene enabled me to look at what I was doing in another way. Also, teaching so much and dealing with young people made me think about how I was doing things as well.

The students in Hong Kong made me think differently about my work. There was already a change going on from having my daughter, and having other kinds of things going on in my life, but the way people thought about art there actually shifted something in the way I thought about my work as well. Moving away from my home country and being exposed to the ways they thought about art helped me to reevaluate the kinds of things I was doing in surprising ways.

It was amazing to me how my students always believed, and not in a simplistic way, that making art was about expressing emotions and expressing what was inside. It was surprising because I didn't think of that as a Chinese quality. Across the board, there was a sense of wanting to express themselves in their work. Maybe that shifted something in the way I worked. I always had an undertone of a dramatic emotional quality in my work, but it was overlaid with a lot of postmodern ideas from studying with Merce, and the Judson, late 1960s idea of not expressing emotion. Those gestures were always there, inside of what I was doing, but moving away from my home country and being exposed to the ways others thought about art made me reevaluate my own approach.

People ask, how were you influenced by living in China for so long? And were you influenced by Chinese art? Yes. I was influenced by the visuals around me, and that entered my work, but, more importantly, it was something about exposing the self and how much I was willing to expose and where meaning was inside my work that was affected. I started to think about where meaning was in my work, and what was meaning.

It was a gradual shift. Having a child, and the primal feeling of what that is and who I am, and what that means to my identity, also began to shift something in how I thought about my work, its meaning and importance. The Chinese students brought something more basic about where they thought art stood within their society: subtlety. Everything there is subtle. It allowed me to take things already in my own work—in terms of the emotional undertones, the humanist undertones that undercut everything I've done and that I had pushed under-neath—and it allowed me more freedom to bring that forward and to express, recognize, and more fully clarify it.

I disbanded my New York company around the time my daughter Rivka was born in 1988. I disbanded it because of my life situation and the company blueprint had become burden-some. Rather than being helpful to make work, the economic pressures to produce in the city were not enabling me to make my best work. They weren't giving me the space, freedom, or possibilities I wanted. It felt like I was stuck within that company format. And the reason to have a company for me was to make work, so when that stopped feeling right, there was no reason for it.

With the dissolution of the NEA funding of individual artists, and the drying up of funds for dance and touring, we were greatly affected. We were still getting lots of work, but it felt like a continuous strain. Everything went into the company: Any money we had went into the company; any extra self that I had went into the company. I'd wake up in the morning, and my grant proposals would be on the kitchen table. That's a hard thing to face. There was no escape. The rejections, the acceptances, it felt like I became wrapped up in that rather than about the reason to do art, so it lost its center.

Right when the company was dissolving, I choreographed an off-Broadway show that went on to Broadway. That was a total trip, unbelievable. It was about the Jews in China, and that was before I ever went to China. It was like some sort of harbinger. I also made work for other companies.

Since then, I've worked from project to project. In Hong Kong, in 1995 or 1996, I started another group called Dance HK/NY, and I had that group all the way through until we left Hong Kong in 2002. A lot of the people who worked with me had been trained by me as students, so they were wonderful collaborators who understood what I was trying to do. They gave me a lot, and that was very satisfying.

In Hong Kong, where I had more facilities to have a group, where it didn't feel like I had to keep them together all the time, I could call them in for projects, and there was more freedom and flexibility. As a result, I got interested in other kinds of projects and works.

Hong Kong is international in terms of business, but having led my whole life in New York where it is so multicultural, Hong Kong didn't feel international at all. It felt Asian and British when we got there. We were there for the handover, and it had all the overlay of British colonialism, but it didn't feel really international. Probably about 99.5 percent of the people are Chinese, and then there's less than 1 percent that are not Chinese. It's gotten even less now. So, it felt like I was in a very unique culture. In order to be a citizen of China— a full citizen—you have to be Chinese. You can't be anything else. I have a permanent resident card in Hong Kong, but I could not be a full citizen there as I'm not Chinese.

It may not have felt international, but it did give me a different perspective on the West. It gave me another way of thinking about how people act towards each other, about social relationships: why people make art, why people are interested in art, a broader perspective. People were still basically people, but the societal pressures, expectations, and rules were really different.

It was interesting being a minority. Perhaps 0.5 percent to 1 percent of the people in Hong Kong are Westerners, so it was very odd to realize that your face is white. You have these features, and you are never going to blend, no matter what; even if you speak fluently, you are always the other. You are always the *gweilo*, the foreigner, the white devil, the white ghost. You're never going to be part of that world, in a true deep sense, and that had a very strange kind of repercussion emotionally.

I would be on a train somewhere out in Kowloon and realize I was the only white face in the car, and it could remind me of what people of color here must feel, because they see your face immediately, and you feel the prejudice against you just because you have white skin, or just because you're Chinese or whatever color your skin is. It takes you aback, and there's a lot of stereotyping because you're white, with expectations and people putting up blocks just because of that, but I think the more you travel around, you see that happening in all kinds of cultures. People have their stereotypes of how other people are going to be.

After we were there for ten years, there was a certain point when I felt if we didn't come back to the West, we would live in Asia for ever. That would be where our life was. I realized I'd always be the ex-pat there, always be the outsider, and it began to have psychological effects. There was a certain degree of isolation; even though I could be really, really close to people, that deep closeness that I could have with someone who has shared experience of postmodernism or my own culture, or who saw certain movies or heard certain things was lacking. It was lonely.

I think it enriched my work to a certain point, but it's not where my stories were. I was always telling my stories from far away. I was never telling my stories from being inside of it. I made a piece, *Scenes from a Mirage*, with Klezmer music that dealt with memory, and times past, and it had elements of a Jewish wedding in an eastern European village. Something about being in Hong Kong made me go back and dig into my own roots. I did research at the Jewish Club in Hong Kong, where I read and looked at many pictures for that piece.

Another piece I made was *Different Trains*, to Steve Reich's music. It had lots of different themes going through it such as the Holocaust in eastern Europe, the war, trains, traveling, and moving. Here I was, in Asia, making pieces that were even more directly related to something in my own background. I found it interesting that it pulled me in that direction.

At a certain point, I was no longer nourished, and I needed to come back to the West. We went to London, England, after that, because it felt like we were coming back to the West, even though that was a very different culture, more foreign-feeling than Hong Kong in a way; but it was a Western culture, and I needed to do that for my work. For multiple reasons, I wanted to get back in touch with the work because I felt like I was outside myself, far away spatially. At Laban, in London, I was the course leader for their masters in choreography; we were there for about a year and a half, and then I went back for a residency a year after that. That was a very interesting experience.

Rosalind Newman's *Scenes from a Mirage*. Photo © Tom Borek.

When I came back from Hong Kong the first time, I made *Out of Dreams*, the solo which was the most successful part of that piece, about my mother, my self, my daughter—three generations of being mothered, of mothering, of birthing. Getting back to some connectedness became more important, maybe from having a child and from being far away from my home. It felt odd, and there was a sense of dislocation. We came back from England two and a half years ago, and there's still a great sense of dislocation, of getting back into this world.

We were gone a very long time. So much has changed here. It was interesting when 9/11 happened, and we were in Hong Kong. The World Trade Center is just five blocks downtown from our loft, and we were watching the whole thing unfold on television in Hong Kong and felt longing to be back here but were far away. To have something like that happen to your home, to your neighborhood, was just incredible, and the longing to come back became more powerful after that. It made me want to be in New York to experience that because this is who I am.

Since I've been back, I'm trying to become located. I'm trying to find a way to adjust to this new world here, because it's very strange to come back. Going to a new place is almost easier, because when you come back to your home country, you think you know something, but you really don't. It's not the same. You turn a corner and say, "Look, I know those stores," but then you don't. There are all different stores. Or the stores might be slightly different, but you don't realize the ways, you don't know the new cues. You think you should because it's your home, your culture, your block, but yet you don't really know it anymore. It is as if you're Rip Van Winkle, and you've been sleeping, and all the things you did, and all the things you learned aren't apparent or there because you haven't been there. In a way, it feels as if you lose whatever those years were that you were away, even though they are there somewhere.

How has the dance world changed? I don't know. I keep going around and trying to figure it out. It feels much more dispersed. Economically, everyone is under great pressure, and it's even more difficult to be a full-time artist here. The situation has always been ridiculous but probably even more for young people coming in. In a way, there's lots of active people doing things on the cheap: poor-man's theater, doing things out in Queens or Long Island City, or in Brooklyn, or doing small things and sharing concerts. The atmosphere feels as if it has gone back to a certain time before, but also more difficult because the cost of living is so high, so the amount of time people can spend working on a dance is so much less. It is so difficult to get a group of dancers together just to rehearse because everyone has ten million jobs here and there. I don't know how young kids do this. I guess they have a lot of energy, hope, and curiosity, but it just seems like an even more difficult life.

When I was in Hong Kong, it became very obvious to me that people weren't looking at America and New York as the center of art anymore. In 1989, Hong Kong students all wanted to come to New York, to America, to study contemporary dance. When I went back to Hong Kong in 1994, it was different. Students didn't want to come to New York; and, as I was there longer, they wanted to come even less. They wanted to go to Europe to study. Australia became more of a force in Hong Kong—they're really exporting their dance to Asia. Somehow, the work that was going on here, or the way we were presenting it to the rest of the world, wasn't generating excitement or interest anymore. The kinds of issues people were dealing with here weren't the issues that were striking a chord there.

Then, when I went to England, I felt even more that the American modern dance being seen, or that people were aware of—of course, there was lots of stereotyping going on from both sides—wasn't interesting to the people there. It didn't have the kinds of meaning that they were looking for in work; people there felt it was just very movement-based (that is, stereotyped), not reflective enough, not dealing with issues, not experimental in the kinds of ways they were interested in being experimental, not conceptual at all or enough, and that hit me in the face very strongly. It is an interesting situation too, because when you think about funding drying up, who was promoted, and who was able to go to Europe, the safe, more established companies went, so that's what they saw, and that's the impression they got.

The kinds of choreographic works have changed here, but I can't get my fingers on where work is going. As I'm starting to see, there are people who are digging deeply, who are looking at things, dealing with issues, perhaps not in quite the same way the Europeans are right now but who are digging very honestly and deeply and trying to do work. They might be out at WAX or might be doing something at the FLEA, somewhere not seen in the same way, so it's much subtler. Again, this is stereotyping and sort of saying that the whole thing is bad, which it isn't. There is deep, reflective, experimental work, or people searching, trying to dig into their own voice here, but it's not being seen by a large audience.

At a certain point, in France, they were putting money into making videos of the companies that were in all those ateliers and really sinking money into making those videos look interesting. Maybe ten to fifteen years ago, they produced a whole series of people not known, and it made people notice and say, "Wow!" People here weren't able to make those kinds of videos. They didn't have the funding. People here were just standing and holding their own camera, hoping they could afford to have someone come and video their work. Most American choreographers couldn't afford that kind of editing or cutting or fancy effects.

The other thing that was very obvious about where America is right now and has been for the past number of years was that, living in Hong Kong, it became very apparent that the German Government was really promoting German dance very aggressively there. The Goethe Institute is a fantastic organization which was right across the street from the Academy, and it energetically promoted German arts, had a library, and gave grants. They actively promoted German choreographers in Hong Kong and China, bringing German companies, showing videos for people to see, and giving grants and scholarships for people to study dance in Germany.

The French Embassy was promoting French art. The British Council promoted their dance by bringing it to Hong Kong and by bringing people back to Britain to perform as well as to study. It felt like the one embassy not at all interested in arts promotion was the American Embassy or the American Government, and that was very disturbing. In order to get the Chinese in Hong Kong interested in what Americans are doing, American dance had to be brought there, but I think Hong Kong couldn't get the American Embassy to be interested or supportive. After a while, I think they realized they would have more luck working with other governments who valued the potential in Asia for people to look at their dance. International sharing of arts has something to do with the way the world envisions your country. Unfortunately, America was totally blank about that.

I think we should look at how we're educating young dancers in universities and what it is like to be an artist right now in our society. There are wonderful places to study dance in the USA, but maybe we should look more closely at the ways we are educating our young artists. Perhaps the models that came out of the 1930s, when dance programs were first becoming part of the university, have to be questioned. Where does choreographic education come into the training of a dancer, and how do we train dancers as well as choreographers?

I don't deal directly with racial issues within my work, but I think my cultural experiences and living in this other environment affected what I'm doing. In terms of a racial mix in my company, I never thought about it. I just took whoever was the best dancer and whomever I connected with in terms of work, the way they worked, and how they worked with me—so it was never an issue for me.

When I was in Hong Kong, the majority of the people I worked with were Chinese, except I had one *gweilo*, an Englishwoman who worked with me for a while, and I always thought that interesting. It was also interesting that I had all these Chinese people doing a dance about a Jewish wedding and culture to Klezmer music.

I remember in Hong Kong I felt I couldn't use Chinese music because I wasn't Chinese, and it wasn't just that I thought that, there would have been a lot of repercussions if I did. It's a hot issue. If you're in the USA and you use African music as a Western person, there can be repercussions as well. I've done that and had negative feedback of appropriating someone else's culture. Those are all questions percolating in this world right now. Even if you do use that music, you still have to be aware of issues that you're raising and choose how you want to deal with them: whether to use the music or not, or whether you don't want to directly refer to those issues, you still must be aware of them. I did feel like Chinese dance and Chinese vocabulary moved into the kinds of things I was doing. I was aware of that. I was interested in it; I studied it; I looked at it; I felt like it was in there but used within my own voice. And I might use Chinese-influenced music for something at some point.

It was always interesting to me that Hong Kong choreographers use all kinds of music in Hong Kong, such things as French songs, or music from any nationality they desired. Those questions for them don't exist in Hong Kong, but when one of the Hong Kong dance companies came to New York this past fall, they felt they had to use Chinese music here. So it raises so many issues. Why did the director feel that? He did that to make a statement for the public because he felt that was what he had to do as a Hong Kong, Chinese choreographer. Yet, it's always amazing to me that in Hong Kong there's a vast array of using whatever is there and is appropriate to their work, and I think that is how it should be as long as you're aware of the cultural context.

I don't feel I deal directly with gender in my work, but in the dance world, in terms of who gets work and who is promoted, gender is more clearly an issue. If you think back to all the female choreographers starting out in the 1970s, 1980s as well as 1990s, who were talented and exciting, and the few male choreographers, then look at who is still around and being promoted, getting grants and money. Who is touring all over the place with large-size, medium-size, and small-size companies? Who are those choreographers? It's males. Go down the list of who is performing and who is touring, and the lack of female names is astounding!

What happened to all those wonderful female choreographers who are still making work? Where are they in terms of their support and their touring? Or perhaps many of them have become discouraged. You just don't see them, and it's amazing! And who gets jobs in universities? The percentage of males is very large compared to those within the field. And here it began as a female art, and if you go to a dance class, there will be ten girls and one boy. The girls have worked really hard, and they're talented and beautiful. What's happened, and what makes us as women promote and hire that one male instead of one of those ten women applicants? What makes us do that to ourselves? That is a really interesting, scary, and sad question.

Women can be so competitive with each other. We will slice each other apart. We have to be more supportive of each other. Dance programs say they want to have a male presence in their departments. Even though there may be ten women to one male, they want to have three male faculty members to every one female faculty member.

In my work, there has been partnering and lifting, with female–female lifting, females lifting males, and males lifting females. A long time ago, I did a Buddy Holly piece, called *Heartbeat*, that had the very traditional gender roles, but we would turn it on its head, and then the women would pick up the men. I have always had females and males doing surprising things, in terms of changing and using lots of different kinds of partnering.

Right now, I am working with four women, with no thought of working with a male dancer, and that hasn't entered into my concept. This is personal work about something internal, and I just want to work with females right now. It came about very naturally. It's what the need is in my work for the moment, for my own creativity. Actually, it's good because there are so many wonderful female dancers, so, for now, this suits me in every way.

There is definite ageism in the dance world, and I think that is across the board everywhere. The emphasis is on youth, who is the flavor of the month, who is hot right now; always the emerging artists, always the new and exciting, rather than the been-there, done-that. If you have some experience, they are not interested in it. We are all aging, and our baby-boomer generation is getting older now, and you really sense it. What do you do with that, and how do you go into that gracefully? How do you work with it, getting older? Dance is particularly cruel because what's impressive to an audience is who has the hottest young body and who can do the tricks.

It is interesting how it comes on you really quick, and you become aged, over the hill. You're sort of going up the hill, you're sort of getting there, and then you go, "Oops, I'm over! Well, it happened!" Yeah, that realization is hard to deal with, and I am in the middle of it.

It makes it harder to do your work. Dealing with aging with your own body brings up questions like: How do you deal with not being as able to jump around? Since you're not able to do what the twenty-, thirty-, or forty-year-olds can do, how do you communicate what you want? How do you take yourself out of the physicality of your work and still make it have vitality, life, and a physical presence?

As a choreographer, I have always been very hands-on, physically trying the movement and doing it, so finding new ways to create and communicate movement becomes a challenge. It has been quite a while since I performed, but who knows when that could change? I became less interested in it and didn't feel like I needed to do that for myself. I always felt like other people could do a better job for me of expressing what I needed to express, I didn't feel like I was the best proponent of what my own work was, but my dancing has never stopped, I feel like physically doing it, and I always go into the studio to work by myself.

As one physically becomes more limited, with more injuries, the degree of being able to dance and the vision change. I think people have to remember that even if an older artist can't do it herself, she still knows how movement behaves. She knows enough about movement, and where it will go, and that knowledge can be very important. There can be great wisdom from being in the field for so many years.

My uncle Irving Burton still dances, and he's eighty-two. He performs his own work as well as with Claire Porter. Irving is extraordinary as a mover and as a performer, and he can still be expressive and make work. I think Claire did a quartet a couple of years ago with Stuart Hodes, Irving, Alice Tierstein, and Shirley Ubell . They are all over seventy-five, and it was very interesting.

Beth Soll is still performing. For her, that is a very important part of what her work is about. For me, I don't feel like my work has to be expressed through my own body, although my interests in my work have been affected by being older. My work is more reflective now, more pared down movement-wise. It realizes the power of pause and simplicity as well as the power of movement. That all comes from being older, more inside myself, realizing that invention is not as important as getting to the meaning. Movement invention is still there, but it is not as high a priority. Aging has affected this, and maybe it's wisdom, but also what your own body knows and the process of becoming more internal.

I have done Authentic Movement and Skinner Releasing Technique as well as other somatic techniques. Getting deeper into the body in a more reflective way has affected my work, whether that's because of age or being affected by other ideas about the body. Authentic movement and the Skinner work switched something in me to look at the body as a site for reflection. Right now, I am in a quieter, more internal place, looking at the body in more poetic rather than athletic ways.

In terms of body image on stage, or how my aesthetic has changed or not changed in the past twenty-five years, it has become clearer to me that I need to work with dancers who are willing to go on the journey with me, willing to go through the process. Maybe it's not really about body type as much as about people who are willing to invest themselves in the work. The people I am really interested in working with are able to become embodied in the work, rather than necessarily having a full extension or having high legs or being able to jump ten feet in the air. It's about how they are able to embody my ideas and concepts and how much they will go for that ride.

Would I ever have a heavy person dance on stage? The way it would enter into my work is how much they could or could not express through their body. I think it wouldn't be the heaviness, per se, but that I am still interested in a certain amount of physical expressivity. If the body was not able to get to that because of the heaviness, or because of a lack of training, then no, I wouldn't be interested, just for the sake of a different body type.

This started a while ago, where you would see a lot of different body types onstage. This makes sense for certain kinds of pieces, but if this is used just to be different or unusual, it can be superficial. To my work, that would be superficial, maybe to someone else's work it would not, because it would be making a statement that is intrinsic to that work. My work demands a certain degree of being able to get internally into the physicality of it. Now, it might work for somebody who has a heavier body type, but I think it would be distracting for what I am doing right now. Maybe in two years I will only want to have that.

I made a piece for a company called Dancing Wheels in Cleveland. It's an integrated dance company of standing and seated (wheelchair) dancers; it wasn't at all a work about limitations. I really, really enjoyed the process and found it so fantastic to work with them, because it opened up and created a whole world of other possibilities, not just of the wheels but also of who these people were, and what the limitation gave them. In taking away, it actually opened up a vast array of other possibilities, giving us a certain kind of freedom in the rehearsal process. The process felt like an opening up for me. So, that is a body type, of someone who can't move in the ways we are accustomed. How do you deal with that? If it is intrinsic within the work, then I am interested in it.

Rosalind Newman's *Ring of Shadows*. Photo © Tom Borek.

I think right now this country is in a pretty odd place. The environment of race, age, economics, geography—it all affects what I do. As I said, I am in a period of pulling in and doing very personal and subjective things. Maybe that's the only way I can cope with the current environment.

The last piece I did was standing on 9×4 yoga blocks, which gave a sense of being cornered and kept in prison. I am dancing in smaller and smaller spaces. Perhaps the environment of censorship is entering into my work in ways I am not even aware.

I was teaching at a university, and one of the students taking my beginning modern dance class said, "You know, modern dance gets a really bad rap in school, nobody wants to do it. Everybody thinks it's really boring." I think many young people think it is very uncool. They won't go near it. I don't think it has a very good reputation out there in the world, and maybe there are reasons for that. Maybe it's something about vitality, or that the work just doesn't interest young people or connect to them.

There appears to be more interest in London from the general audience about what is going on in the arts. People actually go to the Tate Modern in London; it's a really popular place. I guess MOMA is popular, but in London you feel like people are more involved, and all different kinds of people in London often knew about the dance scene. It seemed like people were interested in a different way than here. Dance is part of their cultural heritage; it is even funded in that way.

Here, people seem to go to football and basketball games and to music events, or they watch movies or TV, but they don't think of dance within their realm. Even if they live in New York City, they almost never make use of that possibility, although, if you look at the dance page in the newspapers and magazines, there's a zillion things happening. There was a period of time when it felt like what people were creating wasn't vital to the audience. Contemporary dance wasn't interesting beyond a select group of people who were looking at a particular thing. The work didn't seem to be saying anything to the larger population. Maybe the form began to lead itself down a dead end in some respects. I mean, maybe we all felt that a little bit. Now younger choreographers are trying to deal more directly with meaning in their work. This is a crazy time in dance, and the world is pretty crazy! People aren't as interested in studying modern dance as they used to be years ago. There are still great students, but even modern dancers take ballet or do yoga or Pilates. Modern dance classes aren't as popular.

The way dancers used to make money was to teach in New Jersey, Connecticut, or up in Westchester. We would teach little children, adults, whomever, and that's how we would support ourselves. Now people are teaching Pilates and yoga, which is all good and wonderful, but it's not dancing. There is something different about teaching and studying dance than taking yoga and Pilates. Those things are a healthy supplement to training, but they are not about the art. It's not about musicality, or about teaching people about things like how to make a phrase, how to move to music, or how to move with other people. Yoga is about being on your own little mat.

I think it is really sad that the dancers who are dancing with me, who are all wonderful, aren't making more money being involved with dance. They have to waitress, teach Pilates, yoga, or become personal trainers, and they're not able to keep their fingers in the pot of dance. They're not thinking about how to make up phrases, or what that means, or how to look at another dancer, another body, and critique them. Young dancers aren't getting to be inside the field in that way, and I think a lot of them go into yoga and Pilates because they want to stay with the body, but they are not staying with the body as art.

Today's modern dancer is not prone to supporting the people who are teaching modern dance. Dancers are not interested or feel they need to train in other ways. They want athleticism or a healthy body, but there are other important elements besides a healthy balanced body. With dancing, perhaps you get to a healthy balanced body in a different way. Training is so complex.

I think all of that has changed the field too, and that dancers don't study with the masters anymore. Now, your dancers never study with you. That's why I felt so lucky in Hong Kong. They knew what I was about, and they knew my style and also the underneath of it, what I was trying to embody in it. So much was already there, so it was quicker to get to a much deeper place. I think a lot of work suffers from the fact that the dancers can't do that. Because you can't do that two times a week, rehearsing two hours a session, and then people are running off to teach their classes, and running from this or that. It's part of the whole environment, and that's really discouraging because you know you can only go so far. You have to make work that will only go so far with people, and sometimes that is less interesting, unless you can be Mark Morris, or Paul Taylor, who have their dancers all day.

When I stopped having my company, I started creating more of the movement. I actually think that that strengthened the work more. As a choreographer, I do a great deal of my work, especially early on, but still it is very collaborative, and very much about the dancers having input, but I think early on it was a *lot* of input that came from the dancers. A lot of good experimentation made me learn about how movement could behave. It also made me have dancers who became really good choreographers, and it got them very involved in the work, emotionally, mentally, and in every way. Over time, I began to see that in order to shape the work the way I wanted it to be, without it going off into other tangents, I needed a control. At times, it needed more control and shaping, and at other times, I had to let go and be loose in the studio. I think it coincided to the time around 1988 that I began to go into the studio alone, and it might have been because I didn't have the company to work with as frequently, or have the dancers, so I worked on the movement myself, and then it became closer to what I wanted.

Today, the downtown New York dance scene uses contact improvisation, is very organic, and the movement flows. There's brilliant movement invention, but what does it say? The Europeans and Asians say, "It's delicious dancing." It's so delicious; there is so much dessert, but where are the meat and potatoes? Where is the meaning? There is so much movement invention and physicality for the sake of invention, that much of American dance becomes homogeneous-looking without a distinctive voice inside the movement.

I used to make movement in a very collaborative way, but I was searching for my voice through other people's bodies, and with other people who were in my dream, in my landscape. When I first started to make work in the 1970s, dancers were contributing movement. I always loved improvising and making work.

When I worked with Viola Farber in the early 1970s, my favorite part of the process was improvising. She would give us a phrase, and we improvised from that phrase. Much of the dance remained improvised. In one piece called *Passage*, a very early piece of Viola's, we would go down a spatial diagonal pathway with just one phrase from class. We improvised on that phrase, and the improvisation could get pretty far away from the original phrase. Then we had other pieces, where we had a minute of total free improvisation. At that time, Viola was harking back to some of the very early work of Merce's, of chance with improvisation used inside the chance procedures.

Then I worked with Twyla Tharp in her very early big pieces she did with masses of people. She would teach us the phrase and then we would mix it and do part of the phrase and then reverse it. The head would be one count and the feet would be doing another count, so there was a lot of interactivity. It required putting a lot of yourself into it. It was not free improvisation, so it was still within a strong format, and we weren't bringing what we learned in Merce's class into her dance. We were taking what that person was and then dealing with her style. (Since we trained with these choreographers, there was something in our bodies that already knew what their movement was about.) And with Viola, we weren't going to do a Martha Graham contraction in the middle of that diagonal, or we would be dead! We were going to do a curve.

Maybe in my early work I didn't use those methods, but I did try to explore what I was interested in, and, as I said, the dancers I worked with embodied my ideas, even though they were coming from lots of different places. Now, it might be a bit more frightening to work like that, because it can look too homogenous, but you do improv to get certain things, to open up the field.

I am teaching composition at SUNY Purchase, and I am very impressed with my students there, very impressed with their hopefulness. I thought that because they were such highly technically trained dancers they might be less receptive to new ideas. Their degree of technical prowess is amazing and makes you think, "Whoa, they can do anything!" I am also amazed and delighted at how open they are to ideas and how hungry they are to know about choreography. They want to explore who they are. I love them, and that says something really good about the future.

My experience has been that sometimes, with highly technically trained dancers, their brains can become more closed because of the daily repetition of technique, but somehow that hasn't happened here. Maybe that bodes well for the future. Younger dancers should have a sense of how movement behaves and what the history is; in general, there is a lack of interest about what came before. Maybe it is important to revolt against the past, to get rid of it, but maybe there is knowledge in knowing what came before, and that is how the form is passed on, through teaching.

Friday, March 17, 2006

Gus Solomons jr. Photo © Tom Caravaglia.

Gus Solomons jr

Gus Solomons jr created the title role in Donald Byrd's *The Harlem Nutcracker* (1996–9); directs Paradigm, a repertory dance company for seasoned performers; is an arts professor at New York University (NYU)/Tisch School of the Arts; writes about dance for *Dance Magazine, Gay City News*, DanceInsider.com, *Metro Daily*; has an architecture degree from Massachusetts Institute of Technology (MIT); danced in the companies of Pearl Lang, Donald McKayle, Martha Graham, and Merce Cunningham, et al. In 2000, Solomons won a Bessie (New York Dance and Performance Award) for Sustained Achievement in Choreography; in 2001, he was awarded the first annual Robert A. Muh Award from MIT as a distinguished artist alumnus. In 2004, he received the Balasaraswati/Joy Anne Dewey Beineke Distinguished Teaching Chair at the American Dance Festival, Durham, NC. In 2006–7, he was selected as a Phi Beta Kappa Visiting Scholar, lecturing at seven US universities. He bicycles everywhere.

Changing Steps

During the past twenty years, the thing that has most affected my art has been growing older—and more injured. I don't mind getting older; I just hate getting injured. Most of my physical problems—knees and back—have to do with misuse over long periods of time. When I learned to dance, we didn't know how to do it properly. Body mechanics were not yet a real science, so we just used more muscles and did the steps however we could. No one attended to anatomy or structural problems.

One nice thing about getting older is the wisdom that comes with aging. You outgrow vanity and all those things that stand in the way that made dancing difficult. Getting older has been good in that, with my new company PARADIGM, there is a group of older dancers (the youngest is forty-seven): me, Dudley Williams, and Carmen DeLavallade, and now Keith Sabado, Hope Clarke, Michael Blake, and Valda Setterfield.

Since 1996, we've been demonstrating how older dancers can still be eloquent movers. I made PARADIGM into a company because I perceived the demand for what we were doing would be great. Young dancers especially were looking at us and saying, "Oh my God, what you are doing is so beautiful!" And we are doing so much less physically than they're doing. We do no tricks at all, but we know how to stand still. That presence is something young dancers need to see.

The trend in classical ballet is to find younger and younger dancers and then throw them away when they are seasoned, when they can't jump anymore. Just when they mature into the dancing, they're tossed on the trash heap. Baryshnikov has helped to eliminate that tendency by continuing to dance beautifully after he could no longer do the tricks; he switched to modern dance. But he certainly is the exception.

Ballet is ballet, and it's not going to change, but there's so much more that can be physically expressive. I think the evolution of dancers, especially ballet dancers, has begun to exclude physical forms that aren't adapted to the demands of ballet technique anymore. Back in my day, we forced ourselves into those positions somehow. Now, both genetically and by selection, most successful ballet dancers have that ideal build: turnout, extension, classical proportions.

PARADIGM is commissioning choreographers to make work for us. So far, we've had Robert Battle, who's young and whose work is all about energy, and Johannes Wieland, who is also young, thirty-eight. He worked with the Berlin Opera Ballet, and he is an amazing choreographer. He made a terrific piece for us that has almost no movement, just walking, looking . . . and we did it as a double trio because he made it by working out the movement on his own dancers who then taught it to us. The movement illustrates the difference between the older and the younger. We have other choreographers in mind to make dances; it's just hard to find money to commission them.

Working with the students at NYU, who are the most elite dancers, has taught me a lot, not only about the mechanics of dance but also about the values involved. It has also given me some ideas about what makes dancers and dance interesting. I've made much less work myself. I have to make a piece every year at school for the students. And I've made four pieces now for PARADIGM. *A Thin Frost* in 1996 was the first; *Gray Study* (1998) was the second; *No Ice in Poland* (2002) was the third; and *Royal Court Museum* (2006) is the latest.

I'm doing a lot more improvising in performance now. When I was in Poland in 2001, I met Leah Stein, and we did a very impromptu improvisation performance. We were sitting outside of the theater on a Wednesday, and there was supposed to be a performance on Thursday but one of the companies had dropped out. There was a space to fill on the program, and we were kind of half-joking when one of us said, "Let's do an improv." So we went into the studio for an hour on Thursday morning and just clicked. We made a little map of what we were going to do, and we performed it that night. It was great! It felt beautiful, and the audience loved it. We decided we had to do this some more. The thing is, getting older and losing all that vanity and worry and having all this information makes improvisation less treacherous. I'm no longer afraid of improvisation forms—as long as my body is strong.

My first company, the Solomons Company/Dance, ended in 1995 because I got sick of funding it myself. I was living on day-old bread and wilted vegetables. Every penny I earned went straight into the company accounts. I started realizing I was probably going to have to retire at some point and I'd better start saving up. To a large extent, my company had been my family, and having a place to teach at NYU made having a company less necessary psychologically, because Tisch gave me a community.

I started teaching at NYU/Tisch School of the Arts in 1992 as an adjunct and became full-time in 1994. I had also gotten over my depression—long story—and I thought, "Why am I doing this? I could be having a good time. I now have a disposable income. I can go out to dinner!"

The idea of letting the dancers contribute more and more to the material, to the movement, has been a change in my work that evolved over that period of time. I used to make up all the steps, and, of course, they did them as best they could, so they contributed their own personality to all the steps. Using the dancers' input, both their personalities and their movements, makes the dances richer. They have points of view that I wouldn't think of, which expands my own range.

PARADIGM started as an all-black company. My other company was never all-black and was more than likely to be all-white except for me—for which I got criticism. People would say, "Well you're black, why isn't your company black?" In general, in the dance world, Alvin Ailey's company represents "black dance." And then there's modern dance, which has all colors, black, white, brown, red, and yellow. Ailey gets away with being the "black" company, and, of course, it's not all-black either. But it represents the "black dance aesthetic," which now has proliferated to black regional companies like Lula Washington's LA Contemporary Company, Dayton Contemporary, Dallas Black, and Cleo Parker Robinson's companies.

Then there's Garth Fagan, but he's something different. He's his own creature. He's hard to place. He's not part of that Ailey black aesthetic, and yet his dancers have been mostly African American, with a few exceptions, rather than just being all mixed up like Bill T. Jones's company. So, I guess people like Garth and Bill T. Jones illustrate a kind of non-Ailey mixing of races. Race is not an issue in "downtown" Manhattan. Integrated dancing was started by Martha Graham and became a modern dance tradition. Her company was always extremely mixed. In my case, it certainly wasn't active discrimination; it was just that the dancers I had access to were not black dancers. And that may have been because the black dancers didn't feel welcome or interested in working downtown. I didn't feel compelled to seek them out if they didn't cross my path, because being black is not what I was dancing about.

Gender is more of an issue. Since women's liberation, women have been making more waves about issues of exclusion of women from getting grants and being presented. I think some women make it more of an issue than it really is. I don't think there's overt discrimination against women in dance. But there are more all-women women's companies that focus on women's issues than the reverse. Gay and lesbian issues have come into play. Also, gender non-specificity is a real fundament of postmodern dance. In school at NYU, we have ballet-partnering classes, and modern partnering, which is non-gender-specific: the girls lift the guys, and the guys lift the girls.

In terms of gender awareness in my own choreography, maybe it has changed in the opposite direction. When I had a company from about the mid-1980s on, it was primarily male with women. It was never all-male. Now, there is Carmen, who is a woman. She's not just a dancer, she is definitely a female, and that shapes the way I think about the composition of the company. So, yes, gender has affected the work in that sense. I start always with pure movement, but as soon as she does it, it becomes female, so it changes the expression of the work.

Concerning the relationship of the three dancers together, I am aware of gender, of who manipulates whom, who initiates, leads, or supports, but I think that has less to do with gender than it has to do with physical capacity at this point. For instance, Dudley doesn't lift; he hasn't lifted ever. He told Alvin thirty-five years ago he would come in Alvin's company

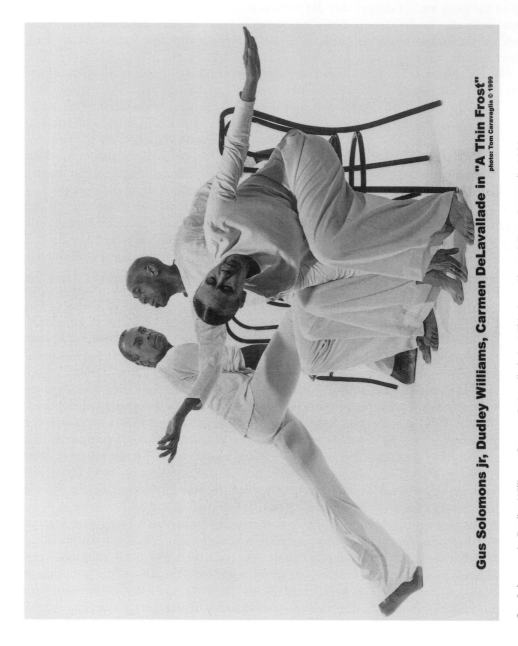

Gus Solomons jr, Dudley Williams, Carmen DeLavallade in *A Thin Frost*. Photo © Tom Caravaglia 1999.

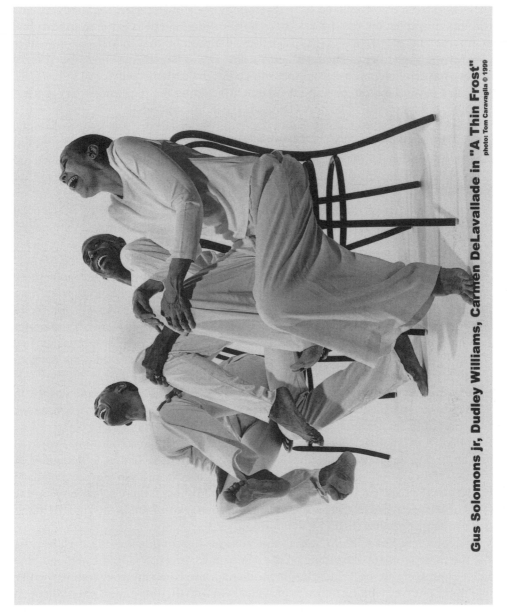

Gus Solomons jr, Dudley Williams, Carmen DeLavallade in "A Thin Frost"
photo: Tom Caravaglia © 1999

Gus Solomons jr, Dudley Williams, Carmen DeLavallade (laughing) in *A Thin Frost*. Photo © Tom Caravaglia.

if Alvin didn't make him do any lifts. Carmen can't lift. I'm the only one of the three of us who can do that, if it gets done. And it doesn't get done that often. So, it's not a gender issue in that sense; it's much more age-related than it is gender-related.

Another trend over the past few years is the mixing of styles, and people have gotten in trouble for that too. White artists are "appropriating" African movement or Capoiera, so that with styles now, everything is eclectic. Everybody's borrowing from everybody. There's cross-pollinizing going on, and I think that's terrific. What happens is the real individual voices emerge and they rise to the top. There will always be that matrix of look-alikes in order for the stars to rise. There's Doug Varone, David Dorfman, John Jaspers, Terry O'Connor. A generation that has from that similar vocabulary emerged as real individuals, people with a strong point of view about what they are doing. So, their vocabulary is going to be similar, but their individual personalities make it different.

I go uptown a lot now to see dance. I love American Ballet Theater. I go frequently to the Joyce, to see a lot of European companies, because I'm not interested in seeing that same old hip-slide, that one-handed handstand, that stuff—those postmodern clichés—which are just as prolific now as the modern-dance clichés that we all broke away from with the Judson Group in 1965.

Has the economic environment changed over the past twenty-five years? I don't know if it's changed. Dance is still at the bottom of the heap. Dancers make the least money among performers. Where I see it more clearly nowadays is that European work is always highly "produced." They have money for sets, lighting, and costumes. American dance is much more stripped down in its conception because choreographers know they aren't going to be able to afford a set, so they make a dance that isn't going to have to have one, or projection, or whatever. That's a result of economic climate, but, as always, dancers will continue to create, whatever the problems. They just forge ahead, and the resulting work is not only a manifestation of the limitations but it's also a solution to those limitations. It has its own kind of energy. There's not much more to look at in American dance than the motion. Movement is much more varied in American dances.

Most European dance comes from a ballet tradition—ballet technique—and departs to various degrees from that; but you always see that same extension of the limbs, whatever the configuration of the movement.

Trisha Brown is uniquely American. People in Europe don't dance that way. People in Holland are trying to, people in Belgium—a little bit—with Anna Teresa De Keersmaeker, so they may finally emerge, but still the vast majority is coming from a neo-classic vocabulary. So, the look of the dancing, the physicality, is different. Although there is less range in the dynamics of European dance, there is a broader range in the expression of the kinds of things they are dancing about and their visual mounting.

My new company, PARADIGM, was almost immune to economics at the start, because none of the three of us are depending on the company for any part of our livelihood; that takes a lot of pressure off me. When you are the director of a company, your company is like your children. They are looking to you to provide them with their rent, and, when you don't have that pressure, it makes things a lot easier. (Now that the company has expanded, that's no longer true; the financial pressures are back—big time!)

With my first company, the dissolution was an economic decision. It just got too tedious and tiresome to fundraise, and I didn't have a manager. We have one now, and that makes things easier. Ken Maldonado, our Managing Director, started out as a Development

Director, raising money, and then he left all his other jobs, because he really loves managing companies. He was Development Director for David Parsons, but now he handles twelve companies. He tours with us and carries the heavy freight, because he's young and strong. He's even learning how to be a production stage manager, and he just enjoys doing what he does, so he's a real blessing.

What do I have to say about our political environment? Politics doesn't necessarily affect my art. The way I relate to people, the way humanity and emotions enter into my work has changed because of the personal change in my own psyche rather than a change in the world outside. I outgrew my depression. I try to think as little as possible now about the politics of what's happening, because I just get angry, and anger doesn't generate work for me. For a lot of people, anger excites them, but it doesn't excite me at all, it just represses me. I have a reverse adrenal response. I go all limp.

NYSCA (New York State Council on the Arts) has never been very good to me, so I've never come to depend on them for anything. I think it's too bad that there's less money available, but I'm not a symphony, and I'm not a ballet, so, selfishly, I don't have such a stake in it. I've always managed to do what I do without a lot of support. We had good support from the NEA when I had a company, and that was helpful. I also have faith that there are enough senators in Congress who have a whit of cultural sense and won't let the NEA die.

Certainly, a lot of artists are hurting, but when the pain gets so deep that people notice, then there will be an outcry. To a certain extent, culture has earned its keep. You can't abstractly say, "Art is good for you, so support art," until you realize what about that concept is hurting you personally.

People say, "Oh there are naked dancers, let's cut out the funding." They forget that their symphony is part of the same family. And ordinary people who wouldn't consider going to a downtown concert listen to NPR or watch public television. When that connection is made, then there will be an outcry. Maybe! And, if not, we'll all have to move to another country.

In general, the American culture is so product-oriented that art hardly has a chance. To be supporting it enthusiastically would be an anomaly in our society. In Europe, where they care about culture, they support it. Art isn't supported in a vacuum without anybody caring about it. In America, we've been trying to support culture relatively in a vacuum.

The geographic environment in this country over the past twenty-five years has changed a lot for dance. There is a lot more of dance happening in more places now, and that's a good thing. There are people who can make a living dancing outside of New York. Well, maybe not a total living. Only a few can manage that: Mark Morris, Merce Cunningham, Alvin Ailey, and Paul Taylor's companies, for example. But there are lots of companies, lots of regional ballet companies, and some regional modern companies that have real presence in their localities. For the most part, they are a bigger presence and are more noticed in their homes than a lot of bigger companies here in New York.

Companies such as Cleo Parker Robinson, Hubbard Street, Lula Washington (she has a really hard time in LA because [a], she's black, [b], she's a modern company, and [c] she's in LA, where they really don't care about noncommercial dancing), and Anne Williams in Dallas, Joan Myers Brown's Philadanco, and Dayton Contemporary Dance are respected companies. So, there are a few. And there's Spectrum in Seattle. Danny Bercheski has a company in Minneapolis. There's a whole lot of dancing in Minneapolis, and a whole lot of money for dance and culture in Minneapolis. I think there is in Buffalo as well. Places like those, where the weather is so bleak, have thriving cultural scenes.

The perception of the quality of the art in the rest of the USA may not have changed over the past twenty-five years. Outside of New York is still thought of as the provinces, but the level of the work has risen. Now there are more well-trained former dancers out there teaching, so the "Dolly Dinkle" schools are getting better. We're getting the results of them at Tisch School of the Arts. Kids come in there at seventeen who have been trained well since they were six, and that's really different than coming in with nothing but bad habits, as used to be the case.

Dance has become both less and more accessible today. It's way too expensive to go the Met to see ABT [American Ballet Theater], but it's affordable to go to the City Center to see ABT now. It's also affordable to see City Ballet if you're not sitting in the priciest seats. Up in the balcony, it's affordable. The Joyce tops at about 35 dollars, and there are lower-price tickets for some events. Sometimes they go as low as 20 dollars a seat, and that's affordable for seeing good stuff. Other theaters have replaced DTW [Dance Theater Workshop] in its price range. As DTW upgrades, more places come in. There's St. Mark's, Danspace Project, Clark Theater at Lincoln Center gets used sometimes, Mulberry St. Theater, the University Settlement. PS-122, the Kitchen, and WAX in Brooklyn (now defunct) present a lot of interesting dance stuff. There's a dance center growing in Brooklyn. They're not coming to the city anymore; they do their own art. And BAM is certainly programming a lot of interesting works.

And what's happening is part of a conundrum; if you program accessible stuff, people will enjoy it and come back. That leaves a lot of the really important, interesting, challenging work behind, but it does increase the audience. For all those years when the NEA was running the touring program, we would send all the arcane work to backwoods towns in Pennsylvania and they didn't have to fill the seats, so there was no marketing, but what they would market was foreign works. Because no one learned how to market, and no one learned how to please the audience to get them to come back, boring dancing proliferated.

Nowadays, programmers and presenters are more savvy about what they need to do to get bums in the seats. To a large extent, it leaves a lot of the important work still underexposed and a lot of the younger choreographers are seeing that and thinking they have to be accessible. More and more of modern dance is becoming about entertainment rather than about art, and that's not good; but more and more average citizens are seeing work that they wouldn't see otherwise.

I use a gauge for that at the gym, where I hear people talking. Granted, that's not a typical cross-section, that's not a blue-collar cross-section; I go to an expensive gym. But a lot of people say, "I went to the ballet last night." And they're not just talking to me. They went to the New York City Ballet or American Ballet Theatre or a dance attraction at City Center or BAM, and they do that regularly. They go to Broadway one week, to symphony next week, to ballet the next week, and to the Joyce the next. So, it's not quite so bleak. It's still not easy to get audiences, but if it were easy, it would be boring.

The dancers in Europe, for instance, are pretty complacent. They just don't care. "Go to class? Why? I'll get paid anyway." "I'll have to rehearse from 9 to 5? Okay, I'll rehearse from 9 to 5." They're very complacent. They don't understand what it is to dance just because you're addicted to it, because you have to dance to get your fix. They get their paychecks and do their steps.

Concert dance today is an alternative to other kinds of show business. Personally, I am studying acting right now, and I get a sabbatical next spring, so I'm thinking seriously about trying to break into show business, to do some more theater, to do other kinds of performing, because I love to perform. I realized a few years ago that I really love performing much more than I love choreographing, and the reason I was choreographing was to give myself something to perform. I think I can do other things, and I want to sing. I even had a fun modeling gig. A magazine, which is the AARP alternative to *Modern Maturity* for people over sixty, wanted dancers to do the spread on winter coats, and they called Dancers Over Forty, the organization, and they recommended me. It's a wonderful spread. I really look like a model. Who knew? So, when I saw that, I thought, "All right, I can do this."

Evolution has always been my forte. I just figured out a way to do the next thing without making a big deal of it. Some people get to these crises because they think, "Oh, I have to change!" Well, that's what you're doing all the time—changing. We keep learning new things, and, if you stay interested, it seems to me, you will have to change just to keep up because otherwise you are doing the same thing over and over again. That's boring. So, in my continuing evolution, I think the next step, now that I have the freedom, is to try other kinds of performing. This is the right moment to be growing older because everyone is doing it and there are more opportunities for being seen.

May 19, 2003

Doug Varone. Photo © Cylla von Tiedemann.

Doug Varone

Doug Varone is a choreographer of contemporary dance for the concert stage, as well as opera, Broadway, regional theater, and film. He is the Artistic Director of Doug Varone and Dancers, which he established in 1986 as an opportunity to explore and process his particular choreographic vision. His work has been singled out for its extraordinary physical daring, vivid musicality, and genius for capturing through movement the nuances of true human interaction.

On tour, the company has performed in more than 100 cities in forty-five states across the USA and in Europe, Asia, Canada, and South America. Stages include the Kennedy Center, Lincoln Center, Brooklyn Academy of Music, San Francisco Performances, London's Queen Elizabeth Hall, Toronto's Harbourfront, Moscow's Stanislavsky Theater, the Venice Biennale, and the Tokyo, Jacob's Pillow, and the American Dance Festivals.

Eleven New York Dance and Performance Awards (Bessies) have been awarded to the company's dancers, designers, and to Varone himself. By any measure, Varone's output is extraordinary for its emotional range, kinetic breadth, and the diversity of platforms on which he stages it.

For New York's Metropolitan Opera, Varone has choreographed new productions of *Le Sacré du printemps*, *Les Troyens*, *Salome*, and the world premiere of Tobias Picker's *An American Tragedy*. Other opera choreography includes *Die Walküre* (Washington Opera); *Il Viaggio a Reims* (New York City Opera); and the American premieres of George Antheil's *Transatlantic* and Ricky Ian Gordon's debut production of *Grapes of Wrath* (Minnesota Opera). As a director and choreographer, he has staged Gluck's *Orfée et Eurydice* and *Il Barbiere di Siviglia* for Opera Colorado and Laurent Petitgirard's *Joseph Merrick: The Elephant Man* (for Minnesota Opera). Varone was awarded a 2006 OBIE for his direction and choreography of Ricky Ian Gordon's *Orpheus and Euridice* at Lincoln Center for its American Songbook series.

Varone's theater credits include choreography for Broadway, at Baltimore's Center Stage, Yale Repertory Theatre, Walnut Street Theatre, Princeton's McCarter Theater, Music Theater Group, the Vineyard Theatre, and Via Theater. He choreographed and directed the Aquila Theatre Company's *The Invisible Man*. Choreography for television and fashion include the dance and underwater sequences of the *The Planets* (for A&E) and designer Geoffrey Beene's couture runway shows in New York City. A collaboration with photographer Michael

Thompson for *W* magazine was featured in its February 2004 issue. Film credits include choreography for the Patrick Swayze film *One Last Dance*.

Varone has created works for the Limón Company, Dancemakers (Canada), Batsheva Dance Company (Israel), Uppercut Danse (Denmark), An Creative (Japan), Dayton Contemporary Dance Company, Bern Ballet (Switzerland), Rambert Dance Company (London), and Chicago's Hubbard Street, among many others. His dances are regularly staged on college and university students.

Born and raised in Syosset, NY, Varone received his BFA from Purchase College where he was awarded the Presidential Distinguished Alumni Award in 2007. Honors also include a Guggenheim Fellowship and two New York Dance and Performance Awards (Bessies) for Sustained Achievement in Choreography (1998) and for *Boats Leaving* (2007). His work has been supported by the National Endowment for the Arts (NEA) since 1988.

Humanity

When I begin creating a new work, it is important for me to take a viewer on a journey that touches them in some way through storytelling. Everything has context and allows that viewer to find a way into the work that relates to his or her own life in some way. What's important for me is that they recognize themselves in the work on some level. I want people to think and feel something the next day, to touch their lives, and to remember the event. I believe that the strength in my work and its vision lie in its emotional context and how that finds its way past the confines of the performance space.

Very often narrative is embraced, whether linear or nonlinear. Always about something, my works employ a sense of dramatic structure that tends not to be abstract in approach. I'm not sure that I've ever made an abstract work, per se.

After making dances for seventeen or eighteen years, the greatest challenge of choreographing now is constantly trying to reimagine and reinvent what I know. The diversity of work I've explored ranges from small duets, larger dance works, and full evening-length theatrical events. In their own way, they are all mining the same territory. When I walk into a studio now, it is about relearning. I have to believe that I've never made a dance before in order for something new to come out. I'm always asking where is the next step I take as an artist and how can I share that in new ways?

I began studying dance when I was very young: tap at the Plainview Conservatory of Dance in Plainview, Long Island, when I was six. That early training has remained a very huge influence in my life. It was a classic "chorus line" tale as I followed my sister to dance class, and when she eventually stopped and I kept studying. Looking at it now in the broader spectrum of my work and the way I hear music, it's easy to recognize the influence of my early tap-dancer rhythms. I feel as if its subtlety is reflected in a lot of the work I create. I studied tap until I was fifteen and performed in a lot of musical theater and summer stock when I was growing up. I was greatly enamored of all the MGM musicals I could catch on TV. I can probably reference whole passages from them that influenced my work. Both Gene Kelly and Fred Astaire remain icons for me in their ease and flow of movement. How they could pass from pedestrian to dancerly prowess in the blink of an eye impressed me so much. It left an imprint that I believe is a seed to the way I move and, as a result, the dances I make.

In high school, I had a wonderful teacher named Jeanne Levine who ran the modern dance club. She was the first person to open my eyes to the art form, as I had never studied contemporary dance. I took classes at the New Dance Group in New York City in my senior year in high school and then went on to study at SUNY Purchase. I studied with wonderful artists, like Aaron Osborne, Mel Wong, Carol Freed, and Kazuko Hirabayashi, and it was the first time I was exposed to contemporary work on a highly professional level. I was overwhelmed by everything that was being thrown at me, as it was so radically different from anything I had experienced. My lack of maturity and self-confidence didn't know what to do with the information. I realize now that this intense environment helped me immensely to grow as an artist and to mature as a human being. Talking to these wonderful artists, learning about their lives greatly influenced me. I began my college years as a tap dancer (Broadway bound!), but, by the end of my freshman year, my passion for contemporary dance changed all that. This was an art form that touched people in a very different way. It wasn't my upbringing but a strange, compelling world to enter.

Prior to Purchase, I had very little formal training. I think Purchase accepted me on faith because I was a guy, and I could move half way decently. I was really kind of dorky. I had glasses and I wouldn't take them off when I took ballet class so I never learned how to pirouette correctly. Trying to adjust to new movement vocabularies was challenging enough, but our dance classes went beyond movement and embraced philosophy and visual art, and, for me, this was a new type of education. Getting used to this was an awkward step-by-step process for so many of us. Many of the students had only studied ballet, and it was a challenge for them to get their heads and heart into a drastically different way of thinking. As I watched them take off their ballet slippers and throw them away, I did the same with much of my life.

Purchase was a major influence on my training because it educated me in a body of ideas and styles. We were trained in the Graham, Cunningham, and Limón techniques, which at that time gave great options to a contemporary dancer. I greatly appreciate that now when I look back on it. As an institution, it prepared me well.

Shortly after graduation, I was incredibly lucky to join the Limón Dance Company. Studying with Aaron Osborne at Purchase was a tremendous inspiration, and it brought me in touch with the Limón work for the first time. It always felt like a style I was meant to dance. There was a beauty to the natural breath-flow of how a body moves. In terms of José's work, I enjoyed the fact that he presented men in a very vulnerable, almost flawed way, and it spoke to the humanist inside me. There was a truth for me in his work. It was 1978, and José had passed away five years earlier, but I was still drawn to the work and wanted to learn from these dances.

When I joined the Limón Company, Carla Maxwell was Acting Artistic Director and the company was going through a huge transition. It was the first major modern dance company whose founder had died and left behind a legacy of dances, without a blueprint about how to pass them on. I found that, as wonderful as it was to do the work and be a part of that legacy, at that particular point in time it was a very frustrating place to be as a young dancer. In order to embrace the truths of José's work, there were constant discussions about the correct version of each step, each gesture. I respected the need for this, but it made me realize that I wanted to have dances created on me, more than restaged.

I was always drawn to Lar Lubovitch's work. I auditioned for Lar and became part of his company in late 1978. For a while, I was actually dancing for both companies at the same time, then eventually focused solely on Lar's. I gave over to being part of someone's philosophy who was making dances directly on me and from 1978 to 1986 I danced for the Lubovitch Company. During that time, Lar built a really beautiful body of work, and it was a very fertile and creative period for him. Through that, I learned a great deal about making dances. I was a part of his process, but I could also sit back and watch the decisions he made. At a certain point, there was a divergence between the direction he was moving and creating and what led me to his work in the beginning. He was searching for a new path, and it seemed obvious that it was time for me to move on. I left the company and wandered for a little bit not really wanting to dance for another company.

I had been creating small dances of my own during my time with Lar and decided to do a concert in New York City. I developed an evening of dances and presented it in September 1986 at PS-122. The event went well, and I was pleased with the work but I wasn't quite sure what to do next. I had just turned thirty, and it felt kind of odd to stop dancing. There was no real dance work I was interested in dancing, and I certainly was not interested in having a company, so I left New York City and went to San Francisco to live, teach, and create. I taught at the Performance Gallery and Footworks. I was part of that environment for several months—six, seven, or eight months—and started making work with the thought that maybe this could be where I would end up.

But I couldn't focus on making dances when I was there; I just wanted to focus on living. There was a drastic difference between New York City and San Francisco, particularly in the 1980s. There was a very different quality of life with different priorities, and it was terrific living in a totally new environment. Ultimately, that never translated into the studio for me. I was struggling to be in the studio every day (San Francisco is just so damn beautiful), and I felt I had lost an inherent edge that New York embodies. Eventually I returned to New York and presented another concert at PS-122, using the same dancers. Once again, the response to the work was very positive. Sitting in the audience was Marda Kirn, who ran the Colorado Dance Festival in Boulder, Col. She approached me at the end of the evening and offered to bring the company to the festival the following summer, 1988. That was the beginning of touring.

From that point on, we began touring the work, nationally and internationally, and I had to start figuring out how to sustain a group of dancers financially. I used my own personal money in the beginning, and then fortunately became part of the Foundation for Independent Artists, an umbrella 501(c) that was administered by Pentacle Management. There were ten companies at that point (including Mark Morris, Eiko and Koma, Bebe Miller, Urban Bush Women, among others) under this umbrella organization, and it was a great way to begin. FIA (as it was lovingly called) began applying for grants for projects, touring, and general operating for us, and it gave us a small sense of financial stability.

But I was finding that it was a very slow progression for me as an artist in the New York dance scene, in part, because the type of work I was creating was not in vogue. There was a similar tone to most of work being created in the mid-1980s by many of my peers. I wouldn't call it abstraction by any means but definitely not narrative in exploration. It was difficult, if not impossible, to get presented in New York City early on. At the time, it was tremendously frustrating, but, as I look back now, I am grateful for the time to grow and mature. I remained dedicated to a vision and was not swayed by the trends, and, for me, that strength has always helped define the work.

When I choreograph, I am very physical in my own body. I want and need to have the movement come out of my body as a starting point. I absolutely embrace the need to bring dancers into the physical aspect of the process, and, within the creation of my work, they do contribute material. Very often it's a way of getting my imagination started. I have been blessed with working with some tremendous creative artists. I always look for people who have information that I don't have, people who move differently yet compliment my style. In building new dances, I love to see what comes out of their bodies based on information or phrases I give them. They naturally come up with movement I could never have thought of, and very often that is the key to getting in the door creatively.

Some of that information finds its way forward into a work. Very often I will use a phrase or use material from the dancers but never by rote. I need to always go back in and change it, develop it into something different, put another stamp on it. I recognize that choreograph-ing is so much more than the development of dance material, but I am not interested in orchestrating someone else's ideas. I have very often not used some amazing material that dancers have created exactly for that reason. The early part of the process needs to be about my ownership of the journey. That's tremendously important to me.

Like a painter, I want to have a handle on the brushes, so I love using the dancers to open up my ideas. The next step is about allowing them ownership over that material, and, in many ways, it is a more liberating and collaborative moment in the process. To be able to work with a dancer over a period of eight, nine, or ten years, and to *not* have to explain every-thing . . . that's the beauty in an ongoing company situation. I will create a phrase, and, as soon as it is in their bodies, it turns into something else extraordinary. They are inside my body and inside my brain and giving them the trust and liberty to explore that material and develop it, morph it so to speak, is a beautiful thing. So, for me, I take the next step and step *away* and watch what they've turned into and how that affects the dance we are making.

Having the luxury of working with dancers for over a length of time allows them to also know things about my creative mind. They intuitively understand the choices I make, and it has made a great difference in the work. It has lent the work a great maturity and honesty, because they know the philosophy behind the style and creative point of view. I don't have to sit there and explain what it is I am trying to create.

It seems odd to reference the old MGM musicals, but honestly, thinking on it, they really are the seed behind my work and style. When I was growing up, age five and six, I would watch all these musicals, and it would blow my mind. As a youngster watching Gene Kelly or Fred Astaire, they would be walking down the street and then all of a sudden they'd break out into this number, as though it was the most ordinary thing. And then, of course, everyone would be dancing. Finally, and all of a sudden, it would start to subside, and life would go on as if nothing had happened. Within that short fantastical moment, so much life was embodied. One of the things I was drawn to in musical theater is how it breaks the boundary between pedestrian and dance moments. That has always stayed with me, and I think that is at the heart of a lot of the work I do. When someone tells me that the work looks spontaneous, I know that I've succeeded in getting a vision across. It's almost as if it is *just* happening, that gesture can start an action and move into an enormous dance, and then, all of a sudden, come back to something quiet with solitude to it.

As choreographers, both Limón and Lubovitch dealt with the idea of community in their larger group works. I feel very attached to their sense of humanity, and, through that, their lineage is clearly at play in my own work. The musicality both José and Lar have was

Doug Varone Company, *Vertical*. Photo © Phil Knott.

significant in hearing and seeing their work, and I was able to learn so much from dancing these repertories. In creating my own dances, I've tried to discover my own voice and style as an artist, teacher, and choreographer. For me, it is very much about finding the things we ordinarily do in life and building movement vocabularies from that. So, my first choreographic ideas were always couched in gestures that developed into movement.

Cantata 78, based on the libretto, was one of my first dances from 1986. The *Bench Quartet* was a short section excerpted from it, and it still remains in our repertory today. It begins with small gestures (each specific to a word in the Cantata's text) normally seen in everyday life and, as the dance progresses, it becomes larger in scope and meaning. My attraction to gestural work led me to create small theater works, like *Home* (1988) and *Care* (1989), that were basically theater scenes or duets about relationships set to music.

My desire to hone my own individual movement vocabulary lived alone in the studio with me for many years while I was continuing to create these gesture-based works. I could never figure out how to translate onto other bodies how I was naturally moving alone. Each time I would try to translate it to other people, generic dance movements came out, and, as a result, the group work I was creating didn't have the same personal feel to it. This vocabulary seemed so particular to my body, I didn't have the tools to explain its genesis to other dancers. In 1993, I couldn't stand it anymore. I went into a studio and started making a dance and vowed not to use anything but my own movement vocabulary, no matter how long it took. I had been working with the same group of dancers for a few years, so together we slowly figured out how to put my movement into their own bodies. The work that was created was called *Rise*. It was a watershed moment, and every other work has developed from that in some way.

Now, I've expanded my ideas into opera, and it's been really fascinating working in a much larger arena. It may be blunt to say that the imagination can be ruled by budget, but having worked in opera I now understand what that means. You get to a certain point in your creative life where you begin imagining larger projects. The dance world can support that to a certain extent but becoming part of the opera world, as both choreographer and director, has allowed me to create on a larger playing field. It has been an amazing journey and has opened up whole other portions of my creative brain. Working with large ensembles, not just the dancers but also chorus members and principal vocalists, forces you to deal with dramatic context, which is always a great challenge. I've learned a great deal about dramaturgy, and that has tremendously helped my own dance-making.

The operas I am most interested in doing now are the works I am choreographing and directing at the same time, because I am trying to create a different type of form. To be sure, there is a great history of dance in opera, but when I take the helm of an opera, bringing my own dancers in or bringing in other contemporary dancers, it is not just to create the dances. I utilize the dancers as a different type of energy within the context of the entire opera. It allows me to turn works that are of great operatic tradition, like *The Barber of Seville*, into dance operas. I am trying to reinvent someone else's wheel, and, as a result, not only bring our art form into a new vision and wider audience but also learn something while bringing that back to dance-making.

Dance as an art form is about the physical nature of how we move. That movement becomes a language, and how we choose to speak that language is an individual human experience. That experience translates into ideas that are tremendously universal in scope. It transcends race and gender. The world is a diverse place, and dance and dancers need to (and I feel very often) reflect upon that truthfully.

I find gender fascinating, and I love that the world has changed so much in the way this topic is viewed. The dance field has really been in the forefront of putting gender awareness out there. It is essential to show the world as it is, and, in doing so, screw around with both traditional and nontraditional roles.

Bel Canto, which dates to 1998, was a turning point for me in that regard and includes two male and one female duet. It was the first time I began exploring a different type of arrangement in terms of partnering and partnerships. And that began affecting a lot of the other types of relationships I put forward, such as how groups are arranged and what the balance is onstage between men and women.

I am very interested in dancers as individuals on stage. I love people who move from their center and move from their heart. They make the work look real, and that is the most important thing for me: finding collaborators and interpreters who embody my work in a very unique way. I am drawn to people who look the way real people look. For fifteen years, a man named Larry Hahn danced with me. He is a big truck driver of a guy, and an amazing dancer. A beautiful dancer named Christine Philian danced with me early on. She always battled with her weight, grew up in ballet, and was told she would never have a career, but she is a gorgeous woman who needs to be in dance. Part of the reason I choose the dancers I do is that they look like real people, so when viewers look at the stage they can see something familiar to them.

I have earned a reputation for not hiring young dancers. It's not that I have a prejudice against younger artists, but I've learned, with the kind of work I make and the type of artists I am interested in creating with, they need to have a lot of life behind them. I don't want to direct dancers as much as have them add their life experience into my work. So I am very particular about what people I take into the company and at what point in their lives they come into the company. I am drawn to mature bodies. I love dancers who are in their thirties; I love dancers in their forties. There is so much more knowledge about bodies now, about how to have longevity in our careers. And the artist who goes on stage at forty, in one of my works, brings much more information to it.

There is a great beauty in mature dancers. Dancers like Larry Hahn, Nina Watt, and Peggy Baker (all who are in their fifties) are continuing to explore not only the drama of what dance is but also the physicality of what it is and what it can be at their point in life. Their artistic knowledge continues to inspire younger dancers.

Regarding changes in the economic environment of dance, it has been very difficult for my generation of dance-makers in particular. We came of age just at the point when the arts environment really began to shift and the Government was trying to justify reasons for continued funding. The funding available to us was couched in initiatives that included extraordinary amounts of outreach work. In order to tour effectively, we needed to develop new skills to communicate on a broader level. Residencies included work in prisons, at-risk centers, and inner-city high schools. At first, my company felt totally unprepared and undereducated for this task. Eventually, we were able to look at the situation as a positive. We looked at the strength of the work and its power to communicate and devised new creative activities that embraced it. We had to discover new skills within ourselves to share our passion and to make it relevant in their lives.

Looking back, I think it really helped focus us as a company. It made me have to be articulate about the work in a new way and to be an advocate for dance in general. The NEA's funding for dance has been cut far back, and fellowships formerly available to younger artists have been eliminated entirely. Private funding remains very difficult still, particularly for young choreographers just starting out. When I look at the generation coming up and the struggles ahead, I feel for them.

However, I think the field itself is beginning to understand how they can proactively take charge in new ways. Organizations like Dance USA, Dance NYC—which in particular deals with the dance field here in the city—have been established to build a network for the community and a solid base for the art form to be seen and heard. These groups are not just for established companies but for young independent choreographers and individual dancers, and they create forums that include all levels of dance and management.

Believe it or not, some journalists are still calling me an emerging choreographer. I find that fascinating, at the age of forty-eight, with a body of work behind me, to still be seen this way in the eyes of dance historians. And I think it is a mindset we put ourselves in. We need to seriously take a look at the landscape of dance and reconfigure it now if we are to survive. There are major artists in our field who have not had the opportunity for growth because the field is saturated with so many dance companies all vying for the same funding. I think we are at a really interesting and defining point. We have watched so many first-generation creators pass away, many of whom defined the art form for all of us and set the standards that we keep holding. The question is, "What happens to these icons, their work and their companies?" I may be in the minority, but I don't believe that a company needs to continue to exist past a choreographer's life.

I think it is very important to see the historical works that are still being reconstructed and performed by companies like Graham and Limón, but not at the expense of a vital young artist. The only way to keep moving forward is to embrace the future. I keep thinking that there needs to be one company established as a repository of all this amazing repertory. Our art form deserves a national company to bring all of these great works together. Building an organization that can create this is a vital step to our growth and certainly deserving of the form. (How do we justify ABT [American Ballet Theatre] staging the works of Paul Taylor and Martha Graham? Will their versions of these styles become definitive over time?)

What do I think about the geographical environment in relation to modern dance during the past twenty-five years? Back in the 1970s, New York was really the center of dance. Dance has decentralized since then, which has only been good for the rest of the country and, ultimately, the art form. As a New York City-based artist, it was difficult at first to also watch funding initiatives be decentralized, but, as a result of that shift, there is now incredible work being done all over the country. Young artists at workshops and universities seem to always chant "I can't wait to come to New York City," and I always ask them "Why?" Part of me is coming from that place that almost moved to San Francisco and recognized it *is* possible to have quality of life and to dance and make work somewhere other than in New York City.

Touring the dances we create is always the dream. I make dances, and I want to share them. As an artist, here in the USA. I am mostly powerless as to where my work is performed. We have many champions for the work but just as many presenters are hesitant about booking us. Not a large enough name, not flashy enough work. I am learning though that the landscape changes over time. The company just went to Pittsburgh for the first time in twenty years due to a shift in the presenting organization. The same thing just happened in San Francisco. I really do feel that choreographers need to become more empowered about their own future and how their work is seen. As far as touring abroad, presenters are just not supporting American dance right now.

Doug Varone Company, *Bottomland*. Photo © Scott Suchman.

When I was touring with the Limón Company and Lubovitch Company, those were great, great years of US State Department touring, and that program is nonexistent now. What an incredible experience it was to bring this American art form abroad and let it be an ambassador for our nation. It reaches out past politics and differences. It lets people understand in a very elemental way that everyone everywhere is the same. There was a real meeting of cultures that enabled us to take huge, giant strides forward. So, particularly having lived through that period, and to watch it fall away, to watch all those programs disappear, and to be in the state we are in now, is both disappointing and aggravating. Sharing our work *can* make a difference. And we could certainly use some innovative diplomacy these days.

I think it is a very sad state of affairs we are in at the moment, and the current administration has eroded any sense of trust in this country. I was in Toronto on Election Day 2004. To be an artist and travel abroad, you get a real sense of what the world thinks of Americans these days. I cherish all the traveling I have done because it has brought me in touch with so many diverse individuals and cultures. Dance is a universal language, and it opens dialogues that other aspects of diplomacy can't achieve.

November 20, 2004

Dan Wagoner. Photo © Marc Ray.

Dan Wagoner

Dan Wagoner was born in the Allegheny Mountains of eastern West Virginia, the youngest of ten in a farm family. After receiving a degree in pharmacy he entered the Army and was stationed in Washington, DC, where he studied and performed with Ethel Butler. With Ethel's guidance, he attended a summer session of the American Dance Festival at Connecticut College and then moved to New York City. He danced with the companies of Martha Graham, Merce Cunningham, and Paul Taylor before forming his own company, Dan Wagoner and Dancers.

For the next twenty-five years, Dan directed, choreographed, and danced with his own company, making over fifty dances. The company toured extensively in the USA as well as Europe, Asia, South America, and Canada with support from the National Endowment for the Arts (NEA), the New York State Council on the Arts (NYSCA), and various private foundations.

The poet George Montgomery, whom Dan met in New York City, became a companion and mentor, helping to choose music and decor for the company and, at times, performing with the company. Many of the dance titles come from George's poetry: *Green Leaves and Gentle Differences*, *Stop Stars*, *Lila's Garden Ox*, and *A Play with Images and Walls*, among others.

Jennifer Tipton designed all the lights for the repertory. Among the costume designers are Santo Loquasto, William Ivey Long, and John Macfarlane. William Balcom and Natalie Gilbert have composed scores for Wagoner.

In 1990 and 1991, he directed the London Contemporary Dance Company, which had annual seasons at the Sadler's Wells Theatre in London. He choreographed two dances for London Contemporary: *Turtles All the Way Down* and *White Heat*.

His work has been performed by companies in China, Canada, England, and Finland, as well as in companies throughout the USA. He has been a guest artist at many universities and is on the faculty of Florida State University.

Dan's work has often been described as deeply American.

Knife Edge of Passion and Delight

Isadora Duncan said that by being an artist, like it or not, you are automatically a revolutionary. I think that is very true. Has my work changed in the past twenty-five years? Oh yes, absolutely! And let's hope that it continues to change even more. All of the backward, conservative attitudes in this country, born out of fear, which I think is antithetical to art—to close doors, to lock everything in, to be safe—ideas can't happen. An artist can't live in that atmosphere.

Over twenty years ago, in 1985, I still had my company in New York City, and the main thrust of my life was choreographing with the company. At that time, I was still touring with the company, having regular seasons, and going to different places to make dances for other companies, especially in London. I made three or four pieces for different companies in England in the late 1980s.

Then I lived at 791 Broadway, still had my studio on 17th Street in New York, and later, down on Broadway between Broome and Grand. In 1989, I went to London. Bob Cohan had wanted me to be the Director of London Contemporary Dance Theatre, and I kept saying "No." Finally he said, "Well, just come look."

I wanted to keep my company in the USA. Coming from Appalachia, West Virginia, very much influenced my work, and I felt that I needed those American roots to know what I was doing. So, I kept resisting, but I did go visit in London. Then some friends advised me very strongly to try it. I think they were prescient about what was going to happen in this country with the NEA and other funding agencies. I went over to try it and directed the company for a couple of years. I was going back to New York and choreographing for my own company at that time. We were doing seasons at the Joyce Theater, usually a week, as well as touring and performing throughout the USA and going abroad part of the time.

I liked London, and I liked the dancers. I made several pieces there, as well as restaging some of my other work, and the company was very successful. We had good box office, and they toured all over England. I went to Moscow with them, to Prague, and Bratislava, and I enjoyed it. They were beautiful dancers and a wonderfully established company, but when they wanted a commitment from me for five years, it scared me. I felt that if I left New York for that long I would lose my way.

When I was in London, I had to make a premiere for my company in New York. Merce came and performed at Sadler's Wells, and I went backstage to speak to him. He knew I had just arrived there to start directing the company, and he said, "How's it going?" I said, "Oh, you know how it is, when you go to a new culture, a new place, it's like starting all over again and questioning everything you've ever done, why or what it means." And he said, "Yes, yes, I know, but we have to just keep plodding along."

I came back to New York, I think, in 1990 (I don't keep a diary). Shortly after that, I did the last season at the Joyce in 1991, and I used that very overly familiar *Symphony in D* of Prokofiev and called the dance *Plod*. I liked that. That was a piece I restaged at Wisconsin last winter, and they had a big success with it and used it also in the opening of a big theater complex that had been built downtown.

When I came back to New York, there were huge cutbacks with the NEA and NYSCA, which were a large part of my support, so I had to give up the company in 1992. There were personal things that intervened as well. My close friend, George Montgomery, who was a poet, a companion, and a mentor in many ways, became very ill. We didn't know until shortly before he died that it was Huntington's disease. It was very hard. Now, with DNA testing, this disease can be diagnosed, but at that time there still was no sure way to know what it was. And the doctors kept thinking it was *not* that, but it manifests itself as madness, so it took a lot of care to keep him out of institutions or mental wards.

Sali Ann Kriegsman, who headed the NEA at that time, came to New York, and we talked. It was during the time of the Mapplethorpe controversy, and there was another thing called *Piss Christ* that had been funded by an umbrella group who had received NEA money. Ultraconservative people in Congress felt that this was taxpayers' money and were outraged at these homoerotic photographs. They almost destroyed the NEA. All my funding was lost. It looked absolutely hopeless and bleak. George was very ill, and it terrified me to try to take care of everything.

How I did it for twenty-five years in New York, I don't know. Living hand to mouth, thinking always, "Can I see it through and somehow find a way to establish myself?" At the time, if I had been able to be level-headed, pull back, and start working on a much smaller scale—to give up my own studio, my own internal administration, to have gotten some sort of an umbrella organization to gently keep the work going—perhaps it would have worked. But it just terrified me to figure out how to do that. It meant taking care of George while trying to earn money to keep the company going. So, I just decided to close up. And it was very sad for me, but I felt helpless and didn't see any way out at the time. Actually, when you know and care a lot about someone who sinks into madness, it's so painful that you can't help but try to lead that person out of blackness and pain. It was devastating. Most of my emotional energy was going towards George at that point, and I didn't have any reserves to try to fight the funding crisis. I closed the studio and put everything in storage.

Sometime in 1994, Lan-Lan Wang, who was at UCLA, called me and said they needed someone as a guest. I ended up teaching about three different quarters at UCLA. In the meantime, she interviewed for the Chair of Dance at Connecticut College and moved there. The moment she moved, she brought all the people who had previously worked with her, and she had me come teach modern dance.

I didn't take a tenured track position at Connecticut College, and, due to that, after a few years I could only teach part time. I taught as a guest at the University of Wisconsin in the winter of 2004. In June, I went to Tallahassee to Florida State University. They created a national choreographic center, and my piece *Dolly Sods: After the Flood* was the first to be selected to be restaged and archived. They presented it in the fall on a dedication program at the Nancy Smith-Fichter Theater. An assistant, Lisa Wheeler, who had been in the original production, taught the dance. I came later to do the final rehearsals. It was the last piece I made in New York, which premiered at the Joyce in 1991.

In West Virginia, there's a very peculiar terrain that's kind of a flat space, up on top of a mountain, and I think it was burnt over probably at the turn of the twentieth century. When it grew back, it was a terrain unlike any that was in the area, a terrain that didn't seem indigenous to that climate, latitude, or longitude. This curious terrain was named for the family that owned it, Dolly. "Sods" meant your farm, or your land, and so it was "Dolly Sods." I had used that title actually, for a piece in London, so instead of *After the Fire*, I put *After the Flood*. It's a poetic name to me, and I like the name *Dolly Sods* very much.

Lisa did a beautiful job, and the dancers were far better than I'd thought they would be. I was pleased with the energy and quality of the dance, and it was interesting to me to see the dance again. Once I no longer had the company, and was not choreographing regularly, I tended not to go back to videos or to revisit my life. It was an education for me to see that dance. It did hold up and actually interested me. And they had quite a success with it, and the dancers danced it beautifully.

I also realized it helped a lot to teach them in class for about five weeks. My way of moving often requires a sense of weight that a lot of current dancers don't understand or know, sharpness, clarity of line, full shift of weight, and speed make for a complexity that interests me. Once the dancers began to do this, they seemed extremely excited and pleased by it.

Also, at Wisconsin, I had to teach a repertory class, having no idea that they were expecting to have it on a program. But at the end of the semester, they insisted the piece, *Plod*, be performed. It wasn't at its best for *me*, but they did it, and, again, they had a huge success with it. There were people who saw it who said they had never seen dancers move in that way, with such power, weight, and speed. It was satisfying that people were still interested in the pieces and seemed to respond to them.

At Connecticut College, I taught the advanced technique and advanced composition. From time to time, I had to do a course called "Conversations of the Arts." I brought, among others, Jennifer Tipton, Tricia Brown, Yvonne Rainer, and Jim Ivory, a film director, from New York City to meet the students. It was interesting. A lot of the students, who are quite bright, weren't even aware of who these people were. Just being in the same room with them brought tangential information. When Jenny Tipton, who is very soft-spoken, came, she absolutely radiated light. And some of these young women wrote, "I was so shocked to see someone who obviously has a passion for what she does, and she makes her living at it." "I thought everybody hated what they were doing."

It's so naive. You'd think that notion didn't exist anymore. But I think it's perhaps even more so now—the pressure to succeed, the high cost of living for all of us, to make money at all costs and at all sacrifices. Most of the students who graduate from Connecticut College go to New York City, and some of them are very talented. Once they begin to get the strength of centering their body, they become empowered. Then, when you encourage them to be outrageous and courageous in their choreography, they begin to do it. They blossom into believing "My God, I can do anything. I can go anywhere." And they begin to do really wonderfully inventive and surprising things.

Young people who find that power touch me. Dance has been my passion and delight, and I have loved all of the work I've done. I have loved performing. I would certainly not have had it any other way.

Dance still holds that deep interest for me. It's harder to warm up, to get myself out of bed. Probably, if I had enough money, I would just collapse and get fat and fade away and die fairly quickly, but young people who want to dance touch me. It makes me think of myself at that age and the delight it brought to me.

I grew up in Appalachia, so I hardly knew what dance was but intuitively wanted to do it. I read every book and *Dance Magazine* I could get as I went to pharmacy school at West Virginia University. I was in the Army, stationed in Washington, and Ethel Butler, who had been in Martha Graham's Primitive Mysteries Company, had a company and taught. I danced with her, and she helped me get a scholarship to Connecticut College in the summer of 1956. I went there and walked into the room to see Martha Graham, Doris Humphrey, Louis Horst,

Dan Wagoner. Photo © Marc Ray.

José Limón, and Merce Cunningham. I was trembling and thought, "Oh my God, these people do exist!" I went to New York City that fall and stayed for forty-one years.

I gave up my New York City loft because there was a fire. Our top floor wasn't damaged, but a woman who had a business on the ground floor owned the building. We were protected by the Artists in Residence rent control. After the fire, she wanted to buy us out, and the rents were skyrocketing. The other two tenants in the building were bought out. I went back, and, the money I would have been bought out with, I used as rent for four years just to stay on in the loft. But it was very changed after the renovation.

It was an old beautiful loft, built in the 1830s. It had fireplaces, old wide pine floorboards, and a tall, pitched beamed ceiling. It was like living in a New England barn. I miss it. I lived there over thirty years. I miss George. He died in 1997. It was a lot of loss for me in 1992 . . . to lose the company and to give up the loft. It's quite wrenching, and I'm probably still not over it.

The only thing that keeps me going now is that I realize I can teach. When I see dancers through a certain period, and I see what they grow into, it inspires me. I get into the dancing, and dancing's a lovely thing; even though now I can't move the way I did because of age. Still, it's a lovely thing to be part of, and it sustains me. I've always done most things in my life instantaneously, on impulse, or on what it felt like. People would say, "Why in the world do you want to dance?" and I would say, "It feels good," which I think is a very legitimate answer.

I tell students, "I view all institutions as the same: penitentiaries, mental hospitals colleges—they're all institutions. In the institution of academia, there's a lot of wonderful information to be had. So, glean it, but don't let yourself be institutionalized, because it's dangerous." When I say these things to students, I am, of course, talking to myself.

How do I think dance has changed in the past twenty-five years? I don't follow the dance world that closely. I go to New York once in a while, if some of my students are in dances downtown. I think today's dancers can't expect to make a living at dancing, and they don't, but still they wait tables, or do whatever they need to do, to try to eke out a living in order to dance.

It seems aesthetically that modern dance has softened very much; softened—meaning in the technique, in the ideas of the dance. Often there will be an implication of political content, gender, psychological motivation, dysfunctional relationships, or families, but it isn't pushed to the extreme. Truly strong, passionate life-ideas are presented, but, movement-wise, they are solved in a very soft-edged way, and often with text.

Whether or not my movement has changed in the past two and a half decades is hard for me to say, because it's a gradual process. I still basically teach technique in the same structure of class. Each day, I try to compose new material, both to keep myself trying new things and to not repeat for the students. I try to give structure in class that's somewhat the same every day but varies enough so they have to sharpen their wits to be aware of it. And then I try to make movement that challenges the dancer in as many ways as possible.

Simply by being older and having practice I can get at ideas quicker. You teach yourself actually. But I still like process and details. I think if my own work, my own dancing, has done any changing, it's gone very much in the direction that it's been pointed at in the beginning, but perhaps now it has more complexity and resonance.

One advantage of getting older is dropping a lot of the tension and fear: "My God, it's two o'clock, the dancers are here, and I've got to produce." Now, I can just sit in the room with them for an hour and not do a thing and not get nervous about it.

I've begun to realize that I can coach dancers, into falls and things on the floor, up and down, and work with them, saying, "Is this possible? Is that possible? Try this, try that." Often, the same way one does with choreographing lifts and support work, I see a configuration and say, "Now, take the thigh underneath, can you flip her over this way?" or, "Can she flip him over that way?"

What resonates emotionally or spiritually in what one does is difficult to get hold of or to see. One has to draw on and integrate both the intellect and the intuitive. The meditative, the erotic, the beast, the Dionysian, must exist alongside the forebrain, the Apollonian. Our culture is terribly dishonest about eroticism. It's not something just to say no to, for it blocks the meridians of energy through the body. Eroticism is not a bad thing, and we are human creatures. There's just such dishonesty about our physical lives. It's too bad. I think it's a reason there's so much obesity, that people don't develop a strong self-image, midbrain sort of thing, and we lose movement through the pelvis. And, of course, pelvic awareness is the very basis of getting centered in your body. The forebrain is for the intellect, the thinking. When you have a smart, intellectual person, who can also let the animal out—you have a dancer!

What's it like to be aging in the dance world? You have no choice. If you're going to keep breathing and face each day and get up, it's essential to listen to your own heart and return to your own passion and delight in order to offset physical loss.

Where is modern dance going? I don't think it's going anywhere. It simply is. And life is not going anywhere; it simply *is* for us all. The main thing for me is to try to be inside each day, each process of making a dance chain of movement, a dance phrase. Not to try to say, "Where is this leading me or taking me?"

Once there was a female British critic, dying to reduce dance into words. She was interviewing Merce. I think the dance they were discussing was *Points in Space*, and she had read that he had devised a plan from physics to make the dance. Then she said, "What did you learn from this?" Merce replied, "I didn't learn anything but it was a lovely experience." Dancers use unspoken information. And I think that answers the whole thing in a way. If the light and passion is gone, then it's wrung dry of its feeling and meaning. Where the real information comes from is when there's a delight: a delight in friendship, in food, in looking at the weather, at the day, in sleep. Through all the pain and all the sadness, one can still find a place to giggle and a bit of delight somewhere. That informs tremendously and provides the ability to go on in an aging body. Certainly, Merce has done that in his own life.

I am very aware of growing older and often complaining or maybe apologizing for it in a way. Most people say, "Oh, you look the same as you did years ago," being very kind and very nice, or say, "Oh that is nonsense, you move better than any of us." I don't think about age at all, and, usually, in working with students, they become my friends and co-conspirators in trying to keep this strange thing called dancing alive.

Almost everywhere I have taught they write me lovely notes, and I don't even think of any difference in age, because I sense they want to go somewhere they're not quite sure of, but they know it can be delightful, thrilling, and exciting. And I know for sure that it can be because I was on that same path at their age. And so, the circle continues. I immediately try to engage them, not as students but as fellow artists who are trying their best to do something interesting with their own life. I like to think of not learning something from it but of having a wonderful experience.

When I first went to New York and met George Montgomery and then Frank O'Hara, Paul Taylor, Merce Cunningham, and John Cage, it wasn't so much like analyzing each other, or thinking, "I'm the master and you are the student." It was how you cook the dinner, what the jokes were, what we laughed at. And there were bits of gossip in the talk, or aesthetics, or ideas, but all of it was in pursuit of a bright, witty, delightful life.

I am used to that, actually, on a different level. Being the youngest of ten, in a farm family, we made up our own games, and my mom joined in and played. All of my brothers and sisters played musical instruments and invented games. The cooking became games, making chocolate fudge at night, or churning ice cream when it snowed. So many of those things created a delightful, rich life. And it was during the Depression, so it was not materialistically a rich life, but it was a rich childhood.

Age doesn't really make a difference. It is the process, the universals, the basics that make a good life. And that same experience can apply both to a six-year-old and to a seventy-year-old.

I made the choice to stop performing because of feeling limitations on my technical skill. I think I felt I wasn't dancing. Now, if I didn't have the hip arthritis and my knees and so forth, I understand my body technically and kinaesthetically better, and I can dance better than ever. I love performing. When I danced in other companies, I got excited but not terribly nervous. In my own work, I got far more nervous in a way, and so probably even if I got to a point of stamina and strength, I still had to tend to everything else—teach the piece, coach the dancers, step back and try to look at it and then put myself in it—it was too exhausting and very trying, and it became too much.

In terms of race and dance, our culture is now more accepting of people of color. The women's movement, the gay movement, has freed young people to a certain extent. Of course, all of the prejudices are still there. Perhaps there is no way for a white person to know about African-American heritage. If you grow up black in this country, probably somewhere along the way, you are made to feel different and outside the Pale, and maybe derogatory things are said, and it would be impossible to let go of those things. To deal honestly with who you are, and where you are within your environment, you would almost have no choice when it comes to art or making a dance. That issue would come up almost every time.

Certainly, a lot of African-American choreographers deal politically with inequality, prejudice, put-down, pain, and, in trying to liberate, often look to Africa as an answer or a way to find dignity and depth in one's own roots and one's own forefathers.

For me, I like abstraction when I look at dance. I like a movement narrative, I like to think of my dance as using energy and bound, percussive, released, or lyrical movement, the juxtaposing of all of these things with the basics of space, time, and energy—energy being, of course, how you release movement: bound, percussive, flowing. I use those basics to build an energy narrative.

I don't start off with a narrative in my own mind. I start off with qualities, textures, and often the music gives the basic impulse, although I have used silence and soundscapes. Often I use high energy, because I am trying to propel myself into another place, into a space-time warp I wouldn't be able to get to with regular everyday mundane movement.

Recently, I mentioned to students that supposedly the Big Bang theory is now accepted as how the universe started. Before it started, the whole universe was contained in matter that was subatomic, that was just a tiny, tiny speck, a tiny mite, and out of that came this whole huge universe. I keep trying to think of myself as this tiny mite trying to explode and push with such a force that it propels me into this glorious, strange, marvelous, and mysterious universe. That is what my own process has been, and it is a rich place for me to go.

Energy propels us to a magical place, and you have to be ready. Of course, that is probably the reason we do it because it is during those few seconds that you know exactly who you are. It may happen three seconds out of the year of long hard warm-up, struggle, rehearsal and class, and technical honing of the body. Those few moments of insight then lead you on to do it another year, to see if you can find again those moments of brightness.

What I was trying to say in talking about race, sexual orientation, gender, is that it all takes its own place when you are on this energy narrative. When the body is honed to a place of skill in moving quickly and slowly and all the different in-betweens, I become color blind. Everything for me then takes its right place. And it happens at moments even now in teaching in the classroom.

There is great diversity of the students here at Florida State University, and it is wonderful to see that and to delve into each person's body, where I can see where they are within their shyness or their overtness, their outgoingness. It is delicious and delightful to point out those things to them and to make suggestions about strengthening their own self-image. They all become beautiful creatures, angels to me. Not all the time, some you want to kick. But it's like entering into a universal world, where annoying misgivings and mannerisms melt away, and you simply see a human creature behaving beautifully.

It is great that one sees more unconventional "dance bodies" than one used to see. Maggie Black, a ballet teacher, once said to me, "Dan, I think if people can align their body, center, and then release it to its full length, it will take the size and shape that is right for them. It is your DNA, it is your blueprint of what you inherited, and you grow into that." Emotionally and technically I think that is true for a dancer. If you can find that place of centeredness, trust yourself, and find honesty in everything you do, it doesn't become decorative, hide behind virtuosity, a conventional shape or beauty. You don't have to think, "Well, should I smile now or should I frown?" The face will take the right countenance for the input of metaphysical or physical awareness that is in the person.

I am very much aware of gender issues in dance. Overtly, I am aware of whether it is a duet of a man–woman, or a woman–woman, or a man with a man. I have learned from young students that they don't have hang-ups about "this is a man's step and that is a woman's step." Even wearing dresses: Men wear dresses and so forth, and all of that has gotten very mixed up. I like it, and it has helped me see in a different way. The idea of playing with gender roles has always been in the back of my mind.

Very purposely, I created a love duet for two women. I did another very tender but swift-moving duet with a man and woman, where, at the very end, the woman carefully scooped up the man in her arms and carried him off, obviously reversing the man–woman thing. I first did that piece in Maine, at Bates, and there was a lot of discussion afterwards about androgyny and the roles of men and women and what they can or cannot do. I remember I really enjoyed that.

I did a dance based on some of George's poems. One of them was,

> There is good luck
> and the return of sexual love
> in the image
> of a black and fertile field.

Natalie Gilbert set it to music and sang it, and I had JoAnn Jansen dance it. She just stood in place and did a treading movement. She wore a little gingham dress tucked up in her

Dan Wagoner. Photo © Marc Ray.

panties so her legs could move freely. And she simply tread, with gorgeous sinewy legs, doing very simple movement, which made me cry.

After that concert, I got a letter from someone, who said, "I know you are from New York and obviously are professionals but why did you have to do that distasteful, sexual thing?" It made me sad that she had not had a good time and paid money to see a performance, because I want to please. But, at the same time, I felt it was very sad that we compartmentalize our lives, and that goodness is here and eroticism is over there and the two can never meet up.

The big thing in all the political campaigns is the word "values," but they never say what kind of values, it is just "you don't have values." But what kind of values? What could be more moral than remaining true to your feelings, to what's in your body? This inward journey is not going to take you into the path of the Devil, it's going to liberate you. By connecting the subliminal, the erotic, the Dionysian, with the forebrain, you get a really intelligent, informed creature. And that's what a dancer needs to be. You have to let the beast out and, at the same time, be just as bright and smart as Einstein.

These are backward times for art and dance. The arts cannot flourish because of fear and conservatism, but paradoxically, at the same time, these movements are going forward. Maybe the general populace accepts it more than they realize, even though there's still opposition.

Gay marriage is a big issue. It is said that the pendulum always swings back, but I feel we are swinging so deeply into obesity of both body and mind . . . how can we get back? And can we get back before there's a complete economic collapse of the system? I don't know. It makes me wonder. I wish our culture were more insightful.

The current environment for dance is pretty dry. It's sad. It's not a culture where people are clamoring to buy tickets to see dance, but there's still a lot of activity bubbling underneath. You have a university with over a 100 dance majors. Young people continue to want to dance, so one has to have hope and faith and keep going, to champion good dance, so that whoever sees it will get the idea and be moved or touched by it. I encourage the young by saying, "We need artists,we need dancers. Be here, get focused, get ready, and demand of yourself every moment of time. That hard work will energize and make life richer. It may sound exhausting but it can take you somewhere you've never been before. You've got to trust that you'll find your way economically, culturally, artistically, and aesthetically into your own power and your own art."

But it's like a knife edge, even at my age. After the loss of George and my company and the loft in New York, I've never gotten over it, and I feel like I'm on a knife edge. I'm just as happy to die and drop off one side, and yet, I know that if I can walk the other side there's this *incredible* universe of magic and wonderment. Frank O'Hara, the poet, said he'd thought of suicide, but then he thought *around* the corner something wonderful might happen, and he'd miss it. So, it's that balance of the dark against the light and the way that the sweet and the sour mix. One has to give in to the delights. If you can learn to take the light, every day find something you can smile or feel good about, it helps raise your own pleasure and expectation of what being alive can be. The sadness swirling around at the same time can make one go mad, but dancing helps put one back. It revives the spirit.

Saturday, March 5, 2005

Mel Wong. Photo © Paul Schraub.

Mel Wong (December 2, 1938–July 17, 2003)

Mel Wong was a choreographer/visual artist who was uniquely involved in exploring the relationship between visual arts and dance in the environment. He established an international reputation, first as a performer with the Merce Cunningham Dance Company and, second, as a choreographer, teacher, and performer with the Mel Wong Dance Company. His educational background included undergraduate work at San Francisco State University and graduate work at the University of California at Los Angeles and at Mills College, where he received an MFA in the Visual Arts and the Catherine Morgan Trefethen Fellowship in art. His paintings and sculpture have been exhibited in galleries and museums throughout the USA. His dance background included professional training in ballet and modern dance in California and New York. He received a Ford Foundation Scholarship to Balanchine's School of American Ballet in 1964 and 1965, and toured internationally with the Merce Cunningham Dance Company (1968–1972). He choreographed and performed his own work beginning in 1970 and formed the Mel Wong Dance Company in New York City in 1975. He choreographed over 190 dances. In 1983–4, he became the first Chinese American to receive a Guggenheim Fellowship in choreography.

Concerned with the interaction between dance and the visual arts, Wong combined elements of both in his mixed-media choreographic works. The Mel Wong Dance Company performed in San Francisco at Summerfest at Cowell Theater (1995, 2000, 2001), at ODC (1998, 2001), "Double Vision"at Footworks (April 1990), and at the Alice Tully Hall at Lincoln Center (1987), at the Asia Society, New York City (1985), the Whitney Museum of American Art at Philp Morris, La Mama ETC (1983), the Dance Theater Workshop series, New York City (1976, 1977), and at universities and arts festivals throughout the USA. Wong was Professor of Dance in Theater Arts at the University of California, Santa Cruz from 1989 to 2003. A faculty member at the State University of New York at Purchase (1974–87), Wong also taught at University of Colorado as Co-Director of Dance (1988–9), Guest Artist at Hong Kong Academy for the Performing Arts (1987–8), at Arizona State University, Sarah Lawrence College, the New Performance Gallery in San Francisco, New York University, Cornell University, Colorado Dance Festival and New Performance (July 1989, 1990, 1991, 1992), the Harvard Summer School Dance Center, for three summers at Quebec Été Danse in Canada, and for three summers at the American Dance Festival at Connecticut College.

In 1990 and 2000, he was a nominee for Outstanding Achievement in Choreography and Reconstruction, Dance Bay Area Isadora Duncan Awards (Izzies). His works have been in the repertoires of companies in Hong Kong, Japan, Europe, the USA, and Canada. From 1980 to 1992, he taught special workshops each year at the 92nd Street "Y" in New York City, and he conducted workshops and master classes throughout the world. Wong received grants and fellowships from the John Simon Guggenheim Foundation, the National Endowment for the Arts (NEA; six in choreography, dance company, and inter-arts), the New York State Council on the Arts (NYSCA; visual and dance), Foundation for Contemporary Performing Arts, Inc., the Ford Foundation, and the Cultural Council of Santa Cruz, among others.

From 1989 until his death, Mel Wong toured his solo work, *Growing Up Asian American in the '50s*, in Hong Kong, Boston, Hawaii, Colorado, San Francisco, Oklahoma, Wisconsin, Connecticut, and New York City.

Meteor of Light

Since Mel Wong died in July 2003, before he could be interviewed, Connie Kreemer, wife, dancer, manager, and Associate Director of the Mel Wong Dance Company, has written this chapter for him, trying to use his words wherever possible.

As Talley Beatty, Donald McKayle, and Alvin Ailey have the distinction of being among the first African-American male modern dancers, Mel Wong stands alone as the first Chinese-American male modern dancer. To achieve this, he had to overcome a lot of opposition, beginning with his own father, who thought it was a "waste of time" to dance. Mel thought dancing was heavenly.

Since the last interview in 1979, many miles were traveled. Mel's company picked up momentum during the late 1970s, early 1980s. He expanded the company to about fifteen dancers, seven of whom were Asian American. Mel was receiving numerous NEA fellowships (six choreography, dance company, and inter-arts), as well as funding from NYSCA (visual arts and dance), and a grant from the Foundation for Contemporary Performing Arts, among others.

As Mel read Buddhist and Taoist books, his interest in Chinese culture grew. I recognized early on that his use of rock, water, incense, and candles was tapping into his Asian roots. One day, we went to the Metropolitan Museum and visited the Asian wing, and, after seeing the Chinese house and artwork, Mel expressed even more enthusiasm for delving into his heritage. As Manager of the Mel Wong Dance Company, I suggested that he apply for the Guggenheim Fellowship to be able to explore his Asian roots. To his delight, in 1983, Mel became the first Chinese-American male to receive the Guggenheim Fellowship in Choreography.

Jade (1983) was the first dance Mel created with conscious intent to reveal his heritage. He used jade as a symbol of a protective stone, bringing good fortune and longevity, by creating a piece, with music by Skip LaPlante, whereby the dancers took turns also being musicians by blowing into bottles and humming. With slide projections, sets, and numerous props, which included phosphorescent jade-colored balls, Mel had a cast of thirty-six dancers for a two-week season at La Mama ETC.

The pressure was on. Having danced in it, I was never able to see it, but, as a dancer, my sense was that it was a massive amoeba with a cast of thousands. Harvey Lichtenstein, from the Brooklyn Academy of Music, came to see it, but, unfortunately, with all the attention towards Mel having just received a Guggenheim, he felt pressured, tried too hard, and the result was mixed. My sense was that it was probably his least successful piece.

We took off in the fall of 1983 for Hong Kong. For three months, Mel choreographed for, and I performed with, the Hong Kong Modern Dance Company. Then, in December, we went to China, first by train to Guangzhou, where we were met by private driver and guide (which was required). We visited Shanghai, Beijing, Xian, Guilin, and Guangzhou, then returned to Hong Kong by boat. In 1983, most people in China were still wearing Mao suits, drab grey or navy blue. It was still early for the Western world to enter, and we were viewed as curiosities. Being the gadget man, Mel loved to tell the story about how people would stop and stare at his large wristwatch and the Nikon camera hanging around his neck. They would look as if they'd never seen such things. I often felt like a movie star with my blonde curls. Curious people would gently touch my hair from behind as we were waiting at a crosswalk.

One day while we were in Beijing, we took a bus tour to the Great Wall. It was cold and windy, and as we walked from the bus and approached the Wall, no one was in sight, except a handful of other tourists. Mel and I walked on the Wall alone for quite some time, until realizing the solitude and opportunity, I said, "Mel, dance on the Wall and I'll take pictures." From that moment, he always wanted to do another site-specific piece on the Great Wall. The tragedy is, he never did.

When we returned to China four years later, in 1987, capitalism had begun. Fashion was thriving, colors prevailed, and technology had entered. Not a second look did we command with our cameras, and, by 1990, when we returned yet again, more people seemed to have cell phones there than in New York!

Mel was deeply moved by being in Asia. He said it was the first time he'd been in a country where he was in the majority race, where people looked like him. To see people eating the same "funny foods" he had grown up enjoying, using chopsticks, kowtowing in acknowledgment to each other as they passed in public, decorative colors, with jade and 24-carat gold embellishing temples and restaurants, ducks hanging in shop windows, and Chinese art everywhere—these things legitimized Mel's sensibilities from childhood, and he felt at home. After that, Mel's affinity with being Chinese, something his family had greatly repressed during his childhood, only continued to increase. He became more conscious and proud of the beauty within Chinese culture, and both his visual art and dance reflected that awareness.

In terms of funding, Mel fell in between the cracks in the 1980s, because he was a visual artist in his own right, who wanted to create his own sets. Both the NYSCA and NEA were funding collaborations between artists. That meant in order to get grants, Mel had to give up doing his own visual art for his performances and find other artists to work with. In 1984, he received a grant from the NYSCA to collaborate with light sculptor Cathy Billian. Mel choreographed *Future Antiquities*, which was performed at the Whitney Museum at Philip Morris. Although it was a successful collaboration, Mel always preferred creating the visuals alone and found it discouraging and discriminatory that he couldn't be recognized as both choreographer and visual artist. Nevertheless, he continued to make drawings as visual

Mel Wong rehearsing on the roof in Hong Kong (October 1983). Photo © Connie Kreemer.

correlations to his dances and usually displayed them in theater lobbies simultaneously with the performances.

His next project was a dance entitled *Buddha Meets Einstein at the Great Wall*, using music by Philip Glass, set by architect Michael Janne, and perhaps the first live computer video art to be presented onstage by artist Ron Rocco. It was performed at the Asia Society in New York City with Mel's drawings in the Clifford Ross Art Gallery near the theater. As always, Mel researched his theme by reading many books about Buddhism, Taoism, combined with readings from Einstein. For the press release, quotes were entered from these sources, showing the relationship and similarities of many of the Chinese Buddhist or Taoist ideas to those of Einstein's.

Imagine my astonishment, when, during intermission, I was summoned by a major dance critic, who asked, "What is Zen Buddhism anyway? I don't know anything about it." The critic apparently decided that without any knowledge of Buddhism (had she bothered to read the press release?) the dance should not be reviewed, nor did one ever appear in the paper. For a dance company trying to get funding, that was tantamount to the performance never happening. It effectively killed the company.

The other fatal blow was that his funding from the NYSCA had been erratic. Being the manager, I saw that many minorities were beginning to get grants through a program called Special Arts Services and decided that, since Mel was a minority, he should apply. The NYSCA told me that Mel didn't qualify. When I asked why, they said he "didn't have enough Chinese dancers in his company" (seven out of fifteen dancers) and he "wasn't doing Chinese dance." When I asked why they didn't make African Americans do African dance, there was no reply. Someone later told me that we probably had a lawsuit for discrimination in our hands, but neither one of us thought in those terms. Infuriated and discouraged, we left the city. A year later, when we returned, that grant category had been eliminated.

The other reason we left New York was because when Mel asked me to marry him, I told him there were two things I wanted: one was to leave New York for cleaner air, and the other was that I wanted children. I told him I was very clear about wanting those two things, and unless he wanted them too, we shouldn't marry. He agreed that both of my desires were also his. We were married in 1984, and I set out finding possibilities for us outside of New York.

In 1985, Mel accepted a guest artist position at Arizona State University, so the two of us went off to teach in Tempe for the academic year. For a few weeks, his company came out to rehearse in the desert near the Superstition Mountains. Mel was enthralled by both the magic of the desert, the air, sky, vegetation, and the Native American culture that permeated the area. He also was amused that even the Native Americans thought he was a "brother."

As a reflection of our desert experience, after returning to New York in May of 1986, Mel created a beautiful, serene piece called *Blue Mesa*, which was filmed in the Petrified Forest National Park by documentary videographer Ted Timreck. The video of the environmental dance was interspersed with dancing on stage to "the haunting score for native-sounding pipes and flutes composed by Rob Kaplan." Jennifer Dunning wrote that it "conjures up wind and ghostly chants" (*New York Times*, March 3, 1987), while Deborah Jowitt said it "evokes a high, windy desert landscape and the integrity of vanished rites" (*Village Voice*, March 24, 1987).

In 1987–8, Mel and I were Guest Artists at the Hong Kong Academy for Performing Arts. Mel taught modern dance and choreography to the Chinese students and choreographed for their performances. He viewed teaching in Hong Kong as another way to connect to his

Chinese heritage and was concerned about sharing ideas about the creative process with the Chinese students. Steadfast in the belief that Chinese dancers should find their own creativity and technique, Mel encouraged them to find their own mode of expression rather than copy Western ideas. It bothered him that much of modern dance in Asia was regurgitating Graham technique. In a 1988 interview with Daryl Ries, published in *Dance Magazine* (December 1988), Mel said, "The East is going through a Western phase [. . .] I see a lot of imitation and it scares me [To Wong, . . . the nurturing of individuality is the key to the future of the artist and to the future of dance in Asia]."

Ries wrote,

> there is a tendency, according to Wong, to be caught up in a "workaholic mentality" as compensation for creativity. "Without a grounding in their own cultural heritage, they may not trust their inner selves, nor understand expression beyond imitation," he says. He continued, "They (Chinese students) want the new technique, but not yet to think for themselves [sic]. They expect discipline, but do not yet respond to freedom of expression [. . .] Dancers should develop their own style and use their heritage to encompass the concepts of dance. [. . .] With this in mind, Hong Kong's dance scene has a world of possibilities.

From Hong Kong, we moved to Boulder, Col., where we were Co-Directors of Dance at the University of Colorado at Boulder from 1988 to 1989. In the summer of 1989, we left Boulder for Santa Cruz, Calif., where Mel was brought in as a full professor and the Director of Dance at University of California, Santa Cruz until his death in 2003. While in Santa Cruz, he reestablished the Mel Wong Dance Company, with six or seven dancers, along with solos performed by Silvia Martins.

Silvia had danced with Molissa Fenley, José Limón, and Mark Morris. He created eleven dances for Silvia. To choreograph again for such an accomplished dancer both nourished and inspired his creativity. It helped him hold on in the desert of dance climate Santa Cruz offered. *Bolero* (1994) was one of his very best dances. About *Bolero*, Tobi Tobias wrote of Silvia's DTW [Dance Theater Workshop] 1996 performance:

> If I told you I saw a marvelous dance to Ravel's Bolero, would you believe me? . . . Wong makes the score new by ditching the easy-orgasm scenario and giving us a portrait of a complex, fascinating, contemporary woman—fierce, sensuous, vulnerable in her daring—who is afraid of something unknown out there in the dark . . . Wong substitutes flowing but short phrases from both classical and modern dance, intercut with vivid freeze-frames of generic Spanish-dance moves. He deploys his mix in a jagged, start/stop rhythm that is unpredictable and arresting. Instead of lulling or narcotizing you into stupefaction, he puts you on the alert.

In 1989, Mel began touring solo works entitled *Growing Up Asian American in the '50s*. Initially commissioned for the Chinese Hawaii Bicentennial Celebration, Mel choreographed *Childhood Secrets*, which he performed with text and yoyo. Mel recounted stories of discrimination during his childhood as one of the first Chinese-American families to move into an all-white neighborhood in Oakland, California. This was his way of humorously presenting painful stories while enthralling the audience with his amazing champion yoyo feats.

Mel Wong with yoyo (1992). Photo © Kevin Bubriski.

Childhood Secrets was the first of a series of five solos about his Asian-American experiences. In 1995, he choreographed a solo for me, entitled *Never Say Never*, where I danced and spoke about living in Hong Kong and taking Chinese herbs and acupuncture to help us get pregnant. The Chinese medicine helped, and we were blessed with three daughters, Anika, in 1989, and, three years later, identical twins, Kira and Suzanna.

Li Chiao-Ping commissioned a solo, *Judgment*, in 1997, and Mel had her dance and talk about other childhood experiences of prejudice and discrimination. About that solo, Mel said in the documentary Men's Project video *six solos: Li Chiao-Ping Dances* (1999) by Douglas Rosenberg:

> In many ways, I'm glad I did it. Because I still think there's a lot of discrimination and prejudice going on in the world. And there's a rise in discrimination and hate crimes [. . .] maybe this solo will help people in understanding what minorities went through [. . .] in the United States, or other parts of the world. 'Cause it's an experience that I think is really hard on the individual going through it.

These solos were performed in Hong Kong, Boston, Hawaii, Colorado, San Francisco, Oklahoma, Wisconsin, Connecticut, and New York.

Mel had a lot to say about racism, and his solos were a way of releasing anger and letting people know, in his own humorous, educational way, how racism had wounded him as a child and how he continued to feel its effects. I found several things he had written about the subject and offer them here in his words:

> I was told to keep my silence but after fifty years, I must speak out! The Naturalization Act of 1790 stated that citizenship was reserved only for whites. That law remained in effect until 1952. The Chinese Exclusion Act of 1882 was directed at the Chinese on a racial basis. The Chinese were excluded from entering the USA. Other racial groups such as Italians and Polish came over by the thousands. This Act was not repealed until 1943. The National Origin Act of 1924 prevented Japanese and other Asians from entering the USA. It also prohibited Asian wives of US immigrants and citizens from migrating to the US to join their husbands. The Cable Act of 1922 stated that an American woman who married an alien, eligible for citizenship would lose her citizenship. During World War II many Chinese men volunteered for the army or were drafted. The irony was that most of these men were not even citizens of the USA. The Japanese were interred during World War II. The irony is that ⅔ of the Japanese were American born. We were also at war with the Germans and Italians, but American-born Germans or Italians were not interred.

Participating in a Society of Dance History Scholars panel entitled "What is American Dance?," February 1992, Mel said the following:

> Before I start, I would like to read to you a review from a well-respected critic in New York City: "I saw two ambitious works in one week, Donald McKayle's *Blood Memories*, and Mel Wong's *Glass*. The dances are nothing alike, but they roused in me a similar feeling of exhaustion, vexation, puzzlement (What's going on here? What's going wrong here?)."

I thought it was very auspicious to find this review in light of today's panel. My choreography has been misunderstood from the very beginning of my career in making dances in New York City in the early 1970s. The critics and panelists from New York State Council on the Arts and the National Endowment for the Arts had problems in viewing my work. I remember a remark from a panelist who said I was "putting them on." I was very upset and mad. I wondered how a panelist or critic could make a statement like this. I worked all year long, saved my money to produce my dance concerts, and would spend over $10,000 on a concert, which would be over in three or four nights. I would be very dishonest with myself and the public if I was "putting someone on." I was very bitter, but I continued to make dances despite the criticism. I had support from the dance community, my concerts were always sold out, and besides, I loved to make dances.

I don't want you to think that I never received support from critics or panelists, because I did, and I am very grateful. The review brought back memories of my New York years and of growing up Chinese in California.

I began to study ballet when I was fifteen or sixteen years old and never felt completely accepted in those early years. The time was in the middle 1950s when one rarely saw a minority in a ballet company. Why? Was it because there were no Asians or blacks around or was it because the ballet world couldn't accept physical types not of European ancestry? I remember I was told I could study ballet but I couldn't join a ballet company—maybe I could be the Chinese dancer in *The Nutcracker*. I was crushed because I wanted to be a prince. It hurt my feelings but I was young and a teenager, full of energy and I was rebellious. I also remember what my grandmother told me, "Work hard, be good at something and people will respect you." So I continued to dance and thought, "The Hell with what people say." This experience, I believe, was the beginning for me to experience, time and time again, negative comments from people about what I do or why I am doing it. I ask myself, "Is it because I am Chinese and people don't understand our ways?"

What is American dance? The first thing that comes to my mind is that dance in America is as varied as the people who live here. In social, folk, or show dancing, the dance is what it is, and usually there are no conflicts about what it means. When dance is considered an art form, especially in modern dance, sometimes conflict arises. What does it mean? Do the rituals mean anything? Why are they dancing on trays of water two or three inches deep? Why are there goldfish in the buckets? There are too many things going on that don't mean anything.

It is the nature of the arts to expose people to new knowledge and a greater under-standing of life. Sometimes people have a difficult time understanding the meaning of art, when a personal point of view is expressed, when there are cultural differences or when artists seek the new ideas and relationships.

I work intuitively so whatever is stored in my subconscious mind comes out in my dances or in my paintings. I was not aware that my dances were greatly influenced by Asian thinking until someone pointed it out to me. She said, "You're very Chinese in your work." All of a sudden everything seemed clear. Many of the critics and panelists were so Western-oriented that they had no clue of the symbolism or rituals I use frequently in my pieces.

My interest in ritual and symbolism can be traced back to when I was growing up, especially between the ages of one to five years old. At that time we lived in an all-Chinese neighborhood. I remember my grandmother would clean house before Chinese New Year and told us that cleaning house on New Year's Day would bring hardship and bad luck to the family. We also performed rituals of offering sweet tea to the elders and in return would receive lucky money or *lee shee* in a small red envelope. Long-life noodles were always served on birthdays. My grandmother would say, "Don't cut the noodles, it will shorten your life." When visiting relatives or friends, we would always bring oranges as gifts or to show respect. Oranges symbolize immortality and good fortune. My family would talk about rearranging the furniture to be in harmony with the Earth's energy (feng-shui). When we visited Chinatown, I would see the Chinese performing their rituals in temples. I would see incense burning and offerings of food for the gods in a red altar in restaurants and other establishments [. . .].

Because I am Asian and express my Asianness, many times I feel I am not understood or taken seriously. This is reflected in the funding as well as the support for [*sic*] the press. I recognize that as an artist, I can't always do good work. But sometimes I have wondered if the critics and panelists have given me a bad review because of the craft of choreography or because of misunderstanding of my Asian sensibility. To cite some examples:

"Clearly *Telegram* was trying to deliver a message. But like the messages in Mr. Wong's other dances, it seemed to be in a secret code."

"But under any conditions, I would have found Wong's piece opaque."

"The dance is so coyly and consciously designed that it's almost impossible to watch. There's too much to look at and listen to, too much perfect dancing without logical structure, too many ideas and not enough magic."

"Your work is not Chinese enough" (NYSCA).

I was very bitter and hurt but as the years go by I am no longer bitter.

We moved to Boulder as Co-Directors of Dance at the University of Colorado at Boulder in 1988. Then in 1989 we moved to Santa Cruz, where Mel was brought in as a tenured Professor of Dance. Having been denied tenure at SUNY Purchase (for political reasons too lengthy to go into), Mel was encouraged when he was brought in as a full professor at University of California Santa Cruz. Unfortunately, just when we arrived, drastic budget cuts began, and Mel soon found himself fighting to save the dance department. He worked there for thirteen years until his death. One year later, the Theater Arts Department did away with modern dance.

For Mel, so much of life revolved around racism. He felt that Asians were the silent minority—people who worked hard, accomplished a lot, but were never recognized. And Mel continued to encounter racism. I remember around 1990, when Mel was being considered for an endowed chair at University of Wisconsin, Madison and was flown in to see the school. As he was walking by some fraternities, some boys surrounded him on the sidewalk and touched their eyes, pulling the skin tight as they chanted, "Ching-chong Chinaman." Mel returned to Santa Cruz saying, "Over my dead body will we ever go there and subject our mixed-race children to their racism."

How did Mel's work change over twenty-five years? I watched his movement soften as it evolved. He increasingly used more breath and flow, more curvilinear movement. Appreciating the influence of capoeira, Mel excitedly tapped into his gymnastic champion roots and experimented with using the floor, going upside-down, doing one-handed handstands and flips, going more and more off axis. As time progressed, his movement got farther and farther away from the linear Cunningham technique he had been often accused of regurgitating. When critics referred to him as "Mercist," he wondered if they bothered to look at his dances.

His choreography changed too. Disliking popular trends, he always went against them. During the height of Sally Banes' postmodern definition of movement for movement's sake, Mel was choreographing movement with abstract-expressionist meaning, rich with metaphor, ritual, and symbolism. In the early 1980s he was an early initiator of the use of props and text, but as that became more the rage, Mel switched back to pure movement.

One constant that never changed was the spirituality projected through Mel's choreography. "With all my pieces, I try to put this eastern thought of otherworldly things. Spiritualism is in all my pieces [. . .] You'll see that these so-called 'mystical' or 'meta-physical' things come out" (*Eye on Dance*, October 1984).

Creating a nonlinear dreamlike state, Mel would use different themes—theatrical, humorous, political, beautiful—combined with highly technical, gestural, quirky, languorous, or alacritous movements. Music choices varied from works composed specifically for his dances (Rob Kaplan composed over thirty pieces, and Skip La Plante was another valued composer) to prearranged music by Philip Glass, Henryk Gorecki, Snittke, Chopin, Frank Sinatra, Laurie Anderson, or the Beach Boys. His way of putting together gesture and dance technique created a meaningful metaphor, imagery that startled the eye, causing the viewer to reflect, using personal imagination.

In 1990, Mel was nominated for an Isadora Duncan Award for Outstanding Achievement in Choreography, and, again, in 2000, he was nominated for another Izzie for Outstanding Achievement in Revival/Restaging/Reconstruction.

About the topic of gender, I was able to find the following statement:

> I take gender into consideration when I choreograph. A lot of times [. . .] in my pieces, male or female could do the same role [. . .] and it wouldn't change it. But then sometimes I have specific . . . you know . . . roles, in my choreography pieces, that are just for women, or just for male. I mean, there is a difference, and yet there is no difference [. . .] It just depends on what I'm trying to express in the piece. I mean, I think the same is true, if you have a heavy dancer, or a tall, thin dancer, or a short dancer—I mean, I think you have to consider all of these elements as your palette. You dance before you go to war. You dance before you get married. You dance, you know, at a funeral. And so dance really is a powerful form, and I still don't quite understand why it's not as respected as other art forms. It's the juxtapositioning of everything in the world, that makes the world go.
>
> (Men's Project Documentary, Douglas Rosenberg)

Mel's work had an asexuality to it, even though it could be extremely sensual. Because he was so concerned with "otherworldliness," he thought of his dances as beyond gender, unless, of course, he wanted to make a statement about a gender role (i.e. women being coy and sexual, men being macho and strong). He often used these stereotyped roles to make an ironic, humorous, or political point. His dances were not about male–female love. They were expressing a love of humanity beyond gender, a love of spirit.

In terms of the question of age, Mel definitely struggled with growing older. Getting older and dancing didn't seem to bother him. He thrived on dancing and worked out religiously every day. He created solos for himself and kept his vitality alive through movement but would comment about how his skin was not as resilient as it once was. What worried him the most was thinking about his age in relation to providing for his three young daughters.

The following statement is taken from what was probably the last videoed interview he gave:

> Yeah, there's a lot of symbolism, like there's a lot of people doing this [puts his palms together], which could represent spirituality, it could represent different religions, different spiritual thought, and the music is quite driving, you know? And it could be that they're doing something they're not supposed to be really doing. Trying to find another meaning in life, trying to find another energy in the universe, trying to relate, you know, bringing nature, people . . . just, the *unknown*—that we want to know. Like, what happens when you die? Or what happens when you go to bed at night? What happens when you listen to, or see something—a powerful art form, that inspires you for a month, two months, the rest of your life? Where are these energies coming from?
>
> (*Backstage Pass*)

Mel found out about these great mysteries on the morning of July 17, 2003 when he went swimming, had a heart attack and collapsed. Now, he is dancing in the cosmos.

October 30, 2005

Jawole Zollar. Photo © Antoine Tempé.

Jawole Zollar

Jawole Willa Jo Zollar (Founder and Artistic Director, Urban Bush Women) was born and raised in Kansas City, mo. She trained with Joseph Stevenson, a student of the legendary Katherine Dunham, and received a BA in dance from the University of Missouri at Kansas City and an MFA in dance from Florida State University. In 1980, she moved to New York City to study with Dianne McIntyre at Sounds in Motion. She founded Urban Bush Women (UBW) in 1984. In addition to thirty-two works for UBW, Jawole has created choreography for Alvin Ailey American Dance Theater, Ballet Arizona, Philadanco, University of Maryland, University of Florida, Dayton Contemporary Dance Company, and others. Her many positions as a teacher and speaker include Worlds of Thought Resident Scholar at Mankato State University (1993–4), Regents Lecturer in the Departments of Dance and World Arts and Culture at the University of California at Los Angeles (1995–6), Visiting Artist at Ohio State University (1996), and the Abramowitz Memorial Lecturer at Massachusetts Institute of Technology (1998). She was named Alumna of the Year by University of Missouri (1993) and Florida State University (1997), and awarded an Honorary Doctorate from Columbia College, Chicago (2002). Most recently, Zollar was recognized with a 2006 New York Dance and Performance Award, a Bessie, for her choreography of the Pearl Primus-inspired dance, *Walking with Pearl ... Southern Diaries*. Zollar has received the Martin Luther King Distinguished Service Award from Florida State University, where she holds a tenured position as the Nancy Smith Fichter Professor in the Department of Dance. Zollar directs the annual Urban Bush Women Summer Institute, an intensive training program in dance and community engagement for artists with leadership potential interested in developing a community focus in their art-making.

Dancing Truth

When I started the company in 1984, I had previously been on scholarship at Dianne McIntyre's Sound in Motion, and she had provided an opportunity for me to choreograph and do studio showings. Out of that experience, I started working with a group of people.

When I decided to form the company, one of the things I realized is that men in dance tend to go to the next better paying gig. I had a group of seven women working with me who were loyal, committed, and focused on the work, so I thought, "Well why not an all-women's company?" I didn't set out to make an all-women's company, but when I found that that was what was happening, I thought, "I'll go with it."

We were working together as people who felt like we didn't fit into the contemporary dance scene. We didn't fit into the Ailey scene; we didn't fit into the postmodern dance scene; we were something else. I was interested in performance, narrative, and emotional quality, and those were things, at that time, the postmodernists were against. They were involved with: "what you see is what you get" and "movement for movement's sake." I was interested in stories, and, at the same time, I was interested in process.

I had taken a workshop with Kei Takei, which had a profound impact on me. Her work told stories, which were beautifully crafted through a sense of ritual and repetition, and I was interested in exploring natural movement. Besides Dianne McIntyre and Kei Takei as women artists who really spoke to what I was thinking about, seeing how Blondell Cummings' work used gesture and then seeing Meredith Monk's and Liz Lerman's work impacted me. Their work helped me make those connections about how I could tell stories in a different kind of way, without the big, grand, sweeping movements but with a more human connection. I was kind of in this "other" place, and there really wasn't a whole lot of support in the dance world, so I found a lot of my support through the women's community and in the theater world.

I first started dancing in Kansas City, mo. at the age of six or seven, in a community dance studio with a man named Joseph Stevenson, who had been a student of Katherine Dunham's. One of the things I now realize was really very powerful about that experience was that he was teaching us what he called "Afro-Cuban dance." I had no context for what that meant. All I knew was that we had drums, and live music, and it was not a technique-based experience in terms of dancing. It was about dancing from the inside out—finding that quality inside yourself and then developing that outward.

I danced with him, and my sister and I performed in something called "floor shows" which were like reviews that were done in black social clubs for events. There would be a comic MC, a stripper, an exotic dancer, a "Flash Act," like the Nicholas Brothers, and we would be the "kiddy" act. So, I was always grounded in the idea that, ultimately, you're entertaining, and that doesn't have to be a bad thing. You want people engaged—it's about engaging people, no matter how far outside their comfort zone you might take an idea. As an entertainer, the idea is that you are still working with an exchange of energy of giving and receiving.

Then I got my undergraduate degree in dance from the University of Missouri, Kansas City, and that was my first experience with both contemporary dance, or what was then called "modern dance," and ballet. After that, I got my graduate degree from the Florida State University Department of Dance, where I'm now back teaching. That was just deepening the training. I didn't start training really, in terms of modern dance and ballet, until I was about twenty, or twenty-one years old, which by many people's impression is a late start. What I believe I got from my first training was a profound sense of rhythm, a profound sense of musicality, listening, and tuning in to the music, and understanding the impulse from where dance comes. I find those things are far harder to teach than technique, so I look at my early training as a very special technique, and one that has enabled me to conceive the idea of UBW.

When I first started my company in 1984, the reason Kei Takei and Blondell Cummings were such profound influences was that I wanted to throw away what I had studied in terms of modern dance, which had been Graham, Cunningham, and Limón, and they had achieved that. I felt like those techniques weren't my voice, and I needed to find my own voice. That was something I saw so clearly in Dianne McIntyre's work, with how she was working with jazz music. In wanting to do that, and also in honoring my other interest, which was theater, I decided to strip away all kind of references to modern technique. So I said, "No, don't point your feet, don't turn out your legs, don't pull up." Actually, for vocal production, if you do that it cuts off your voice as well as your emotional accessibility, so I really threw away a lot of things that did not speak to my voice.

I had studied the Graham, Cunningham, Limón, and Holm techniques at that time, and it was when I saw Twyla Tharp for the first time (I took a summer workshop with her) that I started to realize my voice could be idiosyncratic; it could speak to me as an individual and my experiences, as opposed to the kind of classical modern dance that had been developed. We were just at the precipice of understanding that—what I call becoming more like jazz music. In jazz music there is a distinctive individual voice. Sonny Rollins does not sound like John Coltrane, though they might be influenced. Miles Davis is another, and they each had a very particular point of view. Similarly, I wanted to find and develop what spoke to my experience, growing up in segregation in Kansas City in an all-African-American community. I wanted to find a voice that spoke to those experiences as well as to that of being a woman.

In the beginning, I needed to throw away a certain kind of form. What's evolved in the past twenty years is that now I can let myself be influenced by all of my experiences, including my modern or contemporary dance, and my ballet. I can bring all of those experiences back into the pot, because my voice is strong enough to include those influences. Sometimes in my work, when I was trying to bring those influences back in, perhaps it wasn't gelled or wasn't always clear, but now I'm at a point where I know how to do that.

Now it's about being able to continue to do my work, and the more I produce, the more I learn. My dancers have always been very strongly trained. With the early group I wanted to untrain them to find a particular point of view because the way I was thinking was so unique at that time. What's different now is that I have dancers coming to me, who know about UBW, who know about the vision, who've taken workshops with me, who already are coming with a point of view that's very similar to mine. Now I don't have to break down so many assumptions about what dance is, or vulnerability and strength in the body. They're coming in with that, and it's very exciting.

At the same time, what they're not coming with as much, or what I really seek to find in that dancer is one who is connected to what I would call an "authentic sense of history." One who has connected that in movement, not just in her head, but who has studied certain forms of dance, like the ring shout, or either has had those experiences in church where they can access that, so it's not an indication of the idea, but it comes from some real experience, whether it's observing her grandmother or aunt or coming from a rural background. Those are the things that really lead me to look for very unique individuals.

What major events in my life or in the world have affected my art? I don't know if I can really answer in terms of major events affecting my work. Certainly, with a work like *Shelter*, when I moved to New York and saw the amazing amount of homeless people living on the street, it wasn't an "event" per se, but it was certainly different from my previous experiences coming from Tallahassee. That had a profound effect on me. I thought, "Wow, this is really something. As a society, we talk about who we are, and those people who are anti-choice talk about wanting to protect the most vulnerable in society, but I sure don't see a rallying cry about the homeless, who are extremely vulnerable."

So, I'm not so sure if it's events as much as an ongoing point of view about the world that continues to develop for me. Seeing something like Katrina, where the most vulnerable in society are before our eyes in a way that we can't deny is a real problem, and it's even gotten worse for those people. I know the Katrina–New Orleans situation has deeply affected me. And how that will come out, how that is coming out, I'm not sure, but I am concerned that we can go down a bad path in desensitizing ourselves to the human condition, particularly that which is living right with us and abroad.

Growing up during segregation and growing up with that history as so much a part of my youth, one of the things I'm so aware of is how difficult it was for my mother, father, and grandparents. Due to that, I'm interested in how people find the courage, the strength, the spiritual connection to move forward through their condition. I'm ultimately interested in the transformation. The suffering is part of living on this planet, but the people with strength, who are able to figure something out about that, is what interests me. I don't mean that the ones who survive are the strong ones, but I'm interested in the ones who protest, the ones who say, "No, I'm not going to take this and I'm going to help this person who doesn't have the internal strength to make that stance."

I'm interested in that as well as in how community comes together. I saw that in my own childhood. I grew up at that time where I really did still live in a community, where I ran around the streets and my parents didn't know where I was, but within the community, the neighbors knew and everybody was connected, so they didn't have to know where I was. I'm sorry for children who don't have that sense of freedom.

Community is an important part of our training. To connect as an ensemble is one of the reasons I was attracted to the powerful idea of ensemble-theater because it develops a community that creates together. Running and having a company is hard. I'm concerned that many people are saying it's an outdated model. Their idea is just to work project to project, and they think that's a better model. It might be for some people, but I think the cohesive group supporting the work as well as a sense of familiarity is lost. It's important to grow together, while at the same time to become willing to challenge one another to step out of that familiarity.

In terms of the question of race, I grew up in segregation, so I have a very particular point of view about my experiences. For me, one of the joys of growing up in an all-African-American community was that the culture was really dense. Everything came out of a very strong African-American perspective. Drill teams to majorettes, to almost everything was an incubator for creativity. That was not intended as a good by-product of segregation, but it was something that I felt very strongly. Within the African-American community, everything was contained in the community, I had role models all across the board of what African-American people could do. My father was in real estate. There were just a few stores that were white-owned, but my schoolteachers were all African-American, the lawyers, the doctors, everyone who worked in the hospital, all of those things. Through seeing and experiencing this, I had a really powerful sense of the possibility of achieving.

Race is a difficult subject for this country to tackle, and it will probably continue to be until we come to terms with it. How and why was the construct of race created, and what is

Jawole Zollar's company. Photo © Jennifer W. Lester.

the relationship of slavery to the present day? We have not come to terms with that. Interestingly enough, they're starting to look at that in Europe. I was in Senegal to work on a project there, in collaboration with a woman, Germaine Acogny, who founded a school called Mudras Afrique with Maurice Béjart. It was one of the first contemporary dance schools in western Africa, and her interest is in contemporary African dance. When we were there, she took us to Gorée, which is where the slave dungeons are, and what struck me, besides going in that dungeon, was how many white French tourists there were. There were also a lot of other African tourists.

Germaine said, "Well, Europe is really starting to look at its role in slavery, to come to terms with it. People want to understand what happened and what their historical role was." Other African countries are also now starting to say, "What was slavery? What was our part? What did we do—what did we lose?" And so, being there in the center of that experience where it's not an abstraction, because it's real, and it's there, and you see the chains, and you see this place of horrible human suffering, made me think about it differently.

To say that race has never been a problem in modern dance, I would certainly beg to differ. Dance can't exist outside of society. We can't exist outside of the larger society. We are part of that, and we are subject to all of the same issues that are in the larger society. Racism is white skin privilege, and you can't not have your privilege. You can choose not to act on it. You can choose not to be aware of it, but you can't not have it. It is just there. That's just part of the picture.

In the recent *Ballets Russes* film, there was one black dancer within the US company. They had to send her back home because the Klan was threatening to do something to the theater. I had no idea there was a black dancer in the Ballets Russes. I thought, "Wow, that's a really powerful untold story." So, I think racism in dance has always been there. It's been there in terms of the funding. I think it's been there in terms of how people have felt about Mr. Ailey's work, whether or not it was valid because it has an entertainment part to it. He was not part of the postmodern scene, so there's definitely a huge aesthetic difference.

I could just imagine, if there was a huge power shift, so that the people I grew up with in my neighborhood were the ones in power. I could imagine them at a funding or a presenter meeting saying, "Well, I just don't get the Cunningham Company. There's no movement of the hips, the upper body is stiff, and the dancers don't seem to be able to relate to the music, the aesthetic just seems to be outdated." It could be switched like that. Absolutely it's about power: losing power and who protects that power. If you choose to be unconscious about it, then you do the things that you've done all the time without questioning, "Why am I doing this? Why am I funding this, or why am I presenting this?" And when that power gets challenged, because it rarely concedes itself, it's usually because there's been some challenge that makes people wake up and say, "Okay, I've got to deal with this."

Some people resist and fight it to the death, and other people are saying, "This is really a good thing. I need to look at this. I do need to figure out how to bring in ideas that are different from what I'm thinking." But it's certainly been there in modern dance, and I think that if you were to talk to people like Ailey, even Carmen De Lavallade, you'd learn that they dealt with racism all along.

Carmen De Lavallade has had a different kind of experience because she's had a different kind of privilege based on how she looks and how she's built. There are degrees of racism, degrees of acceptance within the construct. Look at the difference between Pearl Primus and Katherine Dunham. Primus wasn't glamorous. She had dark skin and a short, thick body.

She wasn't glamorous and light-skinned like Dunham. Those racist criteria are still definitely with us.

How have my ideas changed about the body in relation to dance? I don't think they have changed very much. When I started, I was interested in different body types and different ways of moving, and I was very influenced by jazz. The thing I love about jazz is that you have an ensemble of musicians playing together, but each one has their individuality, and, at the same time, they have their commitment to the group. It's not like a ballet kind of unison when you hear people sing together and everything is exactly the same. Within how I work and within jazz, they may all be doing the same step together, but it's more like dances from the African continent, where you see the individuality inside the unity, and that interests me much more. The body types—short, tall, larger, skinny—don't matter. They have never really mattered to me, but I think it's mattered to other people who have seen the work. Sometimes it was disturbing to people, and sometimes it still is disturbing to people. The aesthetic of the "thin is in" is still out in the dance world in full force.

For me, the dancer has to be healthy, and I use the word "authentic," in her body. If someone who's got my kind of bone structure weighs 150 pounds, then they're probably overweight for their structure, and that's more of a health issue that needs to be addressed, rather than an aesthetic issue for me. How are they taking care of themselves and their body? There was one dancer who was in my company who was very petite, but I thought she must come from Samoan stock, because she's got thick legs and thighs, and if she were to diet to get her legs thin, it would be doing herself a disservice because that's her build, and that's her authentic build. She's always going to be thick through her thighs and her calves. She has to honor that and be true to that and find beauty in it. So, I just want them to be in their bodies authentically.

Often people have thought my company was lesbian or that it was our predominant identity. In an audition I don't ask, "Are you gay? Are you straight? Bisexual?" I mean, those aren't things that I ask or care about, but it's been an assumption about the company. I'm not interested in people dissolving that care about their community. I'm interested in them opening up that care to a larger community because the truth is, when AIDS was really ravaging the dance world, had those presenters not been brave and taken a stand and presented pieces like *Still/Here*, there would have been less impact. It was a brave stance, so I absolutely applaud and support that. It can open up.

We have a program called "Project Next Generation," where we commission an emerging female choreographer to set a work on our bush women. We've created a program called "Quantum Leap," which is an apprentice program, but it's also around choreography, and it's not closed to men, it's for whoever comes to the audition. We never say that we're looking for women to audition, We also have a program, again, I think it's all girls, but we didn't set it up to be all girls. We're working in a public-housing place. My stance is, let me do all I can to get women's voices out there. Let me do all I can to support young, emerging choreographers. Rather than complaining about it, let me try to get the playing field a little more level by what I can do. I can't go out and change the whole dance world, but I can have an impact in this corner that will hopefully ripple out. And I think that's what we can do.

Is there still a gender-based feeling across the USA that it's not masculine to dance? Absolutely. When you go to Europe, or other countries, you don't see that. It's a perception here. Certainly, every man in dance is not gay, but it is certainly a perception just in the way that there's a perception that everybody from our company is lesbian. It's a perception, and

I think it's the perception that guides people's actions. There have been periods like when Edward Vilella and Baryshnikov danced, which created a perception that dance could be virile, but overall, until that perception changes, people will continue to believe it's a gay occupation.

Certainly, in the hip-hop scene, it is not the case at all. In fact, Rennie Harris said something really profound. He said, "Every hip-hop dancer is a choreographer because he creates his own style," and I think, as a field, we have inadequately mined that potential. Within hip-hop exists a world of potential choreographers, coming not necessarily into contemporary dance, not suddenly wanting to point their feet and straighten their legs, but coming out of what Rennie started. Let it continue to develop and grow. I wanted to do a choreographic lab for hip-hop dancers, by giving them ideas to challenge ways of thinking, so everything is not in unison in terms of the choreographers but using the forms they know. That's where the men are, a whole bunch of men.

Has the geographical environment changed so that New York City is no longer the center of the dance world? That's the big debate. I don't know enough about the world of dance in other places to make that statement. I think I know enough about dance in the USA to discuss it within our county. I would say it's certainly true that New York is still the center for the USA. There is no other center, there's no other place in the USA right now with the amount of dance activity and companies. Chicago's really starting to come along, but New York is still the center. I hear of amazing things going on in the Netherlands, and in France, but I just don't have a perspective to be able to comment about it.

The interesting thing is, in the USA, we developed the touring mechanisms, and in Europe they developed the creative lab and production values supporting their artists by giving them the time to create and the productions. Now what they complain about is that we've developed something but we don't have anywhere to tour. We don't have the market, so a dance performance might happen only one or two times. What we developed was the market, and now we've got to develop the lab time for dancers and choreographers to create.

We seem to have the trade mechanism. UBW is touring a lot. Not as much as in the past, but we tour. We get out there. We don't just do something once and then run it. There's a presenting base, called the National Dance Project, which supports touring throughout the country. If you're able to tap into that base it helps. We've got those mechanisms in this country, and I think that's something for us to be proud of, too. That's a good thing, and we should continue to strengthen that and develop the time to create.

I hear about European dancers saying they had six months of rehearsal time. I can't think of any artist in the USA (besides possibly Mark Morris) who has his or her group on salary for the whole six months to create a work. I just don't know of that. If that happens here, I need to know about it. We're not going to be able to compete on that level with artists who have that kind of time. Europeans have access to production values as well. To bring dirt and rain, or water onstage is a much harder thing for us to do in this country, but someone should figure out how to do it.

Our artists are not well supported anymore by our government, and the corporations don't do much either. Of course, in Europe, there isn't a lot of corporate support; it's mostly from the governments. There's a lot of wealth in this country. It's not a question of less money; it's a question of how to access it, and I think we've just got to do a better job of figuring that out.

There is an audience in this country that wants to see modern dance, but I don't know that a 2,000-seat house is the best venue for it. I would love to see more 500-seat houses built throughout the country for dance. We were just someplace and there was one of my pieces, which is very gestural, and the dancers were looking at each other. I was standing in the back of the 1,500-seat house and thought it looked like they were not doing anything on the stage. I had to change the choreography for that because my work is built on an intimacy. I think a lot of contemporary dance is built on that intimacy. Some landscape work, as Twyla Tharp calls it in her book *The Creative Habit*, sustains itself in a large theater, but I think a lot of modern dance doesn't.

I've seen some presenters do a really good job of increasing an audience for modern dance. One of them is in California: Ken Foster. He's at Yerba Buena, and when he was at Penn State, he did a great job of educating his audience in a very conservative town, getting them to accept edgy work. That was the artistic brilliance of one presenter. The presenter has to be as brilliant as the artistic director. I've seen places that were absolutely sold out. At the Kennedy Center, we were sold out in January for an engagement in March. Then I see places where there are only a few people in the audience. The presenter has to do that job of figuring out how to market a company and strengthen the base.

It's an exciting time for us. I feel I'm in a nice creative role. We're also going to restage Blondell Cumming's *Chicken Soup*. I don't want us to become a repertory company, but I think there's a way that we can incorporate other works into our productions. When you're a single vision company, there is an awareness at some point in time—hopefully in the very, very distant future—that the choreographer is not going to live for ever, and so, what is that company going to do? What's Tricia Brown going to do? What's Merce Cunningham's company going to do? Now, there's certainly enough work, but at some point, there has to be something new produced, so perhaps we're just bridging that a lot earlier than other companies.

Power bases are difficult to challenge. I think that we just have to be careful that even if I had power with five of my African-American friends, that I don't set up an exclusionary base—and I think it's the human impulse to do that, "I'm going to take care of what I view as my own."

It's what happens with any power base. We certainly see it in Washington. Oh boy, do we see it in Washington with the cronyism! Any power base wants to perpetuate itself until it's challenged. If it's a smart power base, when it's challenged, it figures out that it will be stronger by opening up, not by closing ranks. And you see that with this president; he keeps closing ranks, and closing ranks, and closing ranks, and now what are his numbers? Now his own people are turning on him. The conservative right-wing people are turning on Bush. It's about a power base, and that power base then wants to protect and strengthen itself. What I would say is that it becomes strengthened by opening out, not by closing in.

How has the political environment changed in the dance world over the past twenty years? I'm not sure if I know how to answer that. It was interesting during the whole situation of censorship with the NEA, with respect to Karen Finely and Tim Miller. I thought of supporting that movement, but I don't know if I've ever felt the privilege to be free. So, it was an interesting debate to me, because I don't know that I ever felt the privilege to just say and do whatever I wanted to do.

And that reflects back on race. I never felt free because there are certain things that I'm just not going to be able to get away with as a black woman. You see it on the reality shows.

Jawole Zollar's Sassy Group. Photo © Antoine Tempé.

A strong black woman can't get along with anyone because she's outspoken. That's the stereotype. That's the thing people fear. What might be considered confidence and assertiveness in one area is considered rudeness and overly aggressive in another. I think I have to exist regardless of the political environment, whatever it is. Somebody once asked me to define UBW in one sentence. I said, "A person who is willing to dance their truth, and to speak that truth to power." It means standing up in the face of something more powerful than you and standing in the center of your truth and speaking it, dancing it, owning it, regardless of the environment. That's where I'm coming from.

March 16, 2006

Bibliography

Acocella, Joan. *Mark Morris*. Middletown, Conn.: Wesleyan University Press, 1994.

Adair, Christy. *Women and Dance: Slyphs and Sirens*. New York: New York University Press, 1992.

Adshead-Lansdale, Janet, and Layson, June. *Dance History, an Introduction*. London: Routledge, 1983.

Anderson, Jack. *The American Dance Festival*. Durham, NC: Duke University Press, 1987.

Banes, Sally, ed. *Reinventing Dance in the 1960s: Everything was Possible*. Madison, Wisc.: The University of Wisconsin Press, 2003.

—— *Writing Dancing in the Age of Postmodernism*. Hanover, NH: University Press of New England, 1994.

—— *Terpsichore in Sneakers: Post-Modern Dance*. Boston, Mass.: Houghton Mifflin Company, 1980.

Bellefante, Ginia. "Bill T. Jones Is About to Make People Angry. Again." *New York Times*, September 18, 2005.

Bonoguore, Tenille. "Women's World Is Far from Equal." *The Globe and Mail*, November 21, 2006.

Bremser, Martha. *Fifty Contemporary Choreographers*. London and New York: Routledge, 1999.

Brown, Beverly. "Training to Dance with Erick Hawkins." *Dance Scope*, American Dance Guild, fall/winter, 1971/2.

Brown, Jean Morrison. *The Vision of Modern Dance*. Princeton, NJ: Princeton Book Company, 1979.

Burt, Ramsay. *The Male Dancer: Bodies, Spectacle, Sexualities*. London: Routledge, 1995.

—— "Dance, Masculinity and Postmodernism," in Valerie E. Briginshaw (ed.) *Postmodernism and Dance: Discussion Papers from the Postmodern Dance Summer Schools held at West Sussex Institute for Higher Education, July 1991*. Chichester: Institute of Higher Education, 1991, pp. 23–32.

Butler, Judith. *Bodies That Matter, On the Discursive Limits of 'Sex.'* New York and London: Routledge, 1993.

—— *Gender Trouble*. New York and London: Routledge, 1990.

Carman, Joseph, Sucato, Steven, and Perron, Wendy. "He Said/She Said." *Dance Magazine*, November 2005, pp. 60–70.

Carter, Alexandra, ed. *The Routledge Dance Studies Reader*. London and New York: Routledge, 1998.

Celichowska, Renata. *The Erick Hawkins Modern Dance Technique*. Hightstown, NJ: Princeton Book Company, 2000.

Chatterjea, Ananya. *Butting Out*. Middletown, Conn.: Wesleyan University Press, 2004.

Clark, VeVe A. and Johnson, Sara E. *Kaiso! Writings by and about Katherine Dunham*. Madison, Wisc.: The University of Wisconsin Press, 2005.

Cohen, Selma Jeanne. *Modern Dance, Seven Statements of Belief*. Middletown, Conn.: Wesleyan University Press, 1965.

—— *Doris Humphrey: An Artist First.* Middletown, Conn.: Wesleyan University Press, 1972.

—— ed. *Dance as a Theatre Art.* New York: Dodd Mead & Company, 1974.

—— *Next Week, Swan Lake: Reflections on Dance and Dances.* Middletown, Conn.: Wesleyan University, 1982.

Copeland, Roger. *Merce Cunningham: The Modernizing of Modern Dance.* New York and London: Routledge, 2004.

Daly, Ann. *Done into Dance. Isadora Duncan in America.* Middletown, Conn.: Wesleyan University Press, 1995.

Danto, Arthur C. *Playing with the Edge: The Photographic Achievement of Robert Mapplethorpe.* Berkeley, CA: University of California Press, 1995.

DeFrantz, Thomas F., ed. *Dancing Many Drums: Excavations in African American Dance.* Madison, Wisc.: University of Wisconsin Press, 2002.

—— *Dancing Revelations: Alvin Ailey's Embodiment of African American Culture.* Oxford: Oxford University Press, 2004.

Dell, Cecily. *A Primer for Movement Description Using Effort-Shape and Supplementary Concepts.* New York: Dance Notation Bureau Press, 1977.

Desmond, Jane C., ed. *Dancing Desires: Choreographing Sexualities On and Off the Stage.* Madison, Wisc.: the University of Wisconsin Press, 2001.

Dils, Ann, and Albright, Ann Cooper, eds. *Moving History/Dance Cultures: A Dance History Reader.* Middletown, Conn.: Wesleyan University Press, 2001.

Dixon Gottschild, Brenda. *The Black Dancing Body: A Geography from Coon to Cool.* New York: Palgrave Macmillan, 2003.

Dunbar, June, ed. *José Limón.* New York: Routledge, 2000.

Duncan, Isadora. *The Art of the Dance.* New York: Theatre Arts Books, 1928.

Dunning, Jennifer. "'Moopin,' Where There's Sex, There's Frustration." *New York Times*, September 29, 2006.

—— Obituaries. *New York Times*, April 1, 1988.

Emery, Lynne Fauley. *Black Dance from 1619 to Today.* Princeton, NJ: Princeton Book Company, 1988.

Foster, Susan Leigh. *Reading Dancing: Bodies and Subjects in Contemporary American Dance.* Berkeley, Calif.: University of California Press, 1986.

—— "Closets Full of Dances," in Jane C. Desmond (ed.), *Dancing Desires: Choreographing Sexualities On and Off the Stage.* Madison, Wisc.: University of Wisconsin Press, 2001, pp. 147–207.

Foulkes, Julia L. *Modern Bodies: Dance and American Modernism from Martha Graham to Alvin Ailey.* Chapel Hill, NC: The University of North Carolina Press, 2002.

Franko, Mark. *Dancing Modernism/Performing Politics.* Bloomington, Ind.: Indiana University Press, 1995.

Friedler, Sharon E. and Glazer, Susan B., eds. *Dancing Female: Lives and Issues of Women in Contemporary Dance.* Amsterdam: Harwood Academic, 1997.

Garafola, Lynn, ed. *José Limón: An Unfinished Memoir.* Hanover, NH and London: University Press of New England, 1999.

Gesmer, Daniel. "Festival Keeps Focus on the Fringes." *Los Angeles Times.* December 16, 2006.

Gitelman, Claudio, ed. *Liebe Hanya. Mary Wigman's Letters to Hanya Holm.* Madison, Wisc.: The University of Wisconsin Press, 2003.

Gottlieb, Robert. "Is Morris Feeling Boxed In? His Dynamic Company Shines." *New York Observer, Arts Journal,* available online at <http://www.observer.com/20070129/20070129_Robert_Gottlieb_culture_gottliebdance.asp>.

Graham, Martha. *Blood Memory.* New York: Washington Square Press, 1991.

Hanna, Judith Lynne. *Dance, Sex and Gender: Signs of Identity, Dominance, Defiance, and Desire.* Chicago, Ill.: The University of Chicago Press, 1988.

Haraway, Donna J. Modest_Witness@Second_Millenium.FemaleMan *MeetsOnco Mouse*. New York: Routledge, 1997.

Hawkins, Erick. *The Body Is a Clear Place*. Princeton, NJ: Princeton Book Company, 1992.

—— "What is the Most Beautiful Dance?" in *Erick Hawkins: Theory and Training*. New York: The American Dance Guild, Inc., 1979.

Highwater, Jamake. *Dance: Rituals of Experience*. Pennington, NJ: Princeton Book Company, 1978.

Hohenadel, Kristin. "Dance: The Punk Ballerina Returns, With Souvenirs." *New York Tmes*, November 27, 2005.

Howard, Rachel. "Panel Asks: Just What Is Black Dance?" *San Francisco Chronicle*, Sunday, January 28, 2007.

Humphrey, Doris. *The Art of Making Dances*. New York: Holt, Rinehart, & Winston, 1959.

Irigaray, Luce. *This Sex Which Is Not One*. Ithaca, NY: Cornell University Press, 1985.

Jensen, Robert. *The Heart of Whiteness: Confronting Race, Racism, and White Privilege*. San Francisco, Calif.: City Lights, 2005.

Kendall, Elizabeth. *Where She Danced: The Birth of American Art-Dance*. Berkeley, Calif.: University of California Press, 1979.

Kisselgoff, Anna. "Creation of the World by Hawkins." *New York Times,* July 1, 1979, pp. 12, 18.

Klosty, James. *Merce Cunningham*. New York: Saturday Review Press, 1975.

Kolcio, Katja Pylyshenko, Danitz, Marilynn, and Lehman, Margot C. *Branching Out: Oral Histories of the Founders of Six National Dance Organizations*. New York: American Dance Guild, 2000.

Kourlas, Gia. "How New York Lost Its Modern Dance Reign." *New York Times*, September 6, 2005.

—— "3 Dancers Making a Show of Their Age." *New York Times*, April 3, 2007.

Kostelanetz, Richard, ed. *Merce Cunningham in Space and Time*. New York: Da Capo Press, 1998.

Kraus, Lisa. "Philadelphia's Dance Momentum." *Philadelphia Inquirer*, March 11, 2007.

Kreemer, Connie, ed. *Further Steps: Fifteen Choreographers on Modern Dance*. New York: Harper & Row, Inc., 1987.

Kurth, Peter. *Isadora: A Sensational Life*. Boston, Mass.: Little, Brown and Company, 2001.

Lacy, Madison D. and Adam Zucker (dirs.). "Free to Dance." Video for PBS. A co-production of the American Dance Festival and the John F. Kennedy Center for the Performing Arts in association with Thirteen/WNET New York, 2001.

Lee, Carol. *Ballet in Western Culture: A History of its Origins and Evolution*. New York and London: Routledge, 2002.

Levien, Julia. *Duncan Dance*. Pennington, NJ: Princeton Book Company, 1994.

Long, Richard A. *The Black Tradition in American Dance*. New York: Rizzoli International Publications, 1989.

Lorber, Richard, ed. *Erick Hawkins: Theory and Training*. New York: The American Dance Guild, 1979.

Lowenthal, Lillian. *The Search for Isadora*. Pennington, NJ: Princeton Book Company, 1993.

McDonagh, Don. *The Rise and Fall and Rise of Modern Dance*. New York: The New American Library, 1970.

—— *Martha Graham*. New York: Popular Library, 1975.

McKayle, Donald. *Transcending Boundaries: My Dancing Life*. London and New York: Routledge, 2002.

Major, Geraldyn Hodges. *Black Society*. Chicago, Ill.: Johnson Publishing Company, Inc., 1976.

Manning, Susan. *Ecstasy and the Demon*. Berkeley, Calif.: University of California Press, 1993.

Michaels, Walter Benn. *The Trouble with Diversity: How We Learned to Love Identity and Ignore Inequality*. New York: Metropolitan Books, 2006.

Mitoma, Judy, Zimmer, Elizabeth, and Stiebar, Dale Ann, eds. *Envisioning Dance on Film and Video*. London and New York: Routledge, 2003.

Morris, Gay, ed. *Moving Words: Re-writing Dance*. London: Routledge, 1996.

Murphy, Ann. "The Feminine Mystique." *Dance Magazine.* November 2005, pp. 50–4.

Muschamp, Herbert. "FOURTH floor! Men's lingerie!" *New York Times,* January 8, 2006.

Nagrin, Daniel. *How to Dance Forever: Surviving Against the Odds.* New York: William Morrow & Company, Inc., 1998.

Nikolais, Alwin, and Louis, Murray. *The Nikolais/Louis Dance Technique: A Philosophy and Method of Modern Dance.* London and New York: Routledge, 2005.

Novack, Cynthia J. *Sharing the Dance: Contact Improvisation and American Culture.* Madison, Wisc.: University of Wisconsin Press, 1990.

O'Connor, Barbara. *Katherine Dunham: Pioneer of Black Dance.* Minneapolis, Minn.: Carolrhoda Books, 2000.

Pennella, Florence. "The Vision of Erick Hawkins." *Dance Scope,* American Dance Guild, 12 (2), 1978, pp. 14–23.

Perpener, John O. *African-American Concert Dance: The Harlem Renaissance and Beyond.* Urbana, Ill.: University of Illinois Press, 2001.

Perron, Wendy. "The Lasting Influence of Judson Dance Theater." *Dance Journal/ USA,* 18 (1), 2001, pp. 25–8.

Reed, Cheryl L. "Is Classism the New Racism?" *Chicago Sun Times,* November 12, 2006.

Reese, R. "From the Fringe: The Hip Hop Culture and Ethnic Relations Abstract." Far West and Popular Culture Conference, February 1998.

Reynolds, Nancy, and McCormick, Malcom. *No Fixed Points: Dance in the Twentieth Century.* New Haven, Conn.: Yale University Press, 2003.

Roberts, Sam. "Who Americans Are and What They Do, in Census Data." *New York Times,* December 15, 2006.

Rockwell, John. "The Dance World Has a 60's Flashback." *New York Times,* January 4, 2006.

—— "In the Complex World of Ballet, It's Youth That Soars." *New York Times,* January 18, 2006.

—— "Baby, We Were Born to Dance: The Boss Goes to the Ballet." *New York Times,* January 22, 2006.

—— "A Nude Duet with Twists, Anguish and Eroticism." *New York Times,* February 3, 2006.

—— "Skint. Downton, This Caterwaul's for You." *New York Times,* September 29, 2006.

Ruiz, Don Miguel. *The Four Agreements.* San Rafael, Calif.: Amber-Allen Publishing, 1997.

Senelick, Laurence, ed. *Gender in Performance: The Presentation of Difference in the Performing Arts.* Hanover, NH: University Press of New England, 1992.

Shawn, Ted, and Poole, Gray. *One Thousand and One Night Stands.* Garden City, NY: Doubleday, 1979.

Shelton, Suzanne. *Divine Dancer: A Biography of Ruth St. Denis.* Garden City, NY : Doubleday & Company, 1981.

Siegel, Marcia B. *At the Vanishing Point.* Boston, Mass.: Houghton Mifflin Company, 1972.

—— *Watching the Dance Go By.* Boston, Mass.: Houghton Mifflin Company, 1977.

—— *The Shapes of Change: Images of American Dance.* Boston, Mass.: Houghton Mifflin Company, 1979.

Soares, Janet Mansfield. *Louis Horst: Musician in a Dancer's World.* Durham, NC: Duke University Press, 1992.

Solway, Diane. "When the Choreographer Is Out of the Picture." *New York Times,* January 7, 2007.

Sulcas, Roslyn. "Baryshnikov Takes His Building for a Test Run." *New York Times,* September 25, 2005.

Taylor, Paul. Pr*ivate Domain.* New York: Alfred A. Knopf, 1987.

Thomas, Helen, ed. *Dance, Gender, and Culture.* New York: St. Martins Press, 1993.

Tobias, Tobi. "Wonder Women." *Tutu Revue,* 5, December 14, 2006.

—— "Johannes Wieland." *New York Times,* November 13, 2005.

—— "Enough." *Dance Now,* 15 (2), 2006.

Tynan, Dan. "The 50 Greatest Gadgets of the Past 50 Years." *PC World*, December 24, 2005.

Vaughan, David. *Merce Cunningham. Fifty Years, Chronicle and Commentary,* ed. Melissa Harris. New York, Aperture, 1997.

Wakin, Daniel. "Gambler Shakes Up Land of Tutus and Leotards." *New York Times*, January 8, 2007.

Weil, Andrew. *Healthy Aging.* New York: Alfred A. Knopf, 2005.

Woolf, Vicki. *Dancing in the Vortex: The Story of Ida Rubinstein.* Amsterdam: Harwood Academic Publishers, 2000.

Index

NOTE: Page numbers in bold type refer to a photograph. Works by choreographers discussed in the text are given at the end of their entries.

Related titles from Routledge

Fifty Contemporary Choreographers

Edited by
Martha Bremser

With a new introduction by
Deborah Jowitt

"Bound to become a well-thumbed resource tool"
– Dance Now

Fifty Contemporary Choreographers provides a unique guide to some of today's most important dance-makers. The range of entries is impressively broad, spanning ballet, "contemporary" and post-modern dance, and has an international scope. Each entry locates each choreographer's style and influence within the development of contemporary dance and includes a biographical section; a chronological list of works; a detailed bibliography; and a critical essay.

Choreographers discussed include:

- Michael Clark
- Merce Cunningham
- Mark Morris
- Anne Teresa De Keersmaeker
- Twyla Tharp

Hb: 0–415–10363–0
Pb: 0–415–10364–9

Available at all good bookshops
For ordering and further information please visit:
www.routledge.com

Related titles from Routledge

Rethinking Dance History

Edited by
Alexandra Carter

By taking a fresh approach to the study of history in general, Alexandra Carter's *Rethinking Dance History* offers new perspectives on important periods in dance history and seeks to address some of the gaps and silences left within that history. Encompassing ballet, South Asian, modern dance forms and much more, this book provides exciting new research on topics as diverse as:

- the Victorian music hall
- film musicals and popular music videos
- the impact of Neoclassical fashion on ballet
- women's influence on early modern dance
- methods of dance reconstruction.

Featuring work by some of the major voices in dance writing and discourse, this unique anthology will prove invaluable for both scholars and practitioners, and a source of interest for anyone who is fascinated by dance's rich and multi-layered history.

Hb: 0–415–28746–4
Pb: 0–415–28747–2

Available at all good bookshops
For ordering and further information please visit:
www.routledge.com

Related titles from Routledge

Europe Dancing:
Perspectives on Theatre, Dance and Cultural Identity

Edited by
Andree Grau and Stephanie Jordan

"The most interesting European dance scholars writing today offer rich but succinct accounts full of invaluable insights into developments in dance."
– Ramsay Burt, De Montfort University

"An essential purchase for any undergraduate or research library . . . since nothing truly comparable presently exists."
– *Choice*

Europe Dancing examines the dance cultures and movements which have developed in Europe since the Second World War. Nine countries are represented in this unique collaboration between European dance scholars. The contributors chart the art form, and discuss the outside influences which have shaped it.

This comprehensive book explores:

- questions of identity within individual countries, within Europe, and in relation to the USA
- the East/West cultural division
- the development of state subsidy for dance
- the rise of contemporary dance as an "alternative" genre
- the implications for dance of political, economic and social change.

Useful historical charts are included to trace significant dance and political events throughout the twentieth century in each country.

Never before has this information been gathered together in one place. This book is essential reading for everyone interested in dance and its growth and development in recent years.

Hb: 0–415–17102–4
Pb: 0–415–17103–2

Available at all good bookshops
For ordering and further information please visit:
www.routledge.com